Also by Richard Thompson Ford

The Race Card
Racial Culture: A Critique

Rights Gone Wrong

Rights Gone Wrong

How Law Corrupts

the Struggle for Equality

Richard Thompson Ford

Farrar, Straus and Giroux   New York

Farrar, Straus and Giroux
18 West 18th Street, New York 10011

Distributed in Canada by D&M Publishers, Inc.
Printed in the United States of America
First edition, 2011

Library of Congress Cataloging-in-Publication Data
Ford, Richard T. (Richard Thompson)
    Rights gone wrong : how law corrupts the struggle for equality /
  Richard Thompson Ford. — 1st ed.
        p. cm.
    Includes bibliographical references and index.
    ISBN 978-0-374-25035-5 (hardback)
    1. Civil rights—United States. I. Title.

  KF4749.F65 2011
  342.7308'5—dc22

                                                        2011010705

Designed by Abby Kagan

www.fsgbooks.com

10 9 8 7 6 5 4 3 2 1

For Eloise Berit "Ella" Ford

Contents

Rights Gone Wrong

Introduction

This is the beginning of the twenty-first century's civil rights movement," intoned the Reverend Al Sharpton, addressing a crowd of over twenty thousand people. "We've gone from plantations to penitentiaries . . . they have tried to create a criminal justice system that . . . targets our young black men . . . We're going to change the federal laws . . . We're going to the nation's capital, just like Dr. King did a generation ago." But right then they were in Jena, Louisiana: population three thousand on a typical day; population twenty-three thousand, including the Reverends Al Sharpton and Jesse Jackson and the California congresswoman Maxine Waters, on September 20, 2007.

The extra twenty thousand had arrived to protest the criminal charges brought against six black high school students who had been dubbed the Jena Six. According to the account widely circulated on blogs, websites, chain e-mails, and text messages, and finally picked up by the BBC and the *Chicago Tribune*, the town of Jena was a redneck paradise stuck in the Jim Crow era, where white students had established a "White Tree" under which no black student at the town's only high school dared sit. The black students, consigned to nearby bleachers during school breaks, silently fumed until one brave student, new to town and innocent of the depth of Jena's racism, asked at a school assembly whether he could sit under the White Tree. The school principal warily answered that every student was free to sit wherever he liked.

The next day three nooses hung from the White Tree, meant to illustrate the only way a black student would be allowed under its branches. Racial tensions went from simmering resentment to a rapid boil as whites threatened black students with improvised weapons at parties and once with a rifle in a parking lot. District Attorney Reed Walters addressed the students at Jena High School and threatened, "With the stroke of a pen I can make your life miserable," staring pointedly at the black students. Meanwhile, the whites responsible for these altercations suffered slapped wrists at the most. Jena's racial cauldron boiled over when a white student, Justin Barker, directed a racial insult to the group of black students who would become the Jena Six—talented football players with promising futures. One of the students snapped and attacked Barker; the others joined in or watched. Barker was knocked unconscious, but walked out of the hospital hours later with minor injuries and went to a party that evening. This time, law enforcement responded, not with slaps to the wrists, but with arrests and ultimately an attempted-murder charge. Prosecutor Walters charged Mychal Bell, who would become the public face of the Jena Six, as an adult: if convicted, he would spend much of his adult life behind bars.

The legend of the Jena Six was told and retold in instant messages tapped into BlackBerrys and iPhones on the fly, through bulk e-mail and hastily written blogs, each telling a bit more dramatic than the last. The story seemed straight out of history—or straight out of Hollywood—with its handsome and heroic black football-hero victims, its white rednecks seething with venom and hate, and the power-mad and racist prosecutor who needed only a Boss Hogg white suit and string tie from the costume department to complete the image, flaunting his power before the honest and beleaguered Negroes of Jena: *With the stroke of a pen I can make your life miserable, boy*. It was the perfect rebirth of the civil rights struggle—a stark rebuff to those who had, naively, claimed that race relations had improved in the decades since the Freedom Summers. "For those who have been under the illusion that changes have occurred, this is a wake-up call," the Reverend Jesse Jackson told reporters.

But there was something a bit too dogged about this narrative and something slightly unseemly about the protests, as if people were almost *excited* to have an honest-to-goodness, genuine, unambiguous racial outrage, just like those they had read about in the history books: "This is the first time something like this has happened for our generation . . . You always heard about it from history books and relatives. This is a chance to experience it for ourselves," one college student who marched on Jena enthused.[1]

The facts, however, refused to go retro: they were disconcertingly postmodern—multifaceted and ambiguous. The six young men who became the Jena Six weren't beleaguered subalterns. They were minor celebrities—star football players in a town that was obsessed with its high school football team. Football jerseys sold out at the local markets, town businesses sponsored the team, and townsfolk—whether or not they had kids in high school—turned out in force for the Jena Giants games. Mychal Bell was repeatedly named player of the year by the local newspaper.

According to Jena's defenders, Bell was a serial recidivist who had taken advantage of—and would ultimately suffer because of—his status as a local football hero and the leniency of the liberal juvenile justice system. Bell was the product of a broken home, with an absent father and a mother with a criminal arrest record. According to the African American sports columnist Jason Whitlock, Bell's father "reentered his son's life only after Bell faced attempted-murder charges." Before that, "white people in the 'racist' town of Jena provided Bell with the support and protected his football career long before Jesse [Jackson], Al [Sharpton], Bell's father and others took an interest in Mychal Bell."[2] Bell had been written up for disciplinary problems on a regular basis, and his grades had suffered badly in the year before the Jena Six assault. But even as his behavior careened dangerously toward chronic lawbreaking, Bell was never seriously punished. "You had the judge and DA at those ball games Friday night, clapping them on," said Anlynne Hart, the mother of a young woman Bell had assaulted.[3]

Shortly after the Jena Six rally, *The Christian Science Monitor* published a story written by a journalist from *The Jena Times* titled "Media Myths About the Jena 6."[4] The story directly contradicted almost every element of the Jena-Six-as-civil-rights-violation narrative. According to the article, there was no whites-only tree at Jena High School. Students of all races sat under the tree, and the black student who asked at a school assembly if he could sit under the "White Tree" was making a joke. The "nooses" were not a threat to black students; meant to be lassos, they were an unrelated prank directed at white members of the rodeo team. The students who hung them were guilty only of a baleful ignorance: they didn't know of the history of black lynching and were mortified when they learned how their prank had been interpreted. And they did not get off with a three-day suspension from school: they were sent to discipline court, where they underwent mental health evaluations, spent nine days in alternative school, and served two weeks of Saturday detention. "Media Myths" insisted that District Attorney Reed Walters did not threaten black students. His statement had been taken out of context. His comments were part of an address to the entire Jena High School student body. Walters decided to make a dramatic statement in order to get the attention of some students who were talking on their cell phones rather than listening. "With the stroke of a pen I can make your life miserable, so I want you to call me before you do something stupid," Walters implored—less a threat than an admonishment that students turn to the law rather than to violence to resolve their conflicts.

A central complaint of the Jena Six protest was that law enforcement had treated blacks in Jena more harshly than whites. "Every time the white people did something . . . they dropped it, and every time the black people did something, they blew it out of proportion," insisted one protester. "Media Myths" sought to undermine this claim. A reportedly all-white party from which one of the Jena Six—Robert Bailey—was barred because of his race, leading to an altercation, was actually a racially mixed party to which Bailey had not been invited. A highly publicized attack with a shotgun, for which a white man was not charged, began, according to "Media Myths," with an attack by Bailey and two other black students and ended when the lone white man ran to retrieve the shotgun from his truck in self-defense. Most damning of all, the altercation that led to the criminal charges against the Jena Six was not, as was widely reported, a school-yard tussle blown out of proportion by a racist prosecutor. It was an ambush in which the Jena Six had lain in wait for their victim; blocked his exit from the school auditorium; hit him from behind, knocking him out; and kicked him repeatedly as he lay unconscious on the floor.

These contested facts and ambiguities didn't matter to the protesters, because the Jena Six were more important as symbols of injustice than as flesh-and-blood victims of it. One could dispute the racism of Jena's high school students, police, and prosecutor, but no one could deny the racially disproportionate effect of criminal prosecutions nationwide: according to the Justice Department, while one in one hundred Americans were incarcerated in 2006, one in nine black men between twenty and thirty-four years old was behind bars. The Jena Six symbolized this much larger injustice, just as the "White Tree" symbolized the enduring racial segregation of the nation's public schools and neighborhoods, two of the most severe remaining legacies of America's long and cruel racist history. "Free the Jena Six" became a rallying cry because "Stop Informal Segregation and Prosecutorial Overzealousness That Disproportionately Affect African Americans Here and Elsewhere" wouldn't fit on a T-shirt or a placard.

Donations poured in from around the nation to defend the Jena Six. The rock legend David Bowie donated $10,000 to the NAACP's Jena Six fund, which raised $20,000. The Color of Change, a netroots organization, raised over $200,000. Various organizations and individuals held fund-raisers and sold Jena Six merchandise, with promises to donate the proceeds, and untold thousands of dollars arrived directly in the mailboxes of the Jena Six themselves. By November, people were asking uncomfortable questions about what had happened to the roughly half a million dollars raised to defend the Jena Six. The blogosphere was abuzz with rumors that the parents of the Jena Six had purchased new luxury cars and jewelry; the parents refused to account for as much as $250,000 in accounts that they controlled.[5] Pictures of Robert Bailey, one of the Jena Six, dressed in black gangster regalia—baggy sports jersey, gold jewelry, baseball cap, and shades—rolling on a bed littered with cash, his mouth stuffed with $100 bills, turned up on YouTube. Other members of the Jena Six, Carwin Jones and Bryant Purvis, were photographed mugging like rap musicians at the BET Hip-Hop Awards. As reports of misuse and embezzlement of the donations proliferated, Jena Six supporters squabbled among themselves. "There are definitely questions out there about the money," admitted Alan Bean, the director of Friends of Justice, the group that first investigated the Jena Six prosecutions.[6] These events fed into a now all-too-commonplace idea that civil rights claims had become a racket used by the unscrupulous to get money or other perks and advantages. For instance, referring to the photos of Robert Bailey, the conservative blogger Michelle Malkin quipped: "Some of the [Jena Six] defendants are literally rolling in race-hustling dough."[7]

Unlike the blatant racism of the past, modern racial injustice often has multiple and indirect causes. This makes it a bad target for traditional civil rights activism, which spotlights dramatic instances of bigotry and specific perpetrators. Tellingly, the march on Jena was somewhat unfocused: the demonstrators moved between the courthouse, where Bell was tried for an offense no one denies he committed (the charge had been reduced to aggravated assault), and the site of the "White Tree," which, with all-too-fitting symbolism, had already been cut down, eradicating the one tangible symbol of Jena's racial tensions. As for the rallying cry "Free the Jena Six," at best it relied on the notion that six athletic young men were justified in kicking their lone victim senseless because *other* people who shared his race committed offenses against *other* black students. This sort of racial vendetta is diametrically opposed to the message of social justice and cross-racial understanding that underlay the civil rights movement of the twentieth century. If the Jena Six demonstration marked the beginning of the twenty-first century's civil rights movement, it was an inauspicious start, reflecting a loss of moral purpose, a blurred political focus, and a sadly compromised integrity.

How Have Rights Gone Wrong?

Since the 1960s, the ideas developed during the civil rights movement have dominated American race relations. Courts and governmental agencies enforce legal prohibitions against discrimination; private businesses and universities endeavor to achieve diversity, and individuals think about race relations in civil rights terms: we aspire to the ideal of "color blindness" and condemn the evils "discrimination" and "bias." American civil rights legislation has been a model for other nations, and the American civil rights movement has inspired other important struggles against injustice, such as the South African anti-apartheid movement and the international movement for gay rights.

When it comes to outright discrimination and overt prejudice, civil rights have been an astonishing success. Race discrimination in restaurants, theaters, and hotels was quickly and thoroughly eliminated by the civil rights legislation of the 1960s. Discrimination in employment—while still a problem—has been dramatically reduced and today is widely and roundly condemned. Public figures who make overtly bigoted statements typically suffer widespread contempt and often lose their jobs. As a result of these welcome developments, each successive generation is less bigoted than the preceding one. Barack Obama's election to the presidency demonstrates that race is no longer the insuperable impediment it was in the recent past, and polls suggest that racial animus today is at an all-time low.

But today's most serious social injustices aren't caused by bias and bigotry. For instance, the worst racial injustices stem largely from segregation—a legacy of past racism but not by and large the result of ongoing discrimination—and the many disadvantages that follow from living in isolated, economically depressed, and crime-ridden neighborhoods. Civil rights litigation and activism have hardly made a dent in these formidable obstacles. In fact, sometimes civil rights thinking can distract attention from the real problems, emphasizing dramatic incidents that aren't good examples of the larger injustices.

It's tempting to insist that we just need more of the same—that we've only been too timid in enforcing civil rights laws or too conservative in interpreting them. For many people it seems obvious that civil rights are unambiguously good and more rights, applied to more groups in more circumstances, would be better. Civil rights are widely seen as an emblem of moral progress: societies that extend rights to their citizens are morally superior and culturally more advanced than those that do not, and every society will guarantee a larger number of rights as it matures. Americans are ashamed of our nation's failure to extend civil rights to racial minorities and women in our recent past, and a growing number of Americans are ashamed of our failure to extend civil rights to gay men and lesbians today; similarly, one imagines, our children and grandchildren will be ashamed that we have failed to extend rights to correct a host of social injustices we can now only dimly perceive.

But today, civil rights do too much and not enough at the same time. Opportunists and special-interest lobbying groups have used civil rights laws to get an edge in competitive schools and job markets, demanding special privileges, a disproportionate share of public resources, and even cold hard cash as a matter of civil rights. Civil rights laws prohibiting discrimination have been pressed to perverse and illogical extremes: for instance, laws against sex discrimination outlaw ladies' nights at singles bars, and one litigant even sued to stop Mother's Day. Extremists on both the left and the right have hijacked civil rights, using them to push radical schemes despite democratic opposition, and in some cases even to reverse and undermine the social justice goals civil rights were supposed to achieve.

It's not just that civil rights laws are abused or taken too far: some may be doing more harm than good. For instance, the Fourteenth Amendment to the Constitution was enacted after emancipation to ensure that newly freed slaves would have a chance at a decent and dignified life, and it was the most important constitutional guarantee of equality in the twentieth century, serving as the legal foundation of desegregation in 1954's *Brown v. Board of Education*. But more recently, the Fourteenth Amendment guarantee of equal protection has stymied sensible, if controversial, efforts to correct racial inequality, in direct contravention of its historical purpose. Most dramatically, in 2007 the Fourteenth Amendment was used to block efforts to achieve racial *integration* in the public schools. Today the Fourteenth Amendment's equal protection clause works against equality as often as it furthers it: gallows humor among civil rights lawyers is that its *repeal* might actually be cause for celebration.

Lawyers and judges deserve much of the blame for twisting and perverting the legacy of civil rights, but political activists aren't any better. Today's social protests are often more style than substance, adopting the look and feel of the historic demonstrations of the 1960s whether or not a mass demonstration fits the circumstances. Too often they are both shrill and misdirected, choosing symbolic targets that make for good press even when they aren't good examples of injustice and demanding simplistic and often unworkable solutions to complex social problems. The Jena Six were held up as symbols of the larger problem of racial disparities in the criminal justice system. But as stark and as troubling as they are, these imbalances can't be blamed on the kind of Jim Crow–style bigotry that the Jena Six narrative evoked. These disparities worsened dramatically in the decades *following* the civil rights revolution of the 1960s, but as you would expect, during that same period racial attitudes in society have dramatically improved according to every reliable sociological measure. Unless law enforcement is an island of worsening racism in an ocean of increasing tolerance, today's racial disparities in criminal justice must have more complex causes. For example, civil rights activists justifiably point out that federal sentencing guidelines impose a much more severe penalty for possession of crack than for powder cocaine. Because blacks are more likely to use crack cocaine while whites favor powder, these unequal punishments for similar drugs have contributed to the racial imbalance in our nation's prisons. But was racism behind the disparate penalties? The crack cocaine trade brought with it especially violent turf wars in poor inner-city neighborhoods. Black civic organizations in many cities joined a multiracial call for more assertive law enforcement. An especially harsh penalty for crack cocaine possession was an understandable, if flawed, response. This and other tough law-enforcement policies have caused a dramatic increase in the number of arrests and prosecutions of blacks—especially young black men. This is a gross injustice—the war on drugs has jailed thousands of nonviolent people but has done little to hinder the drug trade—but calling the racial disparity in arrest and incarceration a "new Jim Crow," while rhetorically dramatic, is misleading and distracts attention from the underlying causes of racial inequality.

At the same time, civil rights litigation and activism don't do enough to redress today's most serious social injustices, many of which aren't caused by overt prejudice or simple discrimination.

Inner-city blacks are more isolated from, and less likely to succeed in, the prosperous American mainstream than they were in the
1970s. Joblessness among blacks without a high school education is
higher than at any time in American history: in 2004, 72 percent of
black men who didn't finish high school were unemployed, and
more than half of inner-city black men don't finish high school. By
the time they reach their mid-thirties, roughly 60 percent of these
young men will have been incarcerated.[8] Women still earn about
seventy-five cents for every dollar men earn for comparable work.[9]
The unemployed elderly are more likely to stay that way than
younger job seekers, because of a complex set of economic and
institutional factors. The disabled still often lack access to jobs,
education, and public buildings—things that most of us take for
granted. Gay men and lesbians face widespread hostility and contempt. Despite over forty years of comprehensive civil rights enforcement, numerous new civil rights laws at the federal, state, and
local levels extending entitlements to an increasing number of new
groups, countless costly and acrimonious lawsuits, and the con-
stant drumbeat of civil rights activism, these problems remain stubbornly entrenched.

We should extend new civil rights to some groups, such as gay
men and lesbians, who suffer from prejudice that is often analogous
to that suffered by racial minorities and women. But civil rights are a
poor fit for many social problems, however dire they may be. For instance, the disabled must overcome many impediments to participate in public life and the job market, but most of those impediments
have little to do with bias against them. As a result, laws prohibiting
discrimination against the disabled have been, at best, an awkward
and piecemeal solution to the problems that most disabled people
face. At the same time, they have allowed a few aggressive claimants
to demand personal advantages at public expense. Similarly, civil
rights laws that prohibit discrimination on the basis of age have not
significantly improved the employment prospects of elderly job seekers, but they have distorted the labor market to the benefit of an

already privileged group of older workers—a result that few of the early supporters of those laws could have predicted and even fewer could defend.

Civil rights haven't been a panacea for the illness of social inequality, but like a patient who pops even more pills when the prescription isn't working, we're now at risk of an overdose. Civil rights litigation has exploded, far outpacing the growth in civil litigation generally: in 1991 the federal courts heard about eighty-three hundred employment discrimination cases; in 2000 they heard over twenty-two thousand. Civil rights laws, properly framed and limited, serve a vital social purpose, but too many civil rights can be as bad as too few, and an overused or overly aggressive civil rights regime can be as bad as an ineffectual one.

Rights go wrong when we lose sight of their highest purposes. Too many people think of rights only as entitlements to be exploited to the maximum extent possible, ignoring the civility that is indispensable to a responsible exercise of civil rights. Civil rights make sense only as part of a social contract of mutual respect and cooperation among citizens, where the rights of others and the common good are as important as personal entitlements. And many of today's social injustices are not simple problems of bigotry, and they will not respond to shrill demands or yield to inflexible legal rules. In fact, rigid rules and self-righteous accusations often reinforce the problems. To address these issues, we need more flexible interventions, guided by good judgment, civility, and public-spiritedness. In order to live up to the legacy of the civil rights movement, we must both renew our commitment to civil rights, and move beyond them.

Rights in Recent History

Today's civil rights are a product of struggles for racial justice that grew and matured throughout the twentieth century, and the social upheavals of the 1960s. The social movements of the 1960s challenged prejudices, social hierarchies, and repressive cultural norms in almost every part of American society. Racism, male chauvinism, sexual repression, geopolitical aggression, the Calvinist work ethic, institutional bureaucracy, the mass media, and organized religion all came under withering scrutiny and ferocious attack. The challenges presented by the civil rights movement, the antiwar movement, modern feminism, and what came to be known as the counterculture forced American society to become more inclusive, tolerant, informal, and nurturing. Conservative nostalgia notwithstanding, very few Americans today would wish to live in the society of the 1950s or in the society that would exist today had the social cataclysms of the 1960s not had their effect.

The civil rights that developed in the postwar decades reflected this history. A potent combination of constitutional interpretation and federal legislation dismantled the formal supports of Jim Crow racism. The emergent legal support for antiracism quickly inspired analogous civil rights claims on behalf of women, the disabled, the elderly, and gay men and lesbians. These rights were implemented, with various degrees of success, through judicial interpretation of constitutional principles, federal civil rights legislation, state laws, and local ordinances. Religious liberties were refigured to include nondogmatic and even nontheistic spiritual practices. And at the same time, the separation of church and state was more rigidly enforced to prohibit previously accepted practices, such as prayer in public schools. Sexual liberation and feminism inspired legal rights to contraception and abortion. The long, hot summers of the 1960s led to new rights protecting against police brutality.

But the social changes of the 1960s were not all for the better. The erosion of established, if unjust, hierarchies left people insecure and uncertain of their place in society. Malaise and ennui became widespread. Vague and unfocused paranoid resentment erupted into violence, in antisocial movements on both the left and the right such as the Weathermen, the Symbionese Liberation Army, and the neo-Nazis, and in psychologically demented individuals such as

Charles Manson and San Francisco's "Zodiac" serial murderer. The countercultural critiques of conventional morality, the work ethic, and bureaucracy easily became a justification for self-indulgence and aimless belligerence: the idealistic counterculture of the 1960s aged badly and became the self-righteous and narcissistic "Me Generation" of the 1970s. The decline of mainline organized religion left a void, which was filled by crackpot spiritual movements, exploitative cults, and charismatic charlatans. Widespread antiwar sentiment eroded the prestige of the military—one of the few institutions that could join Americans of all races and social classes in a collective national effort. Civil rights provided ballast to the cultural conservatism, conventional bigotry, and stifling social conformity of postwar America—the rebellious, erotic, and inclusive counterculture was a welcome alternative to the suburban Babbitt and the urban lonely crowd. But countercultural norms also amplified the quixotic radicalism, antisocial aggression, and self-indulgence that grew in American society as unprecedented affluence and mobility collided with widespread anomie and social dislocation.

Meanwhile, throughout the 1970s, 1980s, and 1990s, globalization and automation radically changed America's labor market. Automated manufacturing and offshore labor replaced many secure and good-paying unionized jobs. The new postindustrial economy grew mainly at the high and low ends: polished, college-educated people could find lucrative work in finance, business, and the medical and legal professions. Everyone else scrambled for a dwindling number of good blue-collar jobs, and many were forced into low-wage, part-time, or seasonal work in a growing service sector. Most of these new jobs had less well-defined qualifications than the typical blue-collar job; instead of formal certification or verifiable proficiency, they required "people skills" and an amorphous "professionalism." Layoffs became as common as the change in the seasons, and job insecurity was the norm except among civil servants, tenured educators, and federal judges. These changes coincided with the unraveling of the social safety net. As welfare benefits shrank or were limited during the 1980s and 1990s, long-term joblessness could leave one utterly destitute. Not coincidentally, "the homeless" became a household term as thousands of Americans sought shelter in doorways and under bridges.

Civil rights laws, once the refuge of the most marginal, exploited, and despised, became potential guarantors of job security for millions of formerly comfortable middle-class Americans. Employment discrimination laws effectively formed an incomplete patchwork of protection against wrongful termination: the growing list of prohibited forms of discrimination under federal, state, and local laws, combined with reverse-discrimination cases, meant that almost every employee had a potential civil rights claim. Consequently, civil rights litigation grew at an unexpected pace throughout the 1980s and 1990s: by 2000, employment discrimination cases occupied fully 10 percent of the federal civil docket.[10]

Courts have struggled to limit the growth of civil rights litigation; as a result, employment discrimination plaintiffs lose at trial more often than any other group of civil plaintiffs, and their relatively few victories are more likely than most to be reversed on appeal.[11] As civil rights laws have been stretched thin to cover almost every type of unfairness, they are less able to bear the weight of the most severe social injustices: for instance, after forty years civil rights laws haven't significantly improved job opportunities for unemployed racial minorities, elderly people, or the disabled. Pressed into more widespread service, civil rights law soon lost the once-commonsensical association with the most severe and socially destructive forms of social hierarchy and prejudice. And the more indiscriminate use of civil rights spread from employment to other areas of social and political conflict. Detached from historical context and specific social goals, civil rights were too often used to bypass both market discipline and the democratic process and advance almost any individual interest, political agenda, or partisan scheme.

Inspired by the stylistically tough activism of the Black Power movement, the cushier aesthetics of Me Generation self-actualization, and the romantic nationalism of the nineteenth century, multiculturalists sought to extend civil rights laws to "cultural difference" in the 1980s and 1990s. In its cruder iterations, legal multiculturalism held that racial groups were defined by their distinctive cultural norms and practices: for example, black culture comprised Ebonics, "colored people's time," hip-hop clothing styles, braided hairstyles, and dreadlocks. It seemed to follow that discrimination on the basis of these styles, affectations, and habits was as bad as discrimination on the basis of race. Legal multiculturalism drew on a strong psychotherapeutic strand in civil rights activism, which focused less on tangible economic or political injury than on self-esteem and dignity. Multiculturalists insisted that because minority cultural practices were essential to individual identity and self-worth, a society that favored dominant cultural norms and practices was not only narrow but unjust. Multiculturalists were among the first to grapple with the challenges of porous national borders, global mobility, and an ethnically diverse society, but the civil rights approach to these challenges supplied simplistic and formulaic answers to complex questions. The application of the civil rights model to "culture" treated contestable political conflicts over norms and morality and struggles over the distribution of resources as civil rights violations with perpetrators and victims. Although the legal multiculturalist project was largely unsuccessful in inspiring law reform, it reflected and reinforced the expansion of civil rights laws into domains better managed by the more mundane institutions of the market economy and popular politics.

Why Do Rights Go Wrong?

Rights occupy a special place in American culture and in the American legal system. A right is a distinctive type of legal, political, social, and moral claim. There's a big difference between saying "I deserve this job" and "I have a right to this job" or between complaining "It's not fair that I'm being prosecuted for such a minor offense" and "The prosecutor has violated my civil rights." There's also an important difference between a public policy that's designed to improve the lot of women, racial minorities, or the disabled and a civil right to equal treatment. The distinctive features of rights are an important part of our culture and legal system: rights can provoke needed social change and prevent expedient capitulation to powerful agents of injustice and exploitation. But the distinctive features of rights also make them the wrong tool for many jobs. At their best, civil rights help bring people together as equals, in common projects and shared institutions. At worst, civil rights can hinder or undermine sound policy, fracture society into mutually antagonistic tribes, and encourage selfish and irresponsible individualism. They can even begin to undermine the egalitarian efforts they were designed to further.

Rights as a Secular Religion

Rights are a secular religion for many Americans. Like religious faith, they offer moral certainty and emphasize the importance of individual personality—an antidote to selfish nihilism and chilly materialism. This similarity is no accident: modern legal rights evolved from the natural rights tradition, which first derived rights from theological authority. The earliest and most powerful accounts of human rights are inseparable from religious faith: Thomas Paine defended the French Declaration of the Rights of Man as the codification of "a compact between God and Man . . . [that] cannot be changed, or any ways altered by any human laws or human authority";[12] and of course, the American Declaration of Independence begins with the confident observation that "all Men . . . are endowed by their Creator with certain unalienable Rights." This close connection between rights and religion was obscured, but not broken, by the scientific revolution's corrosive effect on theological certainties and the cultural liberalization and anomie that emboldened

modern philosophers to write God's obituary. The civil rights movement of the twentieth century was an indispensably religious
movement: its most important and charismatic leaders were minis-
ters; its anthems, hymns; its vernacular, gospels; its manifestos,
sermons and scripture. Most of all, the tenacity and courage with
which its adherents pursued justice must be credited to their faith in
a power superior to that which they challenged.

But religion has a dark side: the same faith that inspires great
deeds and unearthly devotion to a cause can also provoke unjustified certainty, inflexible conviction, the blind vindictiveness of the
crusade, and an unexamined deference to all-too-earthly authori-
ties. As a result, quasi-religious activists exploit the desperate faith
of the most vulnerable black communities, using the legacy of the
civil rights movement and the authority of the divine to enrich and
aggrandize themselves at the expense of both civility and those they
claim to represent. Civil rights have inspired some of the most important humanitarian efforts in modern history, such as the abolition of
slavery, the struggle for women's suffrage, and the dismantling of the
Jim Crow racial hierarchy. But more complex and morally ambiguous
social problems require a modesty, intellectual suppleness, and ex-
perimental pragmatism that rights—like religion—tend to discourage. Rights provoke undue faith in categorical thinking and simplistic
"right answers," but the vexing and persistent social justice problems
of today demand context-specific analysis and a careful weighing of
multiple options. When a conflict or problem is defined as a "matter
of civil rights," pragmatic virtues can come to took like moral faults:
willingness to compromise becomes "selling out"; modesty about
one's position becomes a contemptible lack of faith; looking at the
question from all sides becomes a type of apostasy. Civil rights thinking encourages the stiffening of backs and the clenching of fists—a
good stance against spinelessness and cowardice, but the wrong
posture when flexibility and openness are needed.

Rights Offer False Hope of Political
Change Without Politics

Rights can correct discrete and specific social injustices by requiring specific people to do specific things: bigots can be ordered to eliminate discriminatory policies; lechers can be forbidden to extract sexual favors from their employees. But social problems that have multiple causes require far-reaching, complex, and cumbersome institutional reform and choices among controversial alternative policies. Rights offer no guidance for such comprehensive institutional reform; to the contrary, they seem to promise discrete improvements in equity and fairness without the need for holistic social change. In this sense, rights try to split the difference between revolutionary change and timid acquiescence in the status quo. This makes rights attractive to those who find many aspects of daily social and political life disagreeable, but fear or despair of achieving dramatic change. But with rare exceptions, rights cannot change deep-seated institutional and cultural injustices without changing the institutions and culture in which they are rooted. As a result, rights hold out the false hope of political change without the messiness and controversy of politics, yielding either disappointment when the anticipated change doesn't occur or frustration when the discord of politics accompanies it.

Rights Encourage Moralizing at the Expense
of Pragmatic Problem Solving

Americans are pragmatists by temperament: we excel at finding workable solutions to specific problems. We are also a nation of zealots prone to crusades, proselytizing, and moralistic condemnation. At its best, the civil rights movement harnessed the energy of moral outrage to pragmatic legal and policy reform. But sometimes moralism takes the reins and pulls us away from workable policies. When moralism overwhelms pragmatism, we often go to extremes, adopting punitive and ham-fisted measures that make matters worse.

Contrast the ignoble experiment of Prohibition (and the failed war on drugs) with today's more measured and nuanced approach to alcohol-related problems; or consider the abortion controversy, where rigid absolutism on both sides has led to a counterproductive stalemate that leaves many desperate pregnant women without viable options *and* results in preventable terminations of viable pregnancies.

Civil rights advocates, focused on culpable bigots, aggrieved victims, and violated entitlements, too often reject analyses that don't satisfy righteous indignation and eschew potentially effective indirect solutions. For instance, when activists insist that racial imbalances in criminal justice are the equivalent of Jim Crow racism, they reinforce the conviction of the already converted but alienate well-meaning people sincerely concerned about crime; by contrast, a pragmatic approach might focus on the irrational and ineffective drug-sentencing laws responsible for much of the problem. Similarly, racial minorities and women are underrepresented in many jobs and professions, and there's little doubt that discrimination and other subtler biases play a role, but it's unfair to condemn an individual employer without specific proof of wrongdoing. A pragmatic approach would often suspend the moral judgment implicit in current civil rights claims and look to cooperative approaches and public policies that might increase diversity in segregated workplaces.

Rights Encourage Absolutism at the Expense of Common Sense

Rights against race discrimination were designed to reverse the effects of slavery and Jim Crow segregation. Rights against sex discrimination were created to break open bastions of male exclusivity and put the sexes on an equal footing in the modern economy. Rights to religious liberty were developed in response to bloody religious conflicts and ruthless religious persecution. These civil rights are designed to help build an integrated and harmonious society, and they still serve a vital purpose today. But legal rights can come unmoored from such laudable purposes. More so than other laws, rights are especially prone to drift away from their best practical purposes because they are expressed and understood in absolute terms. This allows opportunists to exploit rights for selfish and anti-social ends and leads the credulous to suspend good judgment and common sense for the sake of rigid and inflexible mandates. For instance, some activists insist that the right to be free from sex discrimination means that men and women must share public restrooms, and today the right to be free of race discrimination prevents employers from considering race in order to *avoid* discrimination.

Too often, today's legal culture celebrates the most socially destructive and unreasonable demands. Like a group of drunken fraternity brothers competing to perform the most dangerous and outrageous stunt, lawyers, legal scholars, and civil rights activists strive to outdo each other in developing the most extreme and expansive interpretations of legal entitlements. Too many activists and lawyers attack unobjectionable customs and sensible practices that offend only the most expansive and uncompromising interpretation of the law. In defiance of the ancient prescription *de minimis non curat lex* (the law must not bother with trifles), they make a federal case of minor inconveniences and trivial inequities. They press for changes that will cost far more than they are worth, and they seek to transform carefully moderated regulations into burdensome and crippling mandates.

Rights Encourage Narcissism and Extremism

Over two hundred years ago the English philosopher Jeremy Bentham complained that rights were often little more than "bawling upon paper"—an especially uncompromising and shrill way of asserting a preference. He would find ample evidence for the complaint today. Extremist crusaders and radical zealots, having failed in the marketplace of ideas, press their unpopular social agendas in court. Belligerent crackpots, angry misfits, and resentful losers insist that their rights have been violated when they find themselves at odds with their neighbors and fellow citizens. Antisocial malcontents turn their personal gripes into a federal case if they can find a link—however tenuous—to a legal entitlement. The nation's court dockets are cluttered with silly, trivial, and mean-spirited lawsuits based on ambiguous, perverse, or overbroad interpretations of civil rights. And even people without a remotely plausible legal argument find undeserved solace in newly contrived rights, which they imagine vindicate a growing number of unrealistic demands. Dubious civil rights claims span the ideological spectrum. Radical feminists, conservative activists, multiculturalists, pet owners, bicyclists, competitive students, and wealthy corporate executives all crowd the dockets of the nation's courts and vie for the attention of the court of public opinion, recasting both debatable claims and patently unreasonable demands in terms of civil rights.

The legal culture of rights extremism is reinforced by popular culture. Self-help, personal growth, and self-actualization are as important to Americans today as redemption, virtue, and salvation were to our more religious ancestors. The resulting conflation of self-obsession with personal virtue breeds the solipsism and self-righteousness that inspire wrongheaded claims of right. The powerful and privileged complain of minor and ambiguous slights, and political hacks of all stripes exploit the legacy of the civil rights movement for partisan advantage. The rhetoric of civil rights has provided a convenient vehicle, if not an official apologia, for a culture of entitlement, self-obsession, and self-righteousness that warps popular politics and poisons popular culture. Today, a popular and legal culture of entitlement threatens both social harmony and material well-being. In the courts and on the streets, we all suffer when rights go wrong.

Civil Rights "Occupy the Field" of Social Justice

When a federal law is a comprehensive and exclusive approach to a problem, leaving no room for state or local legislation on the same issue, lawyers say it has "occupied the field." Civil rights have effectively "occupied the field" of social justice, crowding out alternative ways of thinking and new solutions. Rights against discrimination on the basis of age, disability, sexual orientation, height, weight, and physical appearance followed hard on the heels of the right not to suffer race, sex, and religious discrimination created by the omnibus civil rights legislation of the 1960s. Today, it's hard to think of a social cause that isn't framed in terms of rights, and a growing number of social groups seek to define themselves as embattled or despised minorities in order to qualify for civil-rights-inspired public sympathy, if not formal legal entitlements. Civil rights are an important part of many social justice struggles, but they are subject to the law of diminishing returns: rights can offer limited improvements in a narrow set of circumstances, but the effectiveness of the civil rights approach diminishes and its costs increase as it is applied to more novel, complex, and elusive social problems. Those working for social justice all too often eschew the difficult and unpleasant task of popular persuasion, lured by the false hope of a shortcut by way of judicially mandated civil rights. And even policy reform pursued through the democratic process often takes the form of new civil rights. It's now common to think of individual entitlements as the most effective way to attack social injustice. Few remember that when the Civil Rights Act was passed, enforcement by private individuals was a second-best compromise that the act's strongest supporters feared would make the new law ineffectual. They were right to be afraid: the most disadvantaged victims of America's long-lived racial hierarchy, trapped in poverty-stricken ghettos and quarantined in prisons, have enjoyed few of the benefits of civil rights legislation.

What we could call "rights consciousness" occupies a larger part of our culture than ever before. The rights to life, liberty, and the pursuit of happiness seem almost quaint in a field crowded with novel and ambitious new rights. International human rights, conceived as a response to torture and genocide, also aspire to guarantee a smorgasbord of substantive goods and social services, including housing, medical care, dignified employment, and cultural integrity. The Bill of Rights of the U.S. Constitution has inspired the Taxpayer Bill of Rights, the Airline Passenger Bill of Rights, the Consumer Bill of Rights (a telling reflection of our national priorities), and the Pizza Lover's Bill of Rights (ditto). Each of these new rights is inspired by a laudable and important aspiration (with the possible exception of pizza). But is the language and logic of rights the best way to think through or address all of these concerns? And what does it say about public confidence in political institutions and our relationships with our fellow citizens that we pursue so many of our goals and imagine so much of our lives in terms of formal entitlements?

In this book I'll explain in detail how the civil rights tradition took such unexpected and destructive detours—and how we can get it back on course. In Chapters One through Four, I'll look at four wrong turns in today's civil rights thinking, and in Chapter Five, I'll point a possible way back to the straight-and-narrow path toward social justice.

 1. Civil rights are supposed to prevent—or at least counterbalance—the prejudices and discrimination that deny some people a fair chance for a good livelihood and a good life. The unpopular, the despised, and the unsuccessful need rights protecting them from an unsympathetic majority and an unforgiving economy. In a sense, civil rights invert the typical indicia of virtue and merit: social contempt and failure become virtues in the sense that they test society's commitment to rights. For those who suffer contempt because of reflexive prejudice and who fail because of ill-considered social exclusion or exploitation, rights are invaluable and fragile guarantors of social justice. But rights also shelter the truly contemptible and reward those who deserve failure. Rights nurture some of the most antisocial and dysfunctional tendencies in our society, protecting them from the social and economic pressures that would otherwise discourage and contain them. And too often, people use rights to get an edge in the job market or other competitions for scarce resources. Rights go wrong when individuals or political pressure groups use them to bypass the democratic process or to undo the normal incentives and rewards of a market economy. Rather than a guarantee of basic fairness, rights can become an *entitlement to advantage*.

Chapter One will examine the growing number of such entitlements. How can we tell the difference between balancing the scales and putting a thumb on one side? The seriously disabled need special accommodation in order to participate in the mainstream of society, but people with loosely defined and mild learning disabilities have demanded and secured competitive advantages—such as extra time on academic tests and one-on-one tutoring in overtaxed public schools—that give them an edge in a zero-sum struggle for resources and prestige. Bias and unexamined customs make it hard for older people to find work, but age discrimination laws have become a windfall for well-paid older professionals and executives with secure employment while doing little to improve opportunities for jobless older people. In high-stakes competition for good schools, good jobs, and the good life, when is asking for a hand up a way of getting the upper hand?

2. The civil rights tradition encourages us to look at disputes through a lens that is designed to focus on discrimination. In fact, the legal and cultural stigma now attached to "discrimination" is so powerful that the very word is almost synonymous with bigotry. The focus on discrimination made sense in the context of Jim Crow, where racists exploited blacks and established a hierarchy of birth based on a rigid and formal distinction between the races. But today racial injustice is much more complex: formal race discrimination is rare, and the effort to shoehorn problems such as residential isolation, joblessness, incarceration, and a dysfunctional culture of poverty into the category of "discrimination" has made it harder to analyze and address these problems.

Chapter Two will make the case that civil rights shouldn't always outlaw *discriminating tastes*. Emboldened by the early successes of the civil rights approach, lawyers, judges, and activists have tried to make a host of diverse and complex social problems fit the discrimination mold. Describing vexing and complex conflicts over values and resources as discrimination makes it harder for us to address them appropriately. Turning discrimination into a general term of opprobrium leads us to condemn reasonable distinctions based on salient facts. The obsession with discrimination went to self-consuming extremes when in 2009 the Supreme Court said it was illegal race discrimination to consider race in order to avoid discrimination. And civil rights have become so closely tied to discrimination, it seems to follow that anything that can't be blamed on discrimination can't be a civil rights issue.

3. Like a poorly trained guard dog, civil rights have a nasty tendency to turn against their wards, undermining the causes they were supposed to serve. It can be hard to get them back on leash because rights—unlike mundane public policies—are supposed to reflect timeless and immutable moral principles, rather than specific goals that can be revisited and revised in response to changing needs and conditions. And when courts remove contentious social questions from politics, they can short-circuit needed social dialogue and provoke backlash, hindering or stalling more important changes in attitudes and norms. This is why rights can be prime examples of the *unintended consequences of the law*.

Chapter Three will look at the unintended consequences of civil rights laws. The right to equal protection of the laws was originally established in the aftermath of the crimes of slavery and later evoked against Jim Crow segregation in *Brown v. Board of Education*. But a rigid civil rights approach to school desegregation provoked backlash. Worse, it established an inflexible absolutism that now prevents public school districts from pursing racial *integration* and undermines the attempts of Congress and the states to promote racial justice. Laws against sex harassment undermine sexist stereotypes and help women work alongside men as equals. But taken to extremes, they impede cordial relations between the sexes and put women on a protective pedestal, reinforcing Victorian-era notions of female vulnerability and frailty. Civil rights can protect vulnerable minorities from a tyranny of the majority and reverse the damage caused by bigotry. But, like radiation therapy, rights are strong medicine with unpredictable side effects, best used only when milder interventions prove ineffective.

4. As the civil rights movement recedes into the canon of American heroism, it inspires nostalgia for more profound and well-defined challenges and for galvanizing events around which to organize an increasingly fractured black community. As a result, many racial justice activists seek out and even invent racial crises or confrontations, which provide the "look and feel" of the civil rights movement—such as the Jena Six protest—but often without the moral clarity or practical aspirations. The language of civil rights was a comfortable fit for the worst of the excesses of the counterculture and the Me Generation: it wasn't hard for narcissists to see almost any personal belief or selfish desire as sufficiently profound to deserve civil rights protection. Rights against invidious discrimination protected society's downtrodden and persecuted minorities from injustices at the hands of a belligerent majority, but antisocial paranoids of all stripes came to see themselves as a beleaguered minority group. The moralism of civil rights language came loose from its religious moorings and was free to latch onto any ideological conviction or social practice. Americans today have a neurotic tendency to treat *activism as therapy*.

Chapter Four will put social activism on the therapist's couch. The march to free the Jena Six adopted the posture of the freedom riders from the safety of the twenty-first century—more an exercise in nostalgia than a focused social protest. It followed the lead of the Million Man March, which aped the symbolism of 1963's historic March on Washington but lacked the political goals that could make that symbolism meaningful. Such politically aimless activism reaches absurd extremes in "Critical Mass" demonstrations, where bicyclists commandeer the streets of San Francisco and other major cities in a social protest that has devolved into an antisocial indulgence. Demonstrations, marches, rallies, and public protests are a rite of spring on the nation's college campuses and in its major cities—a countercultural affectation as commonplace as ripped jeans and often about as practical. Social protest in the United States has become an interminable psychotherapy session, which yields neither insight nor effective solutions.

Meanwhile, a new generation of black politicians—of whom President Barack Obama is exemplary—have found it better to wield power than to fight it, offering new hope for practical and public-spirited solutions to long-suffered social injustices. Whether they can fulfill their promise remains to be seen, but their cool-headed pragmatism is a welcome change from the attitude of permanent ressentiment that characterizes many social activists.

It's time to rethink and reform the civil rights approach to social justice, which reached its high point sometime in the early 1970s and has been in decline ever since. Conservative judges have watered down or reversed some of its most important practical commitments, and changing race relations have made many of its assumptions anachronistic. Worst of all, civil rights have proven to be utterly inadequate to confront today's most severe social inequities; in some cases, they have been downright counterproductive.

In Chapter Five, I'll explore why today's job markets, popular culture, and politics have left civil rights behind and suggest how some lesser-known civil rights ideas might make them more relevant, less burdensome to legitimate enterprises, and less subject to abuse. If we're willing to put social justice ahead of individual entitlements, we can bring the promise of the civil rights movement into the new millennium. Scaling back individual claims may seem a bitter pill to some, but the costs of self-centered rights gone wrong are even harder to swallow. Today's civil rights are ripe for abuse by extremists and opportunists. They have not provided a clear prescription for social change, and as a result, they have offered false hope to social justice advocates and to the public at large. They have siphoned energy away from more promising engines of progress, and they are increasingly used to undermine the very causes they were originally supposed to serve. We can prevent the abuses and reverse the setbacks if we replace the culture of selfish entitlement with the ethos of social responsibility and common purpose that must underlie any meaningful guarantee of rights. To secure social justice in the twenty-first century, we must put the civility back into civil rights.

1

Entitlement and Advantage

Now you want me to tell you my opinion on autism . . . ? A fraud, a racket. For a long while we were hearing that every minority child had asthma . . . Why was there an asthma epidemic amongst minority children? Because I'll tell you why: the children got extra welfare if they were disabled, and they got extra help in school. It was a money racket . . . Now the illness du jour is autism. You know what autism is? I'll tell you what autism is. In 99 percent of the cases, it's a brat who hasn't been told to cut the act out. That's what autism is . . . Everybody has an illness . . . Stop with the sensitivity training. You're turning your son into a girl and you're turning your nation into a nation of losers.

On July 16, 2008, the radio talk show host Michael Savage managed to offend parents of disabled children, racial minorities, and women in less than a minute and a half—an accomplishment that his rivals Rush Limbaugh and Glenn Beck can only aspire to. The group Autism United demonstrated in front of the New York radio station that carries Savage's program. One of his sponsors, the insurance company Aflac, promptly gave Savage some unwelcome sensitivity training: it pulled its advertising from his program, explaining that the company found "his recent comments about autistic children to be both inappropriate and insensitive." Criticism was almost unanimous among doctors, child psychologists, disability rights advocates, parents, and pundits alike. Several local stations dropped Savage's program in response to public outrage.

Savage is a provocateur—deliberately insulting and extreme, with a loose regard for factual accuracy. According to the clinical psychologist Catherine Lord, autism is "just like epilepsy or . . . diabetes or a heart condition. [Savage's comments are] like blaming the child with a heart condition for not being able to exercise."[1] Savage eventually backpedaled, saying his remarks were "hyperbole," designed to draw attention to the problem of fraudulent diagnosis. He agreed to devote another show to the subject so that parents of autistic children and others could air dissenting views.

Savage, like Limbaugh and Beck, is conservative and contentious, but he is also idiosyncratic—often unexpectedly thoughtful, even cerebral. While Limbaugh and Beck are activists for conservative politicians and causes, Savage is distinguished by a kind of crotchety ennui. As contemptuous of other conservatives as he is of liberals (he called Glenn Beck a "hemorrhoid with eyes"), he treats partisan politics with an aloof disdain: "You'll have to go to one of the other talk-show hosts to get 'Obama's a Ma-a-arxist' and 'McCain is a wa-a-ar hero.'"[2] As a result, where other conservative talk show hosts are annoyingly predictable, Savage's off-the-cuff ramblings and intemperate tirades are often surprising and intriguing, and they often contain at least a grain of truth. For instance, Dr. Lord admitted that mild autism is vaguely defined and can be a catchall diagnosis for children with behavioral problems who fit no other category. A year and a half after Savage's remarks, the psychiatrists in charge of writing the fifth edition of the *Diagnostic and Statistical Manual of Mental Disorders* announced that they were considering folding several types of mild autism—such as

Asperger's syndrome and pervasive developmental disorder—into a single broad category—autism spectrum disorder—reflecting a new understanding that autism is not a single disorder but rather a range of conditions, from severe mental disabilities to mild emotional abnormalities that can come with extraordinary mental gifts.

There's a professional consensus that severe autism is a discrete neurobiological condition, but mild cases can be hard to distinguish from less well-defined conditions, such as attention deficit hyperactivity disorder (ADHD) and other vaguely defined "learning disabilities." Here, diagnosis is difficult and contestable, and expert opinions differ. "We're fairly good about making the diagnosis of kids who are classically autistic, but as you move away from that specific disorder, it gets harder . . . [F]or kids who are of average, close to average or above average intelligence, it is difficult to sort out what is eccentricity versus what is a real social deficit," said Dr. Lord.[3]

Federal law doesn't reflect a continuum that includes mild autism and learning disabilities along with eccentricity and poor concentration. For legal purposes, a disability is a discrete condition: either you have it, and therefore have a right to an array of special concessions and extra help, or you don't. The law doesn't define learning disabilities with precision, but it does provide a partial definition: "a severe discrepancy between achievement and intellectual ability."[4] In practice, this means that learning disabilities are diagnosed, in large part, by identifying a gap between a child's performance in academic settings and the performance one would expect of a child of his or her age and IQ.

Civil rights laws entitle *all* disabled people to special accommodations and services: a blind person might require an exam to be administered orally or written in Braille; a paraplegic might require voice-recognition software or transcription. These accommodations let the disabled reach their potential. Children with learning disabilities are also legally entitled to accommodations and services that other children are not, such as special tutoring and extra time on exams. In theory, just as a blind person needs Braille, a Seeing Eye dog, or a cane to overcome his blindness, a person with ADHD may need extra time to get organized and overcome his inability to concentrate.

But there are some important differences between severe disabilities like blindness and milder learning and behavioral disabilities. First, conspicuous disabilities often trigger reflexive animus or prejudice. Many employers wrongly assume disabled people can't work, and businesses discriminate against them because of squeamishness and irrational aversion. A business that refuses to accommodate a disabled person might secretly wish to exclude him. Milder disabilities don't trigger such reflexive prejudice because, for the most part, they are not conspicuous: typically an employer learns of a learning or an emotional disability only when an employee seeks an accommodation for it. Second, most of the accommodations that people with severe disabilities need wouldn't help a nondisabled person at all. A sighted person wouldn't benefit from having an exam written in Braille; an able-bodied person wouldn't get much of an edge from using voice-recognition software or a professional transcriber. By contrast, people with learning and emotional disabilities often enjoy extra time on competitive exams, costly one-on-one tutoring, and exemptions from discipline for disruptive behavior—things that would benefit anyone. Finally, unlike blindness or a physical disability, many learning disabilities are hard to define objectively; as Dr. Lord admits, they are on a continuum with ordinary "eccentricity." Put these together and you have a recipe for gaming the system: no one would suggest that an eccentric person with a wandering mind has a right to extra time on a timed exam, but someone with ADHD does—and the two can be hard to distinguish. This doesn't suggest that civil rights for people with mild cognitive disabilities are a "racket," but it does suggest that they have the potential to encourage opportunism and can lead to unwarranted advantages.

Suppose two children achieve low scores on a competitive timed exam: one has a diagnosed learning disability, and the other doesn't. Suppose both of the children's scores would improve dramatically if they had extra time to complete the exam. Is it fair to give one student extra time and not the other? Maybe. In theory, the extra time isn't an advantage for the person with a learning disability; it's just the way he copes with his disability. But if the disability is on a continuum with garden-variety poor concentration, then in fairness *anyone* with poor concentration should be entitled to extra time in proportion to the severity of his concentration deficit. This would, of course, defeat the purpose of a timed exam, which is to test not only skills and knowledge but also the ability to perform quickly.

The Harvard medical student Sophie Currier became a heroine to advocates of breast-feeding in 2007 when she demanded and eventually won the right to a breast-pumping break during a medical licensing exam. No hothouse flower, Currier first took the exam—widely considered to be one of the most challenging of all professional qualification exams—when eight months pregnant and came just short of a passing score. Currier chose to nurse her newborn baby as most experts in the medical profession she was poised to join recommend. But she still needed to pass the exam in order to start her residency at Massachusetts General in the fall. So she asked the National Board of Medical Examiners to give her a break—specifically, an extra hour each day to express and store her breast milk. The board refused, informing Currier that it would accommodate only disabilities as defined by the Americans with Disabilities Act.

Currier wasn't the first woman to get a less-than-nurturing reaction to her nursing. Until recently, nursing an infant in public was considered indecent exposure and could result in citation or even arrest. Businesses and employers not only refused to accommodate nursing mothers but often deliberately embarrassed them or asked them to leave. The problem isn't a relic of the era of three-martini lunches and cars with tail fins either. In October 2006, Emily Gillette was flying with her husband and twenty-two-month-old daughter on a Freedom Airlines flight from Burlington, Vermont. Freedom Airlines didn't give Gillette the freedom to feed her baby; instead, a flight attendant barked, "You need to cover up. You are offending me," and thrust a blanket into Gillette's hand. Gillette balked: "No thank you. I will not put a blanket on top of my child's head." The flight attendant kicked her off the flight. In response Gillette filed a complaint against the airline with the Vermont Human Rights Commission. Her story inspired over eight hundred women to stage a "nurse-in" at thirty-nine airline ticket counters nationwide.[5] This wasn't the first time lactation took on the character of social protest: a year earlier women staged a "nurse-in" in front of ABC studios after Barbara Walters spoke unapprovingly about a woman nursing her baby on a flight.

A growing number of women have decided that Mother Nature is a more wholesome provider than Gerber or Nestlé and nurse their newborns for a year or longer. In reaction to social squeamishness about breast-feeding and widespread ignorance of its many virtues, some have become "lactivists," proselytizing to pregnant women and young mothers about the benefits of the breast, lobbying for policy changes to accommodate nursing mothers, and agitating against inhospitable businesses and employers. Their goal is to reverse the decades-long trend toward bottle-feeding, which they see as the result of a conspiracy among hubristic scientists, perverse moralists who eroticize the female breast, and callous industrialists anxious to get new mothers back on assembly lines and behind desks. While breast-feeding was, for obvious reasons, almost universal before the Industrial Revolution, it declined throughout the twentieth century: by 1972 only 22 percent of American mothers nursed their infants.[6] Lactivists reject the notion of better living through technology and cite mounting evidence that breast-fed children are less susceptible to illness and emotionally healthier than those who receive only manufactured formula. Scandals involving contaminated baby formula and conspiracies to foist costly baby formula on an impoverished third world have only strengthened their resolve and increased their numbers.

Medical opinion has shifted decisively in favor of nursing: the American Academy of Pediatrics decided in 1997 to recommend that mothers breast-feed their infants for six months. The U.S. Department of Health and Human Services started a campaign to encourage breast-feeding. Public opinion followed quickly, and today bottle-feeding is tantamount to child abuse among the Bugaboo stroller set. As mothers found themselves caught between the old-school squeamishness of blanket-wielding prudes and a trendy new obligation to breast-feed, some feminists began to wonder whether the new ethos was a totem for women's liberation or a Trojan horse. Hanna Rosin complained in *The Atlantic*: "In Betty Friedan's day, feminists felt shackled to domesticity by the unreasonably high bar for housework, the endless dusting and shopping and pushing the Hoover around . . . When I looked at the picture on the cover of [Dr.] Sears's *Breastfeeding Book*—a lady lying down, gently smiling at her baby and *still in her robe*, although the sun is well up—the scales fell from my eyes: it was not the vacuum that was keeping me and my twenty-first-century sisters down, but another sucking sound."[7]

Nursing requires a significant commitment. Nursing mothers must either feed their children directly or express the milk every several hours; failure to do either can lead to painful engorgement, infections, and a reduction in the milk supply. The National Women's Health Information Center helpfully suggests to working mothers of newborns: "Let your employer know that you are breastfeeding and explain that, when you're away from your baby, you will need to take breaks throughout the day to pump . . . Ask where you can pump at work, and make sure it is a private, clean, quiet area . . . If your direct supervisor cannot help you with your needs . . . go to your Human Resources department to make sure you are accommodated."[8]

Or, failing that, go to court. *Sophie Currier v. National Board of Medical Examiners* wasn't even a close contest in the end. The National Board of Medical Examiners, with their creaky old rules and their hand-wringing about the integrity of their precious exam, didn't have a chance against the sisterhood of virtuous lactation—a powerful fusion of modern feminism and the Victorian cult of pure womanhood, backed by the American Academy of Pediatrics, with Angelina Jolie as glamorous spokesmodel. Currier lost her sex discrimination lawsuit at the trial court but won handily on appeal: Judge Gary Katzmann held that "in order to put the petitioner on equal footing as the male and non-lactating female examinees, she must be provided with sufficient time to pump breast milk."[9]

Pumping breast milk is time-consuming and uncomfortable: a machine must be assembled, the milk must be pumped, the machine must be cleaned so it's ready for next time (which will be roughly four hours later) and disassembled for storage, and the milk must be stored on ice so that it is still fit for the baby to drink later. This could easily consume the entire forty-five-minute standard break for the medical licensing exam, leaving Currier no time to eat or use the restroom. Pumping might not take the entire hour that Currier asked for, but any extra time wouldn't really give her an edge. She couldn't use it to think through or reconsider her answers, because the exam was administered in discrete blocks, and once a block was finished, the examinee could not return to it. The board's concern that the accommodation would compromise the exam seemed unwarranted: after all, Currier wasn't asking for extra time to take the exam itself.

But actually, she was. Currier had been diagnosed with ADHD and dyslexia; as an accommodation, she had demanded and received a full *eight hours* of additional exam time—double the normal limit. The board granted this request because ADHD and dyslexia are recognized disabilities within the definition of the Americans with Disabilities Act. Having failed the exam once even with the extra time, Currier had come back to the board with another demand for an additional accommodation.

It was starting to look as if Currier wanted to keep changing the rules until she passed. This may explain why relatively few feminists or lactivists took up her cause. Pondering the lack of support for Currier, *Slate*'s legal analyst Dahlia Lithwick complained that "if we can't stand up for a woman with a brilliant career who is fighting to care for her babies as she chooses . . . you really have to wonder if we can stand up for anyone at all," but worried that "it's harder to sympathize . . . when we learn that she is already getting a whole extra day to take the test because she has ADHD and dyslexia, or that she received extra accommodation in her schooling as well . . . Suddenly . . . she isn't a pioneer for the rights of working moms. She's a crybaby and an opportunist."[10] This lack of sympathy was widely expressed on blogs and websites devoted to working mothers and lactation rights. "This woman is a disgrace," groused an anonymous commenter on a motherhood blog. "Not only has she failed the exam, she is expecting everyone else to fix her problems for her . . . I am a physician, a working, nursing mom, who passed her general and subspecialty boards (written and oral) while nursing without difficulty." On another site a nursing mother complained, "As a nursing mother who has managed to get through a LOT of daylong exams without whining . . . I can only say there is a limit to special entitlements . . . Ms. Currie [*sic*] is simply an example of entitlement gone too far." Another woman wrote, "While I sympathize with her for nursing . . . keep in mind that she did get lots of extra help [and didn't pass the first time] . . . Is there any chance of passing the 2nd time? Maybe, with the extra 2 days she has been given for a one day test, plus the extra time given for her to lactate . . . In a way, I am glad [she won] . . . now other people will get an awareness and learn how to get . . . perks . . . when going through the educational system."[11]

Doctors, on the whole, were even less sympathetic. One insisted: "The USMLE is a STANDARDIZED test to assess a minimum competency . . . If you don't pass, then the exam is doing what it was intended to do: preventing somebody without a core knowledge of medicine [from] practicing . . . When the patient dies on the table [because the doctor is too slow] who is going to be supporting her when her excuse is 'I needed to breast feed at that moment.'" Another echoed this macabre theme: "When your Father has a heart attack, do you want [someone who] is . . . practicing only because he/she was granted 3 months of time to pass his licensing exam while every other MD passed it in 8 hours?"[12]

Few observers bothered to distinguish between the accommodations Currier received for her disabilities and those she received to pump. Currier's supporters typically treated the extra eight hours she received due to her dyslexia and ADHD as irrelevant: "If a man were to have ADHD and dyslexia . . . [and] were to also have cancer . . . he'd be given accommodations for his ADHD and dyslexia, *and* I would think that additional accommodations would be made for his cancer . . . as well." Her critics thought that each accommodation—regardless of the justification—compromised the integrity of the exam and gave Currier an unfair advantage: "Allowing some students to have a time advantage, no matter the reason, destroys the integrity of the exam."[13]

But there's a big difference between Currier's modest request for an extra break to pump and the extra eight hours of exam time she enjoyed as an accommodation of her disabilities. Perversely, federal civil rights law gave Currier an entitlement to the more extreme accommodation while leaving the modest request open to debate (Currier eventually got her pumping break under Massachusetts state law). Contrary to the complaints of her critics, letting Currier take an extra hour to pump doesn't compromise the exam much, if at all. The extra break is pretty close to the amount of time Currier would actually need to pump and store her milk— leaving her no better off than a non-lactating examinee. You might think that the extra time away from the test would give Currier a recuperation advantage, but any woman who has used a breast pump will tell you that it's not exactly relaxing or rejuvenating. Currier's critics often remarked that she won't be able to ask for extra time in the operating room, but unless she's lactating again when she needs to perform an eight-hour surgical procedure, she won't need to. The break simply compensates for the effects of a temporary condition that would otherwise depress Currier's test results and make the exam an inaccurate measure of her true abilities.

We can't say the same of the legally mandated accommodation for Currier's disabilities. ADHD and dyslexia are not temporary conditions. If they affect Currier's ability to take the exam, they will affect her ability to perform any similar task under time pressure. Of course, an exam isn't a perfect measure of real-life job skills: plenty of people who do poorly on exams excel in real-life situations, and just as many do well on exams and poorly on the job. But when used to test for minimum competence, the exams serve an important function: they are a cheap and efficient way to screen out the ill prepared and the incompetent. You'd be a fool to entrust your health to a doctor just because she had a high score on her medical boards, but you'd be a bigger fool to entrust it to someone who couldn't pass them. Here the morbid fantasies of Currier's critics are relevant: if Currier couldn't focus on a make-or-break professional exam because of her ADHD, will she be able to focus on a life-or-death time-sensitive medical procedure or complete a complex diagnosis? Perhaps Currier will choose a medical specialty where speed and concentration are never required. But if that's the reason to give her extra time, shouldn't anyone willing to limit himself to time-insensitive specialties get extra exam time?

Several federal laws prohibit discrimination against people with disabilities. The most important are the Rehabilitation Act, the

Americans with Disabilities Act, the Fair Housing Act, and the Individuals with Disabilities Education Act (IDEA). Together these laws cover employers, landlords, proprietors of public facilities, public schools, and any other organization that receives federal funding. The Rehabilitation Act and the Americans with Disabilities Act define a disability as a physical or mental impairment that substantially limits a major life activity. The IDEA adopts a similar definition but also specifically defines as learning disabled any child who fails to "achieve commensurate with his or her age and ability levels . . . [and] has a severe discrepancy between achievement and intellectual ability."[14]

The idea behind these laws is that the failure to accommodate a disability is a kind of discrimination. Before the 1970s most disabled people were excluded from meaningful social interaction and gainful employment. Blatant discrimination was the norm, and few institutions made any effort to be accessible to disabled people. The all-too-common view was that if someone was unable to attend school, enter public buildings, or hold jobs because of his handicap, it was a tragic fact of life about which nothing could be done.

Advocates for the disabled, inspired by the civil rights movement, began to challenge this widespread idea in the 1970s. They insisted that disabled people could lead productive lives without science-fiction technological cures if society made an effort to accommodate them. In fact, they argued, many disabled people suffered less from the natural consequences of their physical condition than from discriminatory practices and insensitive policies established in disregard of their needs. Many people were openly contemptuous of the disabled, insulted their dignity with condescension and pity, or avoided them out of an irrational squeamishness. And how different were the myriad subtler decisions made in callous ignorance of disabled people and their needs? A wheelchair-bound architect would never design a building with stairs as the only means of ingress and access to upper floors. A deaf school administrator would make sure teachers provided written as well as oral instruction. Just as discriminatory laws once excluded blacks, discriminatory employment standards, educational policies, and architectural design excluded the disabled.

Congress passed the first major law prohibiting discrimination against the disabled—the Rehabilitation Act—in 1973, prohibiting recipients of federal funding from discriminating. It passed the Education for All Handicapped Children Act banning discrimination in public education two years later. But these laws were too mild and too limited: the disabled remained locked out of the mainstream of the job market and public life. When Congress passed the Americans with Disabilities Act (ADA) in 1990, banning discrimination in employment and businesses open to the public, it found rampant discrimination against the disabled that had resulted in widespread unemployment and poverty in their ranks: "Two-thirds of all disabled Americans between the age of 16 and 64 are not working at all . . . Fifty percent of all adults with disabilities have household incomes of $15,000 or less. Among non-disabled persons [the figure is] only twenty-five percent."[15] The ADA forbids discrimination against people with disabilities and defines "discrimination" to include a failure to make "reasonable accommodations" of their disabilities. The simple nondiscrimination provisions require employers, landlords, and proprietors to treat disabled people as well as they treat people without disabilities. The accommodation provisions require employers, landlords, and proprietors to make special exceptions and take affirmative steps to help the disabled succeed.

The idea that disabled people were limited by laws, policies, and design rather than by their physical handicaps inspired a cumbersome but instructive nominal innovation: the disabled became "differently abled." For instance, the idea that blind people developed their other four senses to an almost superhuman degree was sufficiently mainstream by 1967 to serve as the premise of the Hollywood film *Wait Until Dark*. Audrey Hepburn played a blind woman who is terrorized by criminals looking for smuggled drugs. In the climactic sequence, her character fends off a knife-wielding man by plunging her apartment into darkness, giving her the advantage over her sighted assailant. In the same year the television police drama *Ironside* featured Raymond Burr as the retired detective Robert Ironside, who had been paralyzed by a sniper's bullet. Aided by a modified police van designed to accommodate his wheelchair, Ironside remained an ace sleuth, using his years of experience and intelligence to solve crimes his able-bodied colleagues couldn't crack. Under the right conditions, a handicap could be a strength.

Social movements for the disabled followed the lead of Black Power and turned what had been a cause for stigma into a source of power. And just as black pride matured into multiculturalism, with its vague but consistent implication that any social practice that was sufficiently widespread among a racial group was a part of that group's unique and precious "culture," some disability rights groups came to see their conditions and unique methods of coping as parts of a distinctive and precious culture as well. For instance, activists for the hearing impaired argued for the existence of a "deaf culture" grounded in sign language.[16] Some in the deaf culture movement rejected lip-reading as a demeaning form of assimilation. Some went as far as to reject hearing aids and other medical devices designed to restore lost hearing as an insult to deaf culture: these interventions implied that deafness is a defect to be fixed rather than a condition that gives rise to an equally valid and valuable alternative mode of interaction with the world.

Disability rights laws were inspired by the long-overdue recognition that disabled people could make valuable contributions if given the chance. But the laws could also give effect to a much more questionable claim: that disabilities are not in fact disabling, but simply define different, equally effective modes of perception and interaction. It follows from the stronger claim that any practical impediment to the full and equal interaction of disabled people is the result of some form of invidious discrimination: the wrongful hegemony of bipedal over alternative modes of locomotion prevents a wheelchair-bound paraplegic from easily entering a nineteenth-century building built with grand staircases; the unjust emphasis on concentration and speed keeps a person with ADHD from passing the medical licensing exam.

It can be hard to tell the difference between the natural limitations of a disability and limitations that are imposed or magnified by bigotry, callous indifference, and careless oversight. Until recently, most people assumed that the disabled were simply incapable of making valuable contributions to society, so very few things were designed to accommodate them. Often, minor changes could have accommodated disabled people at relatively little cost. Doors can be widened slightly to accommodate wheelchairs, written materials made available to the deaf to supplement an oral presentation, oral descriptions used to aid the blind. And these changes may inadvertently improve things for a much larger group of people: ramps designed to accommodate wheelchairs also help people with wheeled carts, baby strollers, and wheeled luggage; written supplements to an oral presentation benefit the large number of people who find spoken lectures hard to follow and remember. Rights for the disabled have improved public life dramatically by punishing irrational prejudice and encouraging everyone to rethink habitual practices.

But disabilities are disabling. No amount of design accommodation will allow a blind person to pilot an aircraft safely or help a person with Parkinson's disease to practice delicate surgery. And even when accommodation is possible, disability rights present difficult trade-offs: How much can we afford to change norms, rules, and physical infrastructure to help people with disabilities? Ramps and elevators to accommodate wheelchairs are expensive; remodeling older buildings can destroy their architectural character; Braille translations are costly and hard to acquire; closed-captioning isn't free. We've correctly decided to make the changes in many cases—but not all. The law requires that employers, landlords, and proprietors make "reasonable" accommodations, inviting a cost-benefit analysis. Courts often find that a disabled person is entitled to some accommodation, but not everything that he or she might want. To accommodate a wheelchair, an employer may have to remodel a bathroom but not a staff kitchen. New construction must be designed to accommodate the disabled, but older buildings can remain inaccessible until they are substantially remodeled. Employees must be able to perform the "essential functions of the job" in order to qualify for mandatory accommodations: that rules out the blind pilot and the surgeon with the shakes.

Unfortunately, thinking of these conflicts in terms of civil rights encourages claimants to ignore the necessity of tough decisions and trade-offs. Sophie Currier and her supporters consistently argued that her demands for accommodation were questions of simple fairness, as if there were no downside to changing the rules just for her. Judge Katzmann, for example, insisted that Currier's accommodations just put her "on an equal footing" with other examinees, and another Currier supporter was confident that the accumulation of special breaks didn't matter: someone with ADHD, dyslexia, and cancer should get extra time for all three conditions, she insisted.

There's a reasonable argument that fairness required giving Currier extra *break* time to pump. But there's also a strong argument that giving her two days to complete a time-sensitive exam doesn't put her on an "equal footing" with the examinees who had only eight hours; it gives her an advantage. The argument for this accommodation was that the exam was biased against Currier and the extra time only corrected the bias. But the exam was "biased" only if speedy performance is irrelevant. And in that case the exam is biased against *all examinees* who would have passed if they had had more time. If the speed limitation is arbitrary and misguided, the National Board of Medical Examiners should drop it entirely rather than make case-by-case exceptions.

There's a sound civil rights precedent for such an approach: Title VII of the Civil Rights Act requires an employer to abandon an employment practice that disproportionately screens out members of a minority group *and isn't job related*. But the employer has to drop the practice entirely—not suspend it or change it just for members of the minority group. On the other hand, if the practice *is* job related, the employer can use it regardless of its effect on minority groups.

It's a conceptual sleight of hand to define one person's inability to answer questions quickly and accurately as a disability that society must accommodate in order to reach the merits, when the same inability is considered a lack of merit for other people. This is especially true of a disability like ADHD, which many experts believe differs only in degree from what we might simply call a high-strung or absentminded personality trait. It makes little more sense to insist that exceptions to the normal rules simply "make up" for ADHD than it would to insist that an exam that favors smart people "discriminates" against the less intelligent. We all have unique natural strengths and weaknesses that make us better suited to some jobs than to others. Short people are at a disadvantage in basketball tryouts; socially awkward people typically don't succeed in politics; clumsy people make bad jugglers. Isn't it possible that people who have a hard time concentrating usually don't make the best doctors?

Tom Freston may be best known as the man who discovered music videos. He got involved in cable television in 1979, when it still seemed doubtful that people would pay for television when they could get Big Three network programming for free. Along with the legendary adman George Lois, who designed *Esquire* magazine's avant-garde covers during its golden age in the 1960s, Freston created the now iconic "I Want My MTV" ad campaign that defined shopping-mall chic during the early 1980s. He went on to turn MTV from a cultural phenomenon into a global media empire, launching VH1, Nickelodeon, Comedy Central, and many other cable channels and creating independent programming to edify the masses, including *SpongeBob SquarePants*, *South Park*, and *Beavis and Butt-head*. Freston's MTV Networks invented reality television

with *The Real World*, the first television show to place several strang-
ers in a house together and tape their every move. An arrangement
that would have been an unambiguous violation of professional
ethics if done in the name of science was an unqualified success as
entertainment. He became president of Viacom—MTV's parent
company—in 2004, where he remained until 2006. He left with a
$60 million severance package.

In 1995, after his son Gilbert was diagnosed with ADHD, Freston
enrolled him in the Stephen Gaynor School, a private school special-
izing in learning disabilities. The Gaynor school isn't cheap: one
year there cost $21,819 in 1999. Still, that wasn't much more than
what a typical New York City private school would cost, and few
people with Freston's wealth send their kids to public schools in
New York: private school tuition is simply one of the many extraordinary expenses that wealthy urbanites consider a necessity.

The Individuals with Disabilities Education Act requires all states
that receive any federal funding for special education to provide
all children with disabilities a free and appropriate public education. The law requires that public schools develop "specially designed
instruction, at no cost to parents, to meet the unique needs of a
child with a disability." If the school district fails to provide a child
with an "appropriate" education, the parents are legally entitled to
tuition reimbursement for private schools. Public schools are often
unable to accommodate a child with a rare and severe disability at a
reasonable cost: private placement may be better for the child and
cheaper for the district. And if a district simply fails to offer an appropriate education due to incompetence or neglect, parents should
be able to take matters into their own hands and make sure their
child gets the education he or she needs. The law makes sure that
disabled children have the same access to a free public education as
any other child: the school district must either provide an education
that meets their needs or outsource the job to someone who can.

But what about parents who would never consider public school
for a nondisabled child? Freston asked the New York City Board of

Education to evaluate Gilbert and recommend an educational program suited to his special needs, but nothing the school district had to offer could match the pricey private school Gilbert was already attending. Freston sued the school district for his son's private school tuition in 1997 and 1998, and the district agreed to compensate him. He later argued that this was a tacit acknowledgment that the district had not offered Gilbert an appropriate education; the district insisted that it paid up only in order to avoid litigation. In 1999 the district offered Gilbert a coveted placement in the city's Lower Lab School for Gifted Education with a student-faculty ratio of fifteen to one along with additional tutoring and counseling. But Freston never visited the school or met with any of its staff, and later testified that "it was sort of a moot point . . . I spent the summer in California . . . The down payment [for private school] had been made."[17]

School administrators from coast to coast worried that wealthy parents would game the system to get school districts to pay for private schools—and more. The *San Francisco Chronicle* described the parents of a student with learning disabilities and anxiety disorder who enrolled in a "$30,000-a-year prep school in Maine—then sent the bill to their local public school district." According to the *Chronicle*, "Parents of special education students seek extra-special education at public expense: private day schools, boarding schools, summer camps, aqua therapy, horseback therapy . . . Special education is a growing portion of budgets in many districts, squeezing out services for other pupils." Similarly, *Time* magazine reported that an autistic child's parents "informed Colorado's Thompson school district it had to pick up the bill for Boston Higashi's $135,000 annual tuition." *The New York Times* quoted a Westport, Connecticut, school superintendent who faced special education reimbursement requests for horseback riding and personal trainers.[18] These reports suggested that a law designed to help the disabled and needy had become a giveaway for the rich and greedy. Mainstream media coverage of "extra-special education" echoed the radio talk show host

Michael Savage's claim that learning disabilities had become a "money racket."

New York fought Freston's claim for private school tuition. Joined by a coalition of other large urban school districts, the city argued that "many parents ask public school districts to develop an [educational plan] for their child despite intending from the outset to reject whatever . . . is developed and then claim that the district is unable to provide [an appropriate education] . . . These parents, who never intended to use the public schools, unilaterally place their child in the private school in which they planned to enroll their child all along, and then request reimbursement, hoping for a windfall."[19] The cities pointed out that private schools for the disabled often encourage parents to sue local school districts for tuition reimbursement; some even gave parents a list of "contact information for . . . lawyers and . . . instructions on how to sue the city." The cities insisted that in order to "prevent abuse by parents who never intended to use the public schools," the IDEA allowed parents to seek tuition reimbursement only after their children had tried public schools and they had proven inadequate.

Advocates for the disabled countered that most disabled children do not come from wealthy families; to the contrary, "30 percent of children with disabilities live in foster care . . . Almost 25 percent . . . are living in poverty."[20] The advocacy group Autism Speaks warned that disabled children who are forced to "try out" inappropriate public school placements before moving to an effective private school may miss a critical window of opportunity for development: "The effectiveness of intervention depends on early application . . . When the opportunity presented during this window passes, the squandered potential cannot be regained later."[21] As for the threat of escalating expenses, advocates for the disabled pointed out that private placements accounted for only a tiny fraction of the costs of special education and most private placements involved severely disabled children, whom school districts admitted they couldn't serve. The cases where parents unilaterally put their children in private school and sued the district for reimbursement were trivial in number.

Moreover, the cost of private placement was typically not much more than an adequate public education: in fact, New York City's public schools spent more on average for a disabled pupil attending public schools than Freston had requested in reimbursement.[22] One of the briefs filed on behalf of the City of New York complained that "in one recent school year, public schools spent over 20% of their general operating budgets on special education students."[23] But, as a brief filed on behalf of Freston pointed out, most of that amount was spent on special education in *public* schools—not on tuition reimbursement.[24] Taken together, these arguments implied, perhaps unintentionally, that tuition reimbursement wasn't a unique problem; it was just a dramatic example of the cost of special education generally.

Mark Kelman, my colleague at Stanford, and Gillian Lester, now a professor at UC Berkeley Law School, conducted an extensive study of learning disability claims in public schools. They visited a number of local school districts and talked to local school administrators, teachers, and parents to see how the disability rights laws worked in practice. They came away convinced that treating the education of learning disabled children as a civil rights issue benefited rich families at the expense of the poor and actually made it harder to educate most students—disabled and nondisabled alike.

For nondisabled children, the problem is obvious: the law requires school districts to spend more—often a lot more—on costly special services reserved exclusively for children diagnosed with learning disabilities. This might make sense if the districts were awash in money, or if the special services were uniquely helpful to the children with learning disabilities, the way, say, Braille texts are uniquely helpful to the blind. But in fact many of the special services the schools are required to provide for children with learning disabilities would benefit *any* child: smaller classes with better student-teacher ratios, one-on-one tutoring, immunity from discipline for disruptive behavior, extra time on exams. One administrator Kelman and Lester interviewed worried that only

> maybe half the people we label are "really" LD. The problem is
> that the truly LD kids are irremediable. The 25 percent who eventually show significant changes were probably misdiagnosed. In theory, the LD kids have alternative coping mechanisms, and the
> educator should try to help the kids tap into these alternatives, [but]
> slow learners [who aren't diagnosed as learning disabled] may
> also have untapped abilities . . . The difference between the two is
> merely a matter of degree.
>
> Good teaching, simply, is what makes it work . . . For the LD
> kids or for anyone else, good teaching is good teaching.[25]

Some administrators believe the law requires them to prevent services earmarked for a child with a learning disability from "leaking" over to other, presumably undeserving students who may simply be slow learners. For instance, if a student with a mild learning disability attends class with nondisabled students and receives one-on-one tutoring during the school day, can the tutor also help other kids who have questions about the day's lesson? While some school officials think they must prevent the diversion of special education resources to nondisabled students, others welcome "leakage" as a way to compensate for the inevitably imprecise diagnosis of learning disabilities. "This way, the sharp categories formally exist, but all students who need assistance . . . get it," said one California administrator.[26]

Special education services eat up a growing share of the public school budget in many districts. In 1979 there were 796,000 students diagnosed with learning disabilities; in 2003 there were 2,848,000, and the number continues to grow at a rapid pace. Perhaps too few students were diagnosed with learning disabilities in the 1970s, but as a larger and larger percentage of students are said to have a "disability" that keeps them from learning, one has to wonder whether the cause is truly neurobiological, or whether it's political and social. Under the IDEA, schools that fail to effectively educate disabled children can be made to pay for private school tuition. But the public schools—especially those in large cities like New York— are failing to educate many of their students who aren't disabled too. For instance, in 2006 over 3 percent of *all* the students served by the Washington, D.C., school district were in private placements at a cost, according to *The Washington Post*, of 15 percent of the district's entire budget.[27] But, as two special education experts acknowledged, "the D.C. schools struggle to provide an adequate education to any of their students. Disabled students are entitled . . . to demand an adequate education . . . The nondisabled students . . . lack the same mechanism for exiting failing schools."[28] Contrary to the civil rights theory underlying the IDEA, disabled students who don't receive an adequate education aren't necessarily being discriminated against; tragically, they're often receiving the same- quality education as everyone else.

The civil rights approach to special education also disserved many disabled children—especially those from poor and minority families. Historically, special education has been split along the lines of family income and race. Culturally unsophisticated children— often poor blacks and Latinos and poor people who had moved from rural to urban areas—accounted for the lion's share of children labeled "slow," mentally retarded, emotionally disturbed, or culturally deprived. These students were typically either expelled from school or shunted off into dead-end special ed classes. The problem was so pervasive that civil rights activists in the 1950s and 1960s worried that special ed had become a cloak for racial discrimination and lobbied hard for provisions designed to ensure that minority students were not segregated from mainstream public education.[29]

Meanwhile, the category of "learning disability" emerged due to the efforts of wealthier, predominantly white families in the 1950s and 1960s who saw their underachieving children slip through the cracks of the educational system. Armed with psychological research that had identified discrete neurological causes (such as dyslexia) for certain cases of poor academic performance, they lobbied for a new category that would distinguish their children from the "mentally retarded" and from children who were simply lazy or slow—a recognition of a discrete condition that did not actually decrease intelligence, but only masked it. In studies of children with learning disabilities published in the 1960s and early 1970s, 98.5 percent were white and 69 percent were of middle-class or higher socioeconomic status.[30]

Today's learning disability rights laws are a result of the efforts of these two groups: litigation to prevent the isolation and expulsion of retarded, emotionally disturbed, and hyperactive children eventually led to the Education for All Handicapped Children Act in 1975, now renamed the Individuals with Disabilities Education Act. Special education under the IDEA can range from reimbursement of expensive private school tuition to isolation in a dead-end class with "slow" children. Kelman and Lester worry that poor children typically receive very different treatment under the IDEA mandates than do the children of wealthy parents, who have the wherewithal to pressure school districts for better and more costly options: "The IDEA system . . . permit[s] relatively privileged white pupils to capture high-cost . . . in-class resources that others with similar educational deficits cannot obtain while, at the same time, allowing disproportionate numbers of African-American and poor pupils to be shunted into [dead-end special ed] classes." There was even more reason to worry that the IDEA system benefited the rich at the expense of the poor in the case of demands for tuition reimbursement like Tom Freston's because only wealthy parents could afford to send their child to an expensive private school and sue for reimbursement later. As the coalition of urban school districts warned in its amicus brief: "Every dollar spent on tuition reimbursement is a dollar that can no longer be spent to improve public special education programs . . . [This harms] students with the greatest need for public services, namely those whose families cannot afford to seek services outside the public school system."[31]

Those families face deteriorating schools with large classes and dramatically reduced extracurricular activities. In New York City, kindergarten classes averaged 22 students in 2009, and elementary and middle school classes averaged 25.8 students.[32] In California, budget cuts have made classes of over 30 students commonplace, and many students have to pay for extracurricular activities such as sports and music out of their own pocket—if they are offered at all.[33] It's easy for parents to argue that public school classes don't offer an adequate education to their learning disabled children when they don't offer an adequate education to *anyone*. Given the state of many American public schools, who can blame parents for seeking private alternatives or trying to finagle extra resources for their children? And even the top public schools can't compete with the best that money can buy. New York's offer of a much-sought-after spot at the prestigious Lower Lab School for Gifted Education paled in comparison to the education Gilbert Freston was receiving at the private Gaynor school, where he enjoyed a four-to-one student-staff ratio: the head teacher at Gaynor suggested that the city's proposed class size of fifteen "could be a bit overwhelming."[34]

Freston insisted that he sued as a matter of principle: after taking his case all the way to the U.S. Supreme Court, he donated the tuition reimbursement that he was awarded to tutoring for public school children. But all things considered, Freston's stance is somewhat perverse: What sound moral principle would force cash-strapped public schools to provide a gourmet education for some students while others must make do with a dog's breakfast?

In 2009 students with learning disabilities accounted for almost half the entire population of disabled students receiving special services under the IDEA. It's no accident that the explosion of learning disability diagnoses comes at the same time the public schools are increasingly troubled by overcrowding, spotty teaching quality, and violence. The strongest students manage to learn despite overcrowding and poor teaching, but weaker students don't. So while all students suffer from overcrowding and indifferent teaching, poor performers—whether diagnosed with disabilities or not—suffer most. The parents of such students are right to insist that the schools are failing to help their children realize their potential, and failing them *more dramatically* than they are failing students who learn easily and without much help. In that sense, poor schools are inherently discriminatory: they make any student who has difficulty learning— for whatever reason—worse off than students who learn easily. But of course in this sense any poorly provided public service "discriminates" against the people who need it most: badly run hospitals discriminate against the injured and the sick; incompetent police departments discriminate against people living in crime-ridden neighborhoods; inadequately maintained parks discriminate against people without backyards.

The solution is obvious: better public services for everyone. But the IDEA doesn't make the public schools better; instead, it shifts resources to a small fraction of the larger group of people who need them most. This might make some sense if that small fraction were especially injured by inadequate education or if they would uniquely profit from the extra resources. But if, as many educators believe, these children need the same things that any other student needs— good teaching in small classes—then it's wrong to treat their needs as inalienable civil rights when we treat the needs of other students as luxuries that nearly bankrupt districts can't afford. At any rate, the IDEA doesn't even try to find out whether children with learning disabilities get more out of extra resources than other children would. Instead, the law mandates that some children should have more than others whether or not they need it more or will benefit more from it. All in the name of equality.

Dr. Paul Steinberg, a Washington, D.C., psychiatrist, argues that many students with what we call learning disabilities may in fact simply learn differently than other students and excel in different areas: for instance, "attention deficit disorder" may be a valuable asset in situations that demand spontaneity. "Essentially, ADHD is a problem dealing with the menial work of daily life, the tedium involved in many school situations and 9-to-5 jobs . . . [but] in many situations of hands-on activities or activities that reward spontaneity, ADHD is not a disorder." But in today's economy of technical and professional specialization, concentration is king, spontaneity is less valued, and impulsiveness can be ruinous: "What once conferred certain advantages in a hunter-gatherer era, in an agrarian age or even in an industrial age is now a potentially horrific character flaw."[35] Of course there have always been tasks that required concentration. But in past eras, a lot of things *didn't* require sustained concentration: people we now would diagnose with ADHD could be great hunters, gladiators, knights, traveling minstrels, or rich aristocrats who didn't need to work. During the Industrial Revolution, at least until the era of Henry Ford and modern management science, factory managers expected that workers would daydream and lose focus on the job. By contrast, in the information economy it's harder and harder to find a good job where focus and detail orientation are optional.

This suggests that ADHD—even if it is the result of a discrete neurological condition—isn't really a disability in the way that blindness, paralysis, severe autism, or even dyslexia is. Steinberg suggests we abandon the idea that some people have an attention deficit and instead think of everyone else as blessed (or cursed) with "attention-surplus disorder." He argues that "children . . . with attention disorder may need more hands-on learning. Some may perform more effectively using computers and games rather than books. Some may do better with fieldwork and wilderness programs." Steinberg urges that we "change the contexts in schools to accommodate the needs of children who have [ADHD], not just support and accommodate the needs of children with attention-surplus disorder." Changing the context doesn't suggest case-by-case exceptions to a general rule: it suggests a new pedagogical approach. If some children learn better using computers and fieldwork, we should introduce these teaching methods, and there's no reason to limit them to children with diagnosed learning disabilities. Making viable alternatives available to all children who would profit from them would make the accommodations more equitable, further the important goal of integrating disabled children into regular classes, and eliminate any stigma now attached to "special education."

Of course that's practical only if games, fieldwork, and wilderness programs prepare children for life in the modern economy as well as "tedious" conventional schoolwork. Unfortunately, such ideas are often more attractive as therapy than as pedagogy. Educators tried out similar new and untested pedagogical methods in the 1960s and 1970s: when I was in grade school, for several years we learned "new math" and were graded on the quality of our ideas, regardless of whether they were well composed using proper grammar and sentence structure. The idea behind these new pedagogical methods was much the same as Dr. Steinberg's idea: different children have different learning styles, and many children aren't engaged by conventional pedagogy. These experiments were often short-lived because the new methods didn't teach children as effectively: in order to tackle advanced subjects such as trigonometry, calculus, and college-level composition, you needed to have mastered the "old" math, with its multiplication tables and long division, and the boring old rules of grammar, sentence structure, and vocabulary. Moreover, students needed the mental discipline that the old methods imposed: part of the point of rote memorization was to teach children to focus on a single task for long periods of time.

Dr. Steinberg points out that "each child and adult learns and performs better in certain contexts than others." Of course, this is true whether the person in question is diagnosed with a learning disability or not. It's best to encourage people to pursue interests and careers for which they are well suited. Let's face it: in many jobs a wandering mind isn't a superficial condition that somehow masks an employee's good performance; it's a flaw that makes for poor performance. This is true whether or not the cause is an immutable neurological condition, inadequate practice, or a simple lack of diligence. We should help people with short attention spans find jobs where sustained attention isn't important, not artificially inflate their grades and test scores and kid ourselves that concentration and speedy performance isn't important in jobs where it is.

From the beginning, the precise rationale for disability rights has been unclear. Disability rights enjoyed widespread support among both liberals and conservatives, but for very different reasons. That has made it hard for courts to know how to interpret the law and easy for new claimants to press for expanded application and new entitlements. Liberals typically saw the extra resources and special exceptions for students with learning disabilities as civil rights that advance equality—part of a larger set of egalitarian social welfare policies designed to level hierarchies based on what philosophers might call "morally irrelevant" differences. But it's unclear how far liberals will go in pursuit of this conceptual goal. Arguably *all* differences in innate ability and intelligence are *morally* irrelevant. But of course differences in ability—whether due to disabilities or not—are very relevant *practically*. Disability accommodations have less to do with the mainstream civil rights goal of equal opportunity than with equality of *result*—forbidding even-handed policies and practices that happen to disadvantage the disabled. Requiring employers, proprietors, landlords, and schools to ignore differences in ability and absorb the extra costs of compensating for such differences goes further than simply prohibiting irrational discrimination: it's effectively a redistribution of wealth. In many cases, that redistribution makes sense; for instance, forcing building owners to pay for wheelchair ramps when they remodel or forcing employers to make allowances for blind or handicapped employees gives a long-neglected and disproportionately impoverished group of people a chance to lead fulfilling and constructive lives. But we should evaluate such accommodations as social welfare policies—not categorically accept them as inalienable civil rights.

Conservatives, by contrast, saw the disabled as among a small group of deserving unfortunates who suffer through no fault of their own—unlike the much larger group of losers who have their own shiftlessness and irresponsible behavior to blame for their misfortunes. Disability rights correct for variations in human ability caused by accidents and genetic randomness while leaving more patterned and predictable inherited inequalities firmly in place. Educational accommodations for students with learning disabilities are a conspicuous example: a diagnosis of a learning disability often effectively allows successful parents to pass their advantages in academic accomplishment along to their less successful children. Perhaps this is why many conservatives have supported fairly aggressive disability rights but have opposed much milder civil rights for other groups. To the extent disability rights protect existing socioeconomic statuses, they are consistent with a conservative tradition at least as old as Edmund Burke that places a high value on continuity and social stability. But they are at odds with the more widely accepted libertarian conservatism of today, which emphasizes self-reliance, free enterprise, and the discipline of the market. And they are certainly at odds with the civil rights tradition, which abhors hierarchies of birth and prizes social equity.

Disability rights serve two important purposes: they prohibit discrimination based on irrational aversion or inaccurate stereotypes, and they help to integrate disabled people into the mainstream of society. As for simple discrimination, given the long history of aversion to and prejudice against the disabled, it makes sense to require reluctant employers and proprietors to give disabled people a chance—even when doing so requires some extra effort or expense. There's no doubt that simple prejudice against the disabled is still a serious and pervasive problem. Like race and sex, most disabilities are conspicuous: a blind person with a cane or Seeing Eye dog, a paraplegic in a wheelchair, or a mentally ill person muttering to herself makes an obvious target for the bigoted employer, landlord, or proprietor. But the milder emotional and learning disabilities aren't conspicuous; in fact, they weren't considered disabilities at all until recently. When people with these conditions do poorly in school or at work, they aren't suffering because of irrational prejudice or inaccurate stereotypes; they're suffering from an accurate assessment of their performance.

Disability rights also help to integrate the disabled into the mainstream. Congress noted the isolation and resulting impoverishment of the disabled when it passed the Americans with Disabilities Act in 1990. Again, people with more severe and conspicuous disabilities are the ideal beneficiaries of such an integrationist policy. Without mandatory accommodations, people with severe disabilities would be unable to compete for jobs, unable to communicate effectively, and unable to get around in cities designed for the able-bodied. But mild emotional and learning disabilities don't prevent people from finding gainful employment or making their way in the world. They may prevent some people from getting the jobs they most want, but many, many nondisabled people can't get the jobs they most want because they lack the required skill, temperament, or intelligence—deficits that are at least partially determined by discrete neurological conditions too. That's not a civil rights issue—that's life. Mandatory accommodations for the disabled involve the redistribution of resources—to disabled employees from employers, to disabled customers from proprietors, and to disabled students from the other students who compete with them for teaching resources and high grades. Deciding when such redistribution is justified requires difficult trade-offs between competing policy priorities—not an inflexible legal entitlement.

Rock of the Aged: Civil Rights for Older Workers

Google was one of the few high-tech Silicon Valley firms that emerged from the dot-com crash of 2001 not only unscathed but actually stronger. By 2003 its Internet search engine had become so popular that its lawyers had to worry that the "Google" name might become a generic term for Internet search ("I'll Google it"), jeopardizing its legal status as a trademark. Having conquered web searches, Google moved on to dominate Internet maps, directions, and real-time traffic conditions. It launched an ambitious—some said quixotic—plan to digitally scan every book in the world for a text-searchable database: Google Books collaborated with some of the world's largest libraries and alienated some of the largest publishers and literary agencies, who organized a lawsuit to block the project. Another Google project bested some of the world's most powerful military intelligence organizations: in 2006 a satellite image from Google Earth revealed top secret U.S. operations in Pakistan in a photograph sharp enough to render the painted lines on the tarmac. When Google went public in 2004, the offering was among the most anticipated in Silicon Valley history, although many were skeptical that the company could hold its initial valuation of $27 billion. In 2009, in the midst of the worst economy since the Great Depression, Google was worth $140 billion.[36]

Google had done so much so quickly with a huge team of energetic, talented, and fiercely dedicated employees. The Googleplex—its main offices in Mountain View, California—is a sprawling campus of four large buildings, each surrounded by lawns, courtyards, and, this being suburban California, ample parking. The Googleplex is a cross between a university quadrangle and the ultimate party house. Google offers its employees three free meals a day at eleven cafeterias, free laundry, free hairstyling, a state-of-the-art gym complete with stationary lap pool, a volleyball court, lounges with pool tables, foosball, video games, and replicas of a spaceship and a dinosaur skeleton. Google provides bicycles and Segway scooters for employees to move around its campus, where they work on laptops at informal workstations, "yurts," and "huddle rooms" that encourage collaboration and out-of-the-box thinking. The company provides toys to entertain the children of employees, and dogs are always welcome.

With all of these postmod cons, Google employees never need leave work. "We have a preference for those who like to work hard and play hard and are enthused about working on collaborative global teams," informs each job listing for Google. Brian Reid started working at Google in 2002 as director of operations and engineering. A former professor of electrical engineering at Stanford, Reid was an early Internet pioneer. He helped invent one of the first Ethernet networks at Stanford in 1981 and worked on the first e-mail protocols and on the first Internet search engine—AltaVista—in 1995. Reid was fifty-two years old when he started work at Google—a good two decades older than Google's founders, Larry Page and Sergey Brin. Reid received positive evaluations from his superiors, in which they described him as "very intelligent" and "creative" and complimented his "confidence when dealing with fast changing situations" and his "excellent attitude." But, in what was to prove a foreboding observation, his first performance review noted that "adapting to the Google culture is the primary task for the first year here . . . Google is simply different: Younger contributors, inexperienced first line managers, and the super fast pace are just a few examples."

Reid lasted less than two years at Google. During his short tenure on the company's campus, he was the target of a series of age-related jokes and disparaging comments. His immediate supervisor called him "lethargic" and dismissed his ideas as "obsolete" and "too old to matter." His co-workers referred to him as an "old man" and an "old fuddy-duddy." A CD jewel case served as an office placard for Google managers: some quipped that Reid's should be a vinyl LP. Google's management began to ease Reid out in October 2003 when they replaced him as director of operations with someone fifteen years younger. Reid was moved to a new position in charge of a pilot program that would allow Google's engineers to earn graduate degrees on-site at Google. The new program turned out to be little more than a place to park Reid before driving him out: the degree program was never staffed or funded, and in January of the next year Google's top management worked on "a proposal . . . on getting [Reid] out." On February 13, 2004, the vice president of engineering, Wayne Rosing, told Reid he was not a "cultural fit" in Google's engineering department. Reid applied for positions in other departments but the company's management had already made sure Reid would not find a new home in the Googleplex. Various department heads had coordinated by e-mail to adopt a uniform line with Reid. "My line at the moment is that there is no role for him," wrote the vice president of business operations. "We'll all agree on the job elimination angle," advised the human resources director, Stacy Sullivan. Five months later, Reid sued Google for age discrimination.[37]

Much of Reid's complaint focused on Google's corporate culture. Reid was let go because he wasn't a cultural fit at Google. He argued that the atmosphere at the Googleplex was biased against older workers. Was Google's culture a culture of youth? In many ways it was: Google used physical activities, such as skiing and hockey, as a way of team building; the Googleplex is modeled on a college campus; the decor is bright, colorful, and eccentric, like a dream house designed by MTV; and many of the perks offered to employees—from foosball to table tennis to free T-shirts—are likely to appeal to the young. But it's just these attributes that make Google both a successful business and a beloved employer. Google is widely considered one of the best places to work in the high-tech industry. Its youthful culture is a deliberate attempt to cultivate the fresh, innovative thinking that has made the company a success. Even the age-related comments Reid rightly complained of may have reflected this emphasis on novel, out-of-the-box thinking rather than age-based animus. It's not inconceivable that an older person could fit in at Google; in fact, the company hired Reid with the expectation and hope that he would adapt to the Google lifestyle. Is it a civil rights issue when an employer wants a workforce that's young at heart?

In 1967 roughly half of all private job openings were explicitly closed to applicants over the age of fifty-five; one-fourth were limited to those forty-five or younger. Older people were disproportionately unemployed and stayed jobless longer than younger people. Spurred to action by the pathetic image of a jobless older person reduced to eating pet food in his cold-water flat, Congress passed the Age Discrimination in Employment Act of 1967, or ADEA. Naturally, the ADEA was modeled on the Civil Rights Act of 1964, which prohibited discrimination on the basis of race, color, national origin, religion, and sex. Unlike the 1964 act, the ADEA sailed through a Congress made up overwhelmingly of middle-aged and older people, buoyed by a broad consensus that discrimination on the basis of age was cruel, inefficient, and unjust. "Nobody defends such discrimination, and—it ought to be stopped," declared a labor union representative in his testimony before Congress.

As expected, employers quickly took down the "Elderly Need Not Apply" signs after the ADEA was enacted. But unemployment among the elderly actually *increased* in the ten years after the ADEA was passed.[38] Was the reason lack of enforcement? Did employees not know their rights under the ADEA? To the contrary, there was a "backlog" of age discrimination lawsuits that had grown every year since the ADEA was passed. The problem wasn't in enforcement; it was in the design of the ADEA. Age discrimination was different from discrimination based on race, sex, and religion. It was oddly lopsided: older people suffered discrimination in hiring, but once hired, they fared as well as or better than younger workers. The Department of Labor's commissioner on aging found that older employees were "frequently preferred over the younger" for promotions and received favorable treatment on the job.[39] That's still true today. "If you are old and have a job, you are less likely . . . to be fired," said Alicia Munnell of the Center for Retirement Research at Boston College in 2009.[40] There was really no need for a civil rights law to protect older *workers*; it was older *applicants* for jobs who needed protection. This was still the case over forty years after the ADEA was passed: in the recession of 2009 older people who were laid off were out of work for an average of 22.2 weeks; by contrast, younger people were unemployed an average of 16.2 weeks.[41]

The ADEA didn't do much for job *applicants*, because an unemployed person is unlikely to sue for a job he didn't get. A job applicant has very little information about the hiring process, the decision makers, or the qualifications of other people vying for the same job: it's hard to know whether discrimination or legitimate factors made the difference. Moreover, litigation takes time—time that could be better spent continuing the job search. That's why only about 9 percent of all employment discrimination claims challenge hiring decisions.[42] By contrast, once hired, people become invested in their jobs and are much more likely to sue to keep them and to advance in them. Accordingly, almost 80 percent of all employment discrimination claims involve firing and denied promotions. Unsurprisingly, then, the ADEA encouraged current employees to sue over promotions and termination—where age discrimination wasn't much of a problem. The ADEA empowered older workers who, as a group, were already better off than younger employees, but did little to solve the problem of chronic unemployment among the elderly. In fact, because the law gave older people a new weapon to use against employers—a weapon that they were much more likely to use once hired—the law probably *encouraged* employers to discriminate against older job applicants, making the problem the law was designed to solve worse.

The civil rights solution didn't fit the problem of unemployment among older workers very well. Even when the ADEA was passed, it was well-known that "age discrimination is . . . seldom a matter of blind or arbitrary prejudice which often exists for reasons of race, creed, color, national origin, or sex . . . [It] is a more subtle series of problems . . . a combination of institutional factors and stereotyped thinking."[43] But the civil rights approach focused only on stereotypes, neglecting the subtler institutional factors that are actually the biggest cause of the problem. Congress basically cribbed from the 1964 Civil Rights Act, extending the same civil rights protections to a new group—the elderly—as if age discrimination were caused by irrational bigotry against the aged and inaccurate stereotypes about their qualifications. For instance, Secretary of Labor Willard Wirtz argued that age discrimination reflected outdated attitudes, "a failure on the part of employers to realize how technology and the life sciences have combined to increase the value of older people's work";[44] and William D. Bechill, the commissioner on aging, insisted that "stereotyped attitudes about the ability of older people . . . play a major role in barring older workers from fair . . . consideration."[45]

Stereotypes about older people are a problem, but as the NYU law professor Samuel Issacharoff and his coauthor Erica Harris point out in a detailed discussion of the ADEA, age discrimination is often driven by simple economics. Labor economists describe the typical career path in terms of a "life cycle."[46] The typical employee needs training early in her career, becomes a seasoned and efficient worker in mid-career, and then slows down a bit near the end of her career. If wages and salary perfectly matched the productivity of each employee, most people would receive very low compensation early in their careers, when they are still learning—in some cases the costs of training might be greater than the contribution new employees make, suggesting an "apprenticeship" model where the new employee should work for very little. Then pay would rise very quickly after the employee became accomplished. Finally, pay would level off and eventually drop as the older employee slowed down and thoughts turned from work to a well-earned retirement filled with grandchildren, gardening, and exotic travel (at least that's what *I* hope to be looking forward to at seventy).

But of course this isn't how compensation is usually set. Typically, compensation rises relatively slowly but inexorably: pay cuts reflect a firm in financial crisis or a sanction for unacceptably poor performance. This type of arrangement involves an implicit bargain between employer and employee: the junior employee builds up a debt while being trained, which she pays off as she gains skills, eventually banking a surplus, which she will collect as she ages and her compensation exceeds her value to the firm. Viewed sympathetically, it's a humane and practical model based on a long-term relationship: younger people receive a decent wage and avoid the indignities of apprenticeship, and older workers enjoy compensation that reflects the esteem and respect they've earned throughout a long career—even if it exceeds their current productivity.

But the deferred compensation and cross subsidy inherent in this approach encourage three types of age discrimination. Two are necessary parts of the implicit bargain and therefore defensible if one accepts its terms; one is an indefensible breach of the implicit bargain by the employer.

First, an employer might refuse to hire older employees because they will enter the pay scale at just the point where compensation exceeds contribution, never having "banked" the surplus by working when their contributions exceeded compensation. If the firm pays according to seniority, or guarantees retirement benefits at a certain age, the newly hired older worker will arrive just in time to collect the subsidy. Even an employer that is happy to retain older workers hired early in their careers or in mid-career might not want to *hire* workers already near the end of their careers. Of course, such an employer could hire a senior employee for a wage she's worth—even if it's much less than other workers of the same seniority who have contributed to the firm during their most productive and less well-compensated years. But this would require the firm to be explicit about the implicit cross subsidy involved in the salary structure. An advantage of the employment life cycle is that the subsidies are implicit. Making them explicit would be bad for employee morale: mid-career employees would resent subsidizing older and younger employees, and older employees would lose esteem and respect.

Of course, discrimination in hiring is just what the ADEA was supposed to prevent. But ironically the law may have made this kind of discrimination more likely by giving employers an *additional* reason to avoid hiring older people. Under the ADEA, an employer who hired an older employee on a trial basis would have to worry about a lawsuit if things didn't work out. It's not surprising that employers responded to the ADEA by eliminating conspicuous discriminatory policies while continuing to discriminate against older job applicants in less obvious ways.

Second, a smoothly and inexorably rising pay scale assumes mandatory retirement—a form of age discrimination. At some point the surplus banked in mid-career runs out. Before the ADEA was amended to prohibit the practice, most employers openly discriminated by imposing a mandatory retirement age. The ADEA originally covered only employees between forty and sixty-five, but the upper limit was eliminated in 1986, effectively outlawing most mandatory retirement.[47] As a result, many older workers had the option of staying on at high compensation long after having recouped any surplus they had contributed in the middle of their careers. Many employers adjusted to the new legal regime by replacing "lockstep" compensation based on seniority with bottom-line-oriented compensation such as merit pay and low base salaries supplemented with productivity bonuses. This shift ultimately affected more than compensation: it was part of a change in attitude, the demise of a more collaborative and genteel business relationship and the rise of a more beady-eyed, "eat what you kill" approach. As Issacharoff and Harris put it, "Employees who currently have expectations of wages above marginal output will appear to be an unaffordable luxury in highly competitive markets."[48] For example, an internal

Wal-Mart memo that came to light in 2005 notes unapprovingly that "the cost of an associate with seven years of tenure is almost 55 percent more than the cost of an associate with one year of tenure, yet there is no difference in his or her productivity. Moreover, because we pay an associate more in salary and benefits as his or her tenure increases, we are pricing that associate out of the labor market, increasing the likelihood that he or she will stay with Wal-Mart."[49] Perhaps the atmosphere that Brian Reid encountered at Google reflects this harder-edged employment relationship and the resulting contempt for employees even slightly "past their prime."

Third, an unscrupulous employer may breach the implicit bargain and fire a loyal employee just as she is about to recoup the surplus she built up during her most productive years: a nasty bait and switch. Ironically, the ADEA does not prevent employers from sacking older employees just before their pensions vest—provided they do so out of simple greed and not bias. When sixty-two-year-old Walter Biggins was fired just a few weeks before his pension benefits vested, he sued for age discrimination and won a jury trial verdict, which was sustained on appeal. But the Supreme Court held that Biggins hadn't suffered age discrimination. According to the Court, "It is the very essence of age discrimination for an older employee to be fired because the employer believes that productivity and competence decline with old age . . . on the basis of inaccurate and stigmatizing stereotypes." But in Biggins's case "the decision [was] not . . . the result of an inaccurate and denigrating generalization about age, but . . . rather . . . an *accurate* judgment . . . that he indeed is 'close to vesting.' "[50] Cheating an employee of his pension doesn't involve anti-elderly bias—just evenhanded avarice. As a result, the Court held that age discrimination laws don't prohibit one of the most common tricks employers use to cheat older employees. In fact, the employer's conspicuous avarice was almost a *defense* to the age discrimination claim. "Inferring age motivation . . . may be problematic in cases where other unsavory motives . . . [are] present," opined Justice Sandra Day O'Connor.

But the Court didn't leave Walter Biggins without a remedy. Although his employer didn't discriminate on the basis of age, it did violate the federal Employee Retirement Income Security Act, which regulates employee pension plans. *Biggins* doesn't imply that there's nothing wrong with cheating an employee of his nearly vested pension. Instead, it suggests that much of what we call age discrimination may be better dealt with outside the civil rights framework.

Instead of reducing unemployment among the needy elderly, the ADEA benefited older workers who had jobs—the group that was already "frequently preferred over . . . younger" employees. The ADEA let employees forty and older—and only employees forty and older—sue when they were fired or passed over for promotion: unlike every other civil rights law, the ADEA expressly rules out most "reverse discrimination" lawsuits. Of course, if discrimination *against the elderly* is the problem, perhaps it makes sense to limit the law's protection to older plaintiffs. But such an asymmetry does amplify the concern that a law designed to ensure fair treatment will become a boondoggle for a specific, politically connected group. We've all heard this concern voiced loud and long in the context of race-based affirmative action, which California's former governor Pete Wilson famously condemned as a "racial spoils system." Ironically, the concern is much more valid—though less noticed—in the context of age-based civil rights. Although the ADEA is, strictly speaking, an antidiscrimination law and not an affirmative action law, because of its built-in asymmetry—age discrimination is unlawful only when it disadvantages older people—one could argue that the entire law is a form of affirmative action. And because older Americans *as a group* are not disadvantaged at all, the remedial purpose of these rights is more dubious than for race- or sex-based affirmative action policies. In fact, older people have a vastly disproportionate share of the nation's wealth and political influence, and their fortunes were improving dramatically even as Congress continued to expand and strengthen age discrimination laws. Between 1970 and 1984 the median income of people over sixty-five rose by 35 percent as compared with less than 1 percent for people from twenty-five to sixty-four[51]—yet Congress expanded the ADEA to prohibit mandatory retirement in 1986.

The ADEA looks even more like an age-based spoils system when one looks at its effect on retirement benefits. After the ADEA outlawed mandatory retirement, employers were faced with the prospect of having to retain older, overpaid employees long after they had recouped the deferred compensation earned in their more productive and less remunerated mid-career years. Many tried to buy their way out of the problem by offering older employees a "golden handshake"—a onetime cash payment on retirement. Already this was a huge windfall for older employees: the older life-cycle wage arrangement assumed mandatory retirement at a specific age; outlawing mandatory retirement essentially rewrote the deal in favor of older employees. The golden handshake is the amortized cash value of this imposed revision of the employment contract—a direct transfer of wealth from employers (and, indirectly, younger employees) to older employees.

Employers typically offered the golden handshake to employees who were young enough that they were likely to continue working for many years unless bribed to retire, and offered younger employees more than older employees. In other words, the employers discriminated on the basis of age. But this had nothing to do with animus or negative stereotypes; it was a straightforward reflection of the economics that led employers to offer golden handshakes in the first place. The employer was basically buying older employees out of what had become an unprofitable mandatory employment contract from the employer's perspective. The value of the buyout would depend on the expected length of the employees' tenure. Age was a pretty good proxy for expected length of tenure: older employees would generally retire without inducement earlier than younger employees. Moreover, the golden handshake had to be enough to allow the employee to live comfortably in retirement, and that figure would be higher for younger people, who would have to make it stretch over a longer period of time. Adjusting the size of the golden handshake by age made sense, both from a narrow economic perspective and from a more humane perspective.

The American Association of Retired Persons (AARP) had emerged as a powerful lobby in favor of expanded and strengthened ADEA provisions by 1986, when Congress revised the ADEA to outlaw mandatory retirement. It continued that role, lobbying Congress in the late 1980s to outlaw age-targeted retirement incentives. Its position was that targeted retirement incentives were age discrimination and therefore violated the ADEA per se. But the AARP changed its tune when it realized that a strict prohibition of age discrimination would kill the goose that gave the golden handshakes altogether. Strict application of the ADEA's age discrimination rule would require employers to offer retirement inducements to everyone over the age of forty—or no one at all. As Issacharoff and Harris explain, "No employer could afford to offer retirement inducements to its entire workforce. At this point, the AARP did an about-face and began to lobby heavily for the preservation of [age-targeted retirement incentives] . . . so long as they were offered to everyone over a minimum age . . . When it came to benefiting older workers, . . . violations of the equal treatment principle proved to be more than just acceptable—they were required."[52]

Issacharoff and Harris aptly describe this and other lobbying for expanded age discrimination laws as "wealth-grabbing self-interest" resulting in a "windfall to older workers." It's important to add that only some older workers benefited, and some benefited much more than others. A common argument against mandatory retirement is that changes in society have made it an anachronism. Advances in public health have allowed people to stay healthy and productive well into what would once have been their golden years, and today many people are psychologically invested in their careers in a way that their parents were not. But in fact the average age of voluntary retirement from the workforce has *declined* steadily and steeply since the mid-twentieth century, from about age sixty-eight in the early 1950s to age sixty-two in the late 1990s.[53] The abolition of mandatory retirement makes no difference to the many people who choose to retire early.

The main exception to the trend toward earlier retirement is highly educated professionals and business managers. Because these careers are not physically demanding, people don't "burn out" as readily as in other jobs. And because performance in such careers can be hard to measure objectively, status and reputation play a large role. Perhaps older professionals and managers retire later because they are more likely to be productive later in their careers. But productivity may just be harder to measure in the professions and upper management, allowing today's older employees to use their reputations to hang on to coveted positions when an earlier generation would have "passed the baton" to younger protégés.

The uncharitable might think it telling that the legal profession has been largely exempt from age discrimination laws. For the most part, law firm partners are not considered employees covered under the ADEA, and mandatory retirement is still relatively common: over half of large law firms had mandatory retirement of some form in 2007.[54] This may be changing: disgruntled older law firm partners have sued their firms over mandatory retirement, and the Equal Employment Opportunity Commission has taken up the cause of these unlikely subalterns—a move that has prompted many firms to drop mandatory retirement.[55] But law firms have clung to mandatory retirement for good reasons. Many large law firms are still prime examples of the life-cycle model of compensation, which is responsible for preserving what collegiality remains in the typical Big Law sweatshop. Starting salaries at the more prestigious law firms in large cities are, as I write, as high as $170,000 a year. With all due admiration for the graduates of our nation's law schools, I'm certain that no student fresh from law school or a clerkship can justify these salaries, especially when the costs of inevitable on-the-job practical training are deducted from the balance sheet. It's well-known that many firms lose money on first- and sometimes even second-year attorneys and begin to break even only in the third year. Law partnerships remain lucrative because senior associates and young partners bring in much more than they earn in salary: salaries rise with seniority, but not as rapidly as skill and productivity do. For associates, compensation is typically tied to seniority and to the number of hours billed. But for the most highly compensated partners, compensation reflects the value of client relationships—a partner's "book of business." A partner who brings an important client into the firm will receive a yearly draw that reflects the billings to the client, even if he or she does little of the actual legal work for the client. So some senior partners earn much more than their current productivity would justify, based on the firm's total billings to clients in their "book." In effect, the mid-career lawyers subsidize both the novices and many older partners.

Mandatory retirement is indispensable to such a compensation structure. If partners can keep clients in their accounts indefinitely, the firm will become top-heavy with partners taking more out of the partnership than their current contributions justify. Of course, partners deserve to be compensated for "rainmaking," as client cultivation is referred to in the profession. But not all client relationships are the result of a current partner's rainmaking efforts: many clients have been with the same firm for generations. Traditionally, as partners age, they groom younger partners, to whom they will hand off their client relationships when they retire. But without the predictable and orderly handing down of client relationships that mandatory retirement encourages, partners within the same firm will begin to compete with each other for clients. Junior partners, with little prospect of building their own books of business within the firm, will try to build a book by leaving and then poaching clients they have worked with from senior partners at their old firms. Senior partners will become stingy mentors, guarding their client relationships from the younger lawyers with whom they work. Collegiality, mentoring, and client service will all suffer.

There's no doubt that rigid mandatory retirement deprived businesses and society of talented older employees. But nothing *required* employers to impose mandatory retirement, and nothing prohibited talented older workers who faced mandatory retirement at one job from working elsewhere. At its best, mandatory retirement was an orderly and humane way of ending the employment relationship on a high note—with a gold watch and a party rather than with a bad performance evaluation and a pink slip. It allowed older workers to train and mentor younger replacements without the now-common fear of grooming one's own competition, and it gave younger workers some assurance that coveted high-level positions, department chairs, and client portfolios would eventually be open to them.

The ADEA was first conceived of as a modest intervention to correct a flaw in employment markets that locked many older people in unemployment. It failed to correct that flaw, which continues to injure older people looking for work today. Instead, the ADEA morphed into what Issacharoff and Harris call "a benefits protection regulation for older workers . . . [mandating] open ended obligations to provide older workers lump sum buyouts [and other benefits] without giving any consideration to the economic rationale for these programs."[56] This has contributed to a backlash against employee benefits generally. For example, it's now a commonplace quip among business managers and consultants that General Motors (now radically downsized even after receiving billions in government bailout money) was once a car company that offered employee benefits and is now a benefits company that happens to make cars. In 2005, the Nobel laureate economist Paul Krugman pointed out that GM's health-care benefits alone accounted for $1,500 of the price of every car the company makes.[57] The ADEA is hardly the sole cause of this crisis in employee benefits, but it played a role by disrupting the arrangements that made compensation and fixed-benefits plans economically viable and forcing employers to offer a windfall to a narrow class of older workers at the expense of younger workers, future generations, consumers, and—when the employers go broke and the federally insured pension plans become insolvent—taxpayers.

This has little to do with equality or justice for older people. If the real issue were bias against the elderly or irrational stereotypes, we wouldn't find such ready and compelling economic justifications for so many of the practices the ADEA forbids. If the real issue were the integration of older people into the workforce or the alleviation of material disadvantage, the law would return to its original focus on the *jobless* elderly rather than locking in and increasing advantages for people who are already employed. If the real problem were that discrimination on the basis of age is somehow inherently demeaning or presumptively suspect, then the law would prohibit discrimination against the young as well as against the old rather than limit coverage to people forty and older as the ADEA does. After all, unlike stereotypes about race, sex, or disability, which fall almost exclusively on specific maligned groups, every questionable stereotype about the aged is mirrored by a denigrating generalization about the young: if the elderly are "sluggish," the young are "reckless"; if older people are set in their ways, young people lack wisdom; if the aged are complacent, younger people are naive and inexperienced.

Ironically, civil rights law includes this asymmetry only in the context where it is least justified. Title VII prohibits so-called reverse discrimination as a matter of principle, even though there is no evidence of, say, widespread anti-white or anti-male bias. By contrast, the egalitarian rationale that might justify asymmetrical protection for "protected groups" in the case of race, sex, and religion doesn't apply to age, because older people are disproportionately wealthy and powerful and hence can and do take care of themselves quite well in the market and in politics. The Seventh Circuit judge and University of Chicago Law School professor Richard Posner makes this point well:

> It is as if the vast majority of persons who established employment policies and who made employment decisions were black, federal legislation mandated huge transfer payments from whites to blacks, and blacks occupied most high political offices in the nation. It would be mad in those circumstances to think the nation needed a law that would protect blacks from discrimination in employment. Employers—who . . . for the most part are not young themselves—are unlikely to harbor either serious misconceptions about the vocational capacities of the old . . . or a generalized antipathy toward old people.[58]

Today's age discrimination laws are not "mad." They make perfect sense—as interest-group politics. If age discrimination laws just benefited older people at the expense of the young, any inequity they caused would be short-lived: after all, with luck we will all be old someday. But because age discrimination laws benefit well-off older people—relatively wealthy professionals and business managers—much more than the poor, they are, in effect, a tax on industry levied for the benefit of the relatively rich. Much of this extra income will go unspent, like the inherited advantages locked in by learning disability accommodations, and will pass to future generations. In effect, age discrimination laws have created a sort of reverse inheritance tax, helping well-off upper-level managers and wealthy professionals to have plenty left over to leave to their offspring even after enjoying a lush retirement of travel and comfortable leisure. A bumper sticker popular in places like Coral Gables, Florida, Palm Springs, California, and Leisure World, Arizona, reads, "I'm Spending My Children's Inheritance." Thanks to civil rights laws, some of the nation's richest retirees won't need to.

From Civil Rights to Individual Entitlements

Each of the civil rights laws I've discussed here serves a legitimate purpose. It's wrong and shortsighted to disfavor the disabled or the elderly because of inaccurate stereotypes or irrational aversion. Civil rights laws have an important role to play in making sure such prejudices don't poison the labor market and pollute the public sphere. And prejudice aside, government, employers, schools, and building owners should help isolated and disadvantaged groups join the mainstream of society. But even as they offer a fair deal to the disadvantaged, these laws have also become a perk for the privileged.

We could reduce unemployment and social isolation for the disabled and the elderly without treating them as civil rights issues. The civil rights approach is based on the questionable premise that racial isolation and poverty, gender hierarchy, the isolation of the disabled, and unemployment among the elderly are all diseases caused by a common virus—irrational discrimination. This is plausible only if one has a very capacious definition of discrimination. For instance, in the 1970s Paul Brest, my former dean at Stanford Law School, argued that for legal purposes, discrimination should include distinctions based on not only irrational animus and stereotypes but also what he called "selective sympathy and indifference."[59] This definition of bigotry is familiar enough: *If one of every four young* white *men were languishing in prison, you can bet Congress would have found another approach to law enforcement.* Or: *If men got pregnant, abortion would be a sacrament.* This definition of discrimination reflects a generous notion of collective responsibility and social justice: society has a responsibility to eliminate and avoid not only overt discrimination but also inequality caused by milder forms of bias, such as the inability or unwillingness of decision makers to sympathize with people unlike themselves. But it wreaks havoc when translated into individual entitlements.

If you try, you can make a case that some kind of bigotry—

animus, stereotypes, or selective sympathy and indifference—is behind almost any inequality. Why are black men overrepresented in prisons? Because of racial animus on the part of police and prosecutors. And even if crime rates really do vary among racial groups, tough law enforcement reflects "selective sympathy and indifference" toward the groups with higher crime rates. Why are the lines for the ladies' rooms usually longer than for the gents'? Because architects and building planners are selectively indifferent to the needs of women. Why did most American employers have mandatory retirement at age sixty-five until the 1980s? Because of stereotypes about the productivity of older people and selective indifference to them. Why were older public buildings designed with stairs and not wheelchair ramps? Because landlords and architects were selectively indifferent to the needs of the disabled.

In fact these social problems are quite different from one another: they have different histories; they are perpetuated by different institutions in different ways; and they are justified by different misconceptions (and in some cases, valid concerns). It's not very helpful to insist that they all involve "discrimination" and deserve condemnation for that reason. Discrimination, strictly speaking, is often both necessary and just. Exams are *supposed* to discriminate between people who have acquired the necessary skills and mastered the relevant material and those who haven't. Discrimination on the basis of age made sense and was reasonably fair given the old life-cycle model of employment where compensation rose with years of service rather than productivity. Of course, it's possible that certain exams don't measure the right skills, and it's possible that the life-cycle model of compensation should be discouraged and employers should be forced to tie compensation more tightly to job performance. But both of these questions demand distinctive, fact-specific inquiries and controversial judgment calls.

Instead of making the necessary inquiries and judgment calls, civil rights thinking equates all discrimination with bigotry and assumes that inequalities between groups must be the result of bigotry against the less fortunate groups. If we assume the problem is bigotry, then all of the tricky questions of implementation (how can we best address the real causes of inequality?) and distributive justice (who should pay?) disappear, and the answers seem simple: we should eliminate bigotry, and the bigots should pay. Driven by the unexamined presumption that exams that disfavor students diagnosed with learning disabilities are "biased" against them, the law demands that those students receive special exceptions. But no one asks whether the exams accurately measure relevant skills and knowledge generally, because garden-variety poor performers aren't a discrete group against which educators could be biased or about which they might harbor stereotypes. Age discrimination law condemns mandatory retirement as a reflection of "stereotypes" about the aged, despite its fairly obvious practical function of offering older workers with declining productivity a dignified exit from the workplace. But it allows an employer to breach the implicit employment contract and cheat his older employee of an almost-vested pension—one of the most common hazards for older employees—because the bait and switch is motivated not by stereotypes but by simple avarice. Shoehorning such a wide range of social problems into the discrimination framework has made it harder to remove the impediments that trip up many disabled and elderly people, even as it's made it easy for people to turn civil rights into selfish entitlements—and feel justified in doing so.

2

Discriminating Tastes

In 2008 a California man filed a civil rights lawsuit to stop Mother's Day. On May 8, 2005, the California Angels baseball team held a Mother's Day celebration, which included a "#1 Angels Baseball Mom" contest and a Mother's Day tote bag giveaway. According to the court that heard Michael Cohn's lawsuit, "due to the difficult logistics of discerning which women were mothers in the heavy traffic of entry to the game, the Angels decided to generalize 'mothers' as females 18 years old and over" and give them—and only them—the Mother's Day gifts. Cohn didn't fit that description, and so he didn't get a fetching Mother's Day goody bag. Angry that he was denied a gift because of his sex, the disappointed Cohn sued. Mothers may rest easy: the court dismissed the lawsuit, and the Golden State remains safe for celebrations of maternity. The California Court of Appeals pointed out that the Angels did not in fact intend to denigrate or disadvantage men; instead, the team wanted, as the scripture admonishes and as loving children have done for millennia, to honor mothers. "The intended discrimination," the court insisted, "is not female versus male, but rather mothers versus the rest of the population." The court noted, "It is a biological fact that only women can be mothers . . . The Angels did not arbitrarily create this difference."[1] In other words, it was not the Mother's Day celebration that discriminated against Michael Cohn; it was Mother Nature, and her policies are not subject to the court's jurisdiction.

But the Angels *did* discriminate on the basis of sex, whether that was the goal or not. A strict application of civil rights laws favored Cohn's complaint, even if nature's law did not. So far, Mother's Day has survived legal challenge. But the zealous guardians of sexual equality have had success in other struggles against the menace of matriarchy.

The modern, anonymous, cosmopolitan singles scene is tricky under the best of circumstances. Office romances are professional suicide. Internet chat rooms are filled with trolls, adulterers, perverts, and pimply junior high school students, all of whom can use the anonymity of the medium to hide their deficiencies. Mixers are often glorified cattle calls. So dewy coed and rumpled hipster, weathered bachelor and middle-aged divorcée alike turn, in hope and in desperation, to Cupid's watering hole: the singles bar. Many of these establishments deter the thrifty and indigent with a sizable cover charge and repel the impatient with a velvet rope and queue. The singles bar presents unique challenges for women, who often must run a gauntlet of wolves looking for an easy score, repressed misogynists, and married conventioneers. Little surprise, then, that men tend to outnumber women in most such venues, and hence the institution, celebrated in song, on signpost, and in newspaper advertisement, of ladies' night.

Viewed charitably, ladies' night is an admirable form of chivalry in an era when few courtesies survive the cold logic of markets and the competitiveness of the concrete jungle. Viewed cynically, ladies' night is itself a beady-eyed response to a competitive market: if one is selling romantic and sexual opportunities, one needs to offer a wide field of compatible partners and reasonable odds of success. The practice has a whiff of patriarchal condescension, and the ethics of a fisherman baiting a hook. But ladies' night is certainly no worse—in terms of sexism or exploitation—than the singles scene is generally.

It is, however, blatant and unapologetic sex discrimination. And that gave the New York attorney and men's rights activist Roy Den Hollander his opening. In June 2007 he filed a sex discrimination lawsuit against five Manhattan nightclubs that charged women less than men as part of their ladies' night promotions. "What I'm trying to do now in my later years is fight everybody who violates my rights," Den Hollander explained to a *New Yorker* magazine reporter.[2]

Den Hollander was not the first man to strike out against the scourge of ladies' night. In 1979 an Anaheim, California, student, Dennis Koire, saw the ugly face of discrimination when he was excluded from a bar that admitted his female companion. He began to notice female chauvinism everywhere: car washes offered women discounts on discriminatory "ladies' days," and nightclubs waived cover charges for women. When Koire sought to assert his equal rights, not only was he rebuffed—he was ridiculed. "Come back when you're wearing a skirt," quipped one car wash manager. "So *sue* me," dared a nightclub proprietor. Koire did just that: with the help of the Orange County ACLU he took his complaint all the way to the California Supreme Court, and in 1985 the court held that ladies' nights violated the Golden State's Unruh Civil Rights Act, which in unequivocal language entitles anyone in the state to "full and *equal* accommodations, advantages, facilities, privileges, or services in all business establishments of every kind whatsoever."[3]

Koire's lawsuit was the beginning of the end for ladies' nights in states across the nation. In 1998, David Gillespie filed a complaint with the New Jersey Division on Civil Rights against the Coastline Restaurant, which occasionally waived a $5 admission charge and offered drink discounts exclusively to women. The division sided with Gillespie and dropped the gavel on ladies' night.[4] In 2006, Steve Horner sued a Denver nightclub over its ladies' night policy. Horner explained his opposition to the unfair advantages women enjoy in American society: "Women are growing up these days feeling they're entitled to favors. I believe that this entitlement mentality is counterproductive to the social goals of an egalitarian society." He then added, apparently without irony, "I'm going to ask for every dollar I'm owed to the letter of the law, which is $500"—this as damages for the $5 admission charge he was forced to pay as women entered gratis.[5] In 2007, Todd Phillips, a lawyer specializing in gender bias, sued a Las Vegas gym that offered women a discount on initiation fees and a separate workout area.[6] Courts in Iowa, Pennsylvania, Connecticut, and Hawaii have found that ladies' nights and similar promotions or discounts are unlawful sex discrimination. And in 2007, the California Supreme Court reaffirmed its opposition to ladies' night, finding for the Glendale lawyer Marc Angelucci of the National Coalition of Free Men—a "men's rights" organization—in his lawsuit against a Southern California club that occasionally waived its $20 entrance fee for women. Angelucci was awarded $4,000 in damages for each violation.[7]

Although the law in several states apparently prohibits ladies' night, popular opinion echoes the approval of Kool and the Gang: "It's ladies' night and girl the feeling's good." After the New Jersey Division on Civil Rights banned ladies' night, Governor James Mc-Greevey condemned the decision as "bureaucratic nonsense . . . It . . . reflects a complete lack of common sense and good judgment."[8] New Jersey later amended its civil rights laws to allow ladies' nights. Conservatives condemned the rulings as yet another example of government intermeddling in the private sphere: a column in the *National Review* insisted that "the ruling—however absurd—is emblematic of the growing arrogance of a government caste that seeks to micromanage every aspect of Americans' lives."[9]

Liberals complained that the decision distorted the true purpose of civil rights laws and diverted resources from real injustices. Rita Haley, president of the New York City chapter of the National Organization for Women, remarked, "I am concerned that he [an anti-ladies'-night plaintiff] is looking for discrimination in all the wrong places."[10] The less ideologically minded lamented the death of chivalry and a misguided step toward an androgynous culture. One commenter on a website chat room quipped: "Ban Ladies Night? Oh dear . . . What's Next? Ban Fun? Ban Drinking? Ban a Good Time? As a bloke, my heart goes out to the person who feel that ladies shouldn't get special treatment."[11] A legal commentator remarked: "Bars rivaling a Star Trek Convention [in the ratio of men to women] are no fun for anyone."[12] The *National Review* column queried, "What's next, ticketing men for opening doors or giving up their seats on the bus?"[13]

Could be. The California Supreme Court chief justice, Rose Bird, insisted in the *Koire* case that "the legality of sex-based price discounts cannot depend on the subjective value judgments about which types of sex-based distinctions are important or harmful." Another lawyer was adamant that ladies' nights had to go, even if the offending bar also had a "men's night" when it gave the same free perks to men. Comparing ladies' night to the racist contempt of apartheid and the Jim Crow era, she insisted that "one act of discrimination does not cancel out another . . . If a bar had a 'Whites' Night' followed by 'Blacks' Night' no one would blink an eye before denouncing . . . each night."[14] The George Washington University law professor John Banzhaf, who has encouraged his students to sue to stop ladies' nights, argues that ladies' night is in principle indistinguishable from discriminatory customs that denigrate women: discrimination is discrimination.[15] Under this kind of logic, offering your seat on the bus to a woman because of her sex is just as bad as making black people stand in the back of the bus because of their race.

Most of the time, people pressing for new legal rights have good intentions and are addressing serious social problems. Professor Banzhaf, who sued to ban ladies' night and plans more litigation over inequitably long lines for women's restrooms, has also helped women fight discriminatory pricing for services, such as laundry services and hairstyling. Many laundries charge more than twice as much to launder and press a woman's blouse as for a man's shirt. Although they may claim that the higher charge reflects the additional work required to manage ruffles, bows, and other feminine details, many apply it to women's blouses even when the garment in question is almost identical to a man's except for size and color. Similarly, some hair salons charge women more than men for a cut and style, even when the women have short and simple haircuts and the men have long and elaborately styled tresses. These practices reflect outdated, habitual prejudices. Common stereotypes cast women as more fastidious about their appearance and women's clothing and hairstyles as more elaborate than men's; as a result, businesses lazily discriminate on the basis of sex, even though those stereotypes grow less valid with each passing year and even though they could easily discriminate based on the actual garment or hairstyle rather than on the sex of the customer.

These types of sex discrimination aren't necessarily the work of bigots intent on keeping women down, but they are based on dubious stereotypes about how women do and should behave. And although each in isolation isn't a big deal, they add up. Imagine receiving a handful of change compared with the dollar a man earns for similar work, facing unspoken barriers on the job, and getting the cold shoulder (or, worse, the wandering glance and groping hand) in the professional social circles that offer your best shot at networking and mentoring. On top of these indignities, imagine you also had to wait in long lines every time nature called and pay a premium to have the clothing you need for work laundered or to have your hair cut (apologies to my female readers, who probably have no need to imagine these things, having experienced them).

One can see why some people might conclude that *every* sex-based distinction is a civil rights issue.

But do we really have to ban Mother's Day and ladies' night in order to address these obvious injustices? If a civil rights crusader like Professor Banzhaf really can't tell the difference between invidious prejudice and innocent or prudent distinctions, will he stop after equalizing the queues for the restrooms? What if the ladies' room is bigger, or cleaner, or has more attendants or a comfy sofa, while the men's is just a wall of urinals with a sticky floor and dirty sink? Shouldn't we sue to eradicate those inequalities too? For that matter, even if the men's and women's restrooms were identical in every respect, could the lofty ideal of equal rights abide separate but equal restrooms? Surely no one would blink an eye before denouncing a business that had a whites-only restroom and a separate but equal blacks-only restroom. If, as Justice Bird insisted, legality cannot depend on subjective value judgments about which types of sex-based distinctions are important or harmful, then doesn't equality require men and women to be integrated in one unisex bathroom? The practical impediments could be overcome—at least in theory. After all, don't sex-segregated bathrooms reflect an outdated obsession with sexual modesty? *Sure, people will be uncomfortable sharing bathrooms with the opposite sex at first, but they'll just have to get over it; after all, men were once uncomfortable sharing corporate boardrooms with the opposite sex too.* And the privacy issues can be mitigated: everyone enters and exits closed stalls fully clothed; a unisex loo could simply eliminate urinals and with them the problem of modesty around the opposite sex.

Is there more than outdated modesty behind separate men's and women's bathrooms? Imagine a lone woman entering a train station bathroom late at night to find a man loitering inside, or an aggressive male suitor following a woman into the bathroom to continue his failed attempt at seduction, or a woman running a gauntlet of drunken men on her way to the toilet at the end of a baseball game. After reading about Professor Banzhaf's planned litigation,

I conducted an informal survey of about fifty smart professional women to see what they thought should be done about the issue of bathroom queue equity. Almost all of the women I asked were well to the left on the ideological spectrum, and many were committed feminists and champions of women's rights. Still, precisely two women—or 4 percent—embraced the absolutist position that separate men's and women's bathrooms violated civil rights. In fact, most were adamant that the sexes should be separate but equal in the realm of personal hygiene. One worried that "a formal right to parity, or a regulatory agency deciding who pees where, is kind of gross . . . and I think if you force people to go unisex, that will lead to pressure for more private stalls for modesty reasons . . . why spend money on that?" Another said, "Gee, this seems such a wrong fight to me . . . Tremendous resources involved . . . but mostly off the point of improving [things] for everyone involved, men and women." Eliminating urinals would require costly remodeling of thousands of bathrooms. Moreover, urinals are almost universal fixtures in men's bathrooms for a practical reason: they're cheap and don't take up much space. Eliminating urinals in coed bathrooms would almost certainly mean fewer places to pee for everybody. These practical considerations were uppermost in the minds of most of the women I talked to, but they don't figure in a rigid equal rights analysis.

Today most people agree that sexist rules and customs that keep women down and perpetuate dusty old stereotypes of female frailty, passivity, and incompetence should be prohibited in the workplace and expunged from the public sphere. But only a handful of extremists would extend laws against sex discrimination to forbid chivalry or ban a time-honored tradition like Mother's Day or an innocent custom like ladies' night. Of course, read literally, without the mediating influence of good judgment or common sense, the laws that prohibit truly demeaning and invidious sex discrimination apply to ladies' night promotions and to the use of the female gender as an expedient proxy for mothers in a Mother's Day giveaway.

Rights go wrong when propelled beyond the boundaries of good sense by abstract and scholastic thinking. Justice Bird's admonishment notwithstanding, legal prohibition *must* depend on value judgments about which practices are important or harmful. Not every distinction—even if based on race or sex—is invidious. Some are practical: sex-exclusive restrooms prevent avoidable embarrassment, harassment, and assault. And some are innocuous: ladies' night is a fairly harmless practice designed to make male-dominated nightclubs more inviting to women. Judges shouldn't blindly apply rigid rules, heedless of practical consequences; it's their job to tell the difference between legitimate challenges to antediluvian prejudices and the trivial, spiteful, and extreme claims that make rights go wrong.

For Discrimination

In the decades since the landmark social movements and civil rights laws of the 1950s and 1960s, civil rights have both narrowed and intensified their focus to zero in on the problem of *discrimination*. The legal and cultural stigma now attached to "discrimination" is so powerful that the very word is almost synonymous with bigotry. But "discrimination," stripped of the moral connotations that now surround the term, simply means making and acting on distinctions. Sometimes it makes perfect sense to discriminate—even on the basis of race or sex. When my doctor tells me to cut down on salt and fatty food because black men are statistically more likely to suffer from hypertension and heart disease caused by salt and fat, he's discriminating on the basis of race and sex. And I should be glad that he is. Unfortunately, the civil rights focus on discrimination leads people to condemn reasonable, prudent, and innocent distinctions.

Worse, faced with inequities that are not caused by discrimination, modern civil rights law is impotent, and civil rights activism is unfocused and often misguided. The narrow civil rights focus on discrimination has encouraged many people to oversimplify the problems of inequality and illegitimate hierarchy and misdiagnose social maladies, condemning benign actions that involve making group-based distinctions and ignoring malignant practices that don't involve discrimination.

Civil rights haven't always been so obsessive or so limited. The historic March on Washington in 1963 led by Martin Luther King Jr. focused on "*jobs* and freedom," reflecting a decades-old civil rights agenda to expand substantive economic opportunities for blacks, who faced both overt prejudice and systematic disadvantage. No one in 1963 thought that civil rights required the elimination of all racial distinctions: when King hoped for a world where people would "not be judged by the color of their skin, but by the content of their character" (perhaps the most abused quotation in the history of American oratory), he advocated a social ideal of equal respect, not a rigid and impractical rule that would condemn the acknowledgment of salient social divisions. During the early 1970s, as the omnibus civil rights legislation was first being interpreted by courts, there was a robust debate about the appropriate meaning and scope of civil rights. Few thoughtful people argued for the rigid and simplistic antidiscrimination law that so many lawyers and judges accept today. For instance, the Yale Law School professor Owen Fiss argued that the Fourteenth Amendment guarantee of equal protection required courts to look askance at laws that disadvantaged certain downtrodden groups, of which blacks were the paradigm.[16] My former dean at Stanford, Paul Brest, argued that equal protection forbade not only overt discrimination but also laws and policies that looked evenhanded but reflected "selective sympathy and indifference."[17] In the 1960s and early 1970s few thought intentional discrimination was the defining feature of social bigotry: many thought the intent of decision makers was inevitably too obscure to be the object of legal scrutiny, and many others thought discriminatory intent was important largely because it led to unequal consequences.

This period was no golden age of enlightenment: many of the ideas advanced then seem misguided today, and many more have proven to be incoherent, quixotic, or unworkable. But the legal, legislative, and popular conversation involved serious and honest grappling with practical questions: How can we change bigoted social attitudes? How can we best integrate isolated racial groups into the mainstream of society? How can we ensure that job opportunities aren't limited by racial and ethnic cartels? How can we prevent government from acting on and reinforcing old prejudices? None of these questions are less relevant today, but over time practical and substantive concerns were lost from view as the civil rights lens concentrated its focus on discrimination.

Of course, discrimination has always been *one* of the main targets of civil rights, and for good reason: historically, people expressed their prejudice openly, in the form of overt discrimination, which in turn isolated women and minorities and limited their job opportunities. But eliminating discrimination came to dominate civil rights—both in the courts and on the streets—at the expense of other means to social justice. Not surprisingly, this narrow focus was largely successful in eliminating overt discrimination, just as a lens that concentrates the rays of the sun onto one spot on a leaf will eventually burn the spot away. This focus on discrimination worked to eliminate the most conspicuous evils of Jim Crow, but such a narrow civil rights approach is no longer the right way to deal with many of the nation's worst social injustices.

America's history of systematic exclusion and exploitation based on race has left us with troubled, racially segregated neighborhoods where job opportunities and successful role models are rare; as a result, a subculture of gray-market hustling is pervasive, and serious crime is common. Even relatively successful black families often aren't part of the informal social networks that provide job opportunities and mentoring for many of their white—and increasingly also their Asian—peers.

Women also face distinctive obstacles to career advancement.

Although a large and growing number of American households need two incomes to make ends meet, in most families women still take on the lioness's share of household work and child care. This isn't just the result of chauvinism among employers (although of course that plays its part in limiting women's opportunities); instead, it's the result of deep-seated social expectations that lag behind a rapidly changing economy. The job market, far from adjusting to the new need for shared domestic responsibility, is becoming more and more demanding. Working men and women alike need a stay-at-home spouse to handle child care, laundry, cleaning, and social planning as they log the long hours on the job that were once the exclusive burden of the ambitious working stiff. The old roles of male breadwinner and female caretaker die hard for both men and women: many women want to fulfill the traditionally female domestic roles, and many men are happy to let them do so. And because gender norms are contested and in flux, the professional woman's every small decision is a potential blunder: from clothing and grooming options to posture and comportment, women in the workplace walk a narrow path between coming across as unprofessionally girlish and titillating and as off-puttingly gruff and masculine. "Discrimination" doesn't capture these pervasive impediments and double binds, and as a result, a law that targets discrimination often misses the mark.

The Harrah's operating company runs hotels and casinos in Las Vegas, Atlantic City, New Orleans, Lake Tahoe, and Reno. Its properties offer lodging and entertainment for conventioneers, stag-party goers, and pleasure seekers of all incomes and tastes: high rollers can experience Caligulaean excess at the luxurious Caesars Palace, while middle-income tourists and conventioneers can book moderately priced rooms overlooking a miniature Eiffel Tower in the petit bourgeois arrondissements of the Paris Hotel and Casino. Harrah's properties in other cities are typically less elaborate, but sybaritic

indulgence is a common theme: while Caesars Palace features gourmet restaurants and designer boutiques, the less exclusive hotels feature all-you-can-eat buffets and souvenir shops. In the legendary Las
Vegas tradition, the Harrah's family of hotels emphasize forbidden
pleasures: gambling, drinking, and sex. This includes Harrah's Reno,
where, according to the company website, guests are invited to "sip
on a variety of cocktails made with only the best liquers" (to say
nothing, one imagines, of liquors and liqueurs) while listening to the
"sexy, seductive Sapphire Sirens heating up the Sapphire Lounge
with intoxicating dances and sensual vocals."[18]

Image is everything in the hospitality-cum-sin business: Caesars
Palace features cocktail waitresses clad in Roman togas cut off at
mid-thigh; Paris is staffed by cancan girls wearing short ruffled
skirts. Bally's Las Vegas is home to "the last authentic showgirl revue," *Jubilee*, which features a chorus line of "50 topless dancers,"
who, in the course of the evening's performance, don over a thousand Bob Mackie–designed costumes featuring sequins, feathers,
false eyelashes, and theatrical makeup. "Hundreds of Thousands
of Rhinestones, Covering Practically Nothing," boasts the hotel's
advertisements. Nor are the titillating outfits confined to showgirls
and dancers: many Las Vegas casinos require cocktail waitresses
to wear stiletto heels during their long hours serving drinks. The
Harrah's-owned Imperial Palace was sued for sex discrimination in
1996 because it required cocktail waitresses to have "a sexy and glamorous appearance" and accordingly moved pregnant women into
less visible—and lower-paid—positions when they began to show.[19]
In June 2001, casino cocktail waitresses organized the Kiss My Foot
campaign and staged a protest outside Las Vegas's Venetian hotel
against rules requiring high-heeled shoes.[20]

What happened in Vegas didn't stay in Vegas: in 2000, Harrah's
implemented the "Personal Best" and "Beverage Department Image
Transformation" program, requiring staff at all of its properties
to meet new grooming and appearance standards. Like Greeks
sequestered inside a statue of a horse, the rules came disguised as a

gift: Harrah's paid for each employee to get a $3,000 professional makeover, including hair and makeup. To make sure the gift kept on giving, employees were photographed in their uniforms and new, improved hair and makeup, a visual memento of their "personal best." Each employee was required to maintain that standard—hair, makeup, and weight—from then on.

Harrah's Reno employees took to the streets to protest the new grooming policies. Roughly fifty people marched with signs reading "Harrah's Makes a Lousy Pimp" and "Harrah's Hooks Women to Make an Extra Buck." The protesters handed out leaflets comparing Harrah's grooming requirements with those of the Moonlite Bunny Ranch brothel—Harrah's rules were more strict. The Bunny Ranch's owner, Dennis Hof, the self-described "pimpmaster general of America," happily took up the cause of the Harrah's employees: "I'm in the sex business . . . and yet I'm not concerned about makeup. Harrah's is not selling sex but they want their girls to be all made up."[21]

Compared with the glitz required of showgirls and cocktail waitresses, the new image for bartenders was downright staid. A standard uniform consisted of black pants, white shirt, black vest, and black bow tie. Grooming rules forbade "faddish hairstyles or unnatural hair colors" and required "tasteful and simple jewelry only: no large chokers, chains or bracelets." No long hair or makeup for men. For women: "Hair must be teased, curled, or styled every day you work. Hair must be worn down at all times, no exceptions. Stockings are to be of nude or natural color consistent with employee's skin tone. No runs. Makeup (face powder, blush and mascara) must be worn and applied neatly in complimentary [sic] colors. Lip color must be worn at all times."

Harrah's had always encouraged female employees to wear makeup, but now it was mandatory: apply the lipstick or apply for a new job. Darlene Jespersen had worked as a bartender at Harrah's in Reno, Nevada, for twenty makeup-free years when the image transformation edict came down. According to the deposition taken as part of her sex discrimination lawsuit against Harrah's, Jespersen found makeup demeaning and degrading. Wearing makeup made her so uncomfortable she couldn't do her job. Rather than compromise her self-image by wearing makeup, Darlene Jespersen defied the new grooming policy and was fired.[22]

Harrah's policy required women and only women to wear makeup and styled or teased hair. It obviously discriminated on the basis of sex, strictly speaking. But the federal courts that heard Jespersen's case and appeal both held that the policy did not discriminate on the basis of sex, legally speaking. Why not?

The short answer is that these courts did what the California chief justice Rose Bird would not and made a value judgment about which types of sex-based distinctions are important or harmful. In doing so, they followed decades of established law that *allows* sex-discriminatory grooming standards and dress codes. Consider the rejected complaint of the television reporter Christine Craft. Like Darlene Jespersen, Craft had bad experiences with makeup. She worked her way from a small local station in Salinas, California, to San Francisco and then to a network job hosting the "Women in Sports" segment of *CBS Sports Spectacular*. CBS made Craft dye her hair blond and wear heavy makeup on the air, but despite these efforts the "Women in Sports" segment was discontinued after thirty weeks. In January 1981, Craft was hired as co-anchor at KMBC in Kansas City, Missouri, as part of an effort to "soften" the news presentation. Craft was apparently willing to serve as the softer side of the evening news, but she insisted that she didn't want to go through another "makeover" like the one at CBS. Management agreed in principle, but added that they did work with image consultants who might have a few ideas about Craft's appearance and dress.

Having lured her to Kansas City, KMBC management and the image consultants then set in to transform Craft from duckling to swan. They applied her makeup, gave her a "dress for success" book, and arranged for a new Macy's wardrobe and wardrobe consultation for her. To no avail: a focus group's reaction to Craft's appearance was "overwhelmingly negative." Craft asked to be released from her contract so she could return to field reporting in California, but KMBC management convinced her to work on her image instead. But the results of a survey confirmed that Craft had not won the hearts of the viewing audience: in comparison with female co-anchors at KMBC's competitors, Craft trailed in almost every category of evaluation. KMBC's consultants advised that the station replace Craft; in August, KMBC demoted Craft to reporter. Craft sued KMBC for sex discrimination.

There's no doubt that KMBC discriminated on the basis of sex. But some of its sex discrimination was to Craft's advantage: the station hired Craft in the first place, in part, because of her sex. Having done so, they insisted on sex-specific grooming, and they evaluated her by comparing her with other women using sex-specific standards. The federal district court and the Court of Appeals for the Eighth Circuit found, following a substantial line of cases, that "appearance regulations making distinctions on the basis of sex" do not violate the law as long as "the standards are reasonable and are enforced as to both sexes in an evenhanded manner."[23]

Title VII allows employers to discriminate when sex is a bona fide occupational qualification (BFOQ), although it allows no such exception to its prohibition of race discrimination. This reflects a widely held belief that sex differences are likely to be relevant to certain jobs. Most BFOQ exceptions involve privacy and modesty: public restroom or locker room attendants, for instance. But sometimes the exception allows an employer to yield to widespread public attitudes, even when those attitudes are objectionable. For instance, one influential case involved a female prison guard who applied to work in a men's prison: because of the risk that a woman would be the target of harassment by prisoners, potentially undermining the authority of the prison guards, the court held that male sex was a BFOQ for the position.

The BFOQ exception is and should be a narrow one. If wide-spread public attitudes about sex difference alone were enough to trigger the exception, the law would mirror social prejudices rather than remedy them. Does this leave us with no alternative but to ban all sex-based distinctions? Most courts have tried to find a middle ground, banning sex discrimination when it's demeaning or harmful to women, but allowing reasonable distinctions that reflect the overwhelming social consensus that some differences between the sexes are both inevitable and desirable. This necessarily involves some difficult and controversial judgment calls.

If you're looking for demeaning grooming and dress codes, there are more obvious targets than Harrah's or the evening news: for example, the Hooters restaurant chain, which allows only well-endowed young women to don the company uniform of tight tank tops and bright orange hot pants and serve its deep-fried diner fare. The chain hires men for other jobs, but table service is reserved exclusively for the "attractive, vivacious Hooters girls."

Hooters doesn't just have different rules for men and women; it has an entirely segregated job category. The Hooters employee handbook advises:

> The essence of Hooters is the Hooters Girl . . . Customers can go to many places for wings and beer, but it is our Hooters Girls who make our concept unique. Hooters offers its customers the look of the "All American Cheerleader, Surfer, Girl Next Door." The essence of the Hooters Concept is entertainment through female sex appeal, of which the LOOK is a key part. When you are in the Hooters Girl Uniform you are literally playing a role . . . you must comply with the Image and Grooming Standards that the role requires.
>
> Hair is to be styled at all times. No ponytails or pigtails . . . No bizarre hair cuts, styles, or colors are acceptable . . .

Make-up is to be worn always to best accentuate your features. Hooters Girls are to be camera-ready at all times . . .

The Hooters Girl uniform shirt . . . must be sized to fit, *NO BAGGINESS.*

Only approved Orange Hooters Girl Shorts are to be worn, sized to fit . . .

Pantyhose are a required part of the uniform and are to be worn any time the Hooters Girl uniform is worn . . . If the panty-hose run or snag, they must be immediately replaced with a new pair for you to continue your shift . . .

Failure to comply with Image or Grooming Standards may result in discipline up to and including termination.[24]

Many women find the Hooters concept demeaning, but it's been men who have taken legal action against the company for sex discrimination. Hooters claims that sex is a bona fide occupational qualification for the job of Hooters Girl. The company compares its policy with that of the Playboy Club, which employed an exclusively female staff of scantily dressed "Bunnies" to serve drinks and food. In 1971 the New York State Division of Human Rights held that sex was a BFOQ for the job of Playboy Bunny.

Hooters's website presses its point by including, in a website gallery of attractive young Hooters Girls, Vince "the Hooters Guy": a burly man with a mustache and hairy chest wearing a tight white tank top and blond wig. "In 1995, HOOTERS . . . needed help to communicate how ridiculous it was for the Federal EEOC to try and force HOOTERS to hire guys as HOOTERS Girls," reads the accompanying text. Hooters's legal justification may be as skimpy as its uniforms. When Southwest Airlines, billing itself as the "love airline," made a similar argument in defense of its policy to limit flight attendant and ticket agent positions to women, a federal court found it liable for sex discrimination. Like Hooters, Southwest had made sex appeal its competitive advantage: "Unabashed allusions to love and sex pervade all aspects of Southwest's public image. Its T.V.

commercials feature attractive attendants in fitted outfits . . . while an alluring feminine voice promises inflight love."[25]

Hooters apparently isn't confident enough to test its legal theory in court; instead, the company seems willing to buy off disappointed male job seekers in order to keep its girls and their unique attractions front and center. In 1997, Hooters settled a sex discrimination lawsuit filed by disappointed male job seekers for $3.75 million: the company agreed to hire men as hosts, kitchen staff, and bartenders, but the settlement allowed Hooters to continue to limit waitstaff positions to women.[26] The deal didn't satisfy everyone: in 2009, a Corpus Christi man, Nikolai Grushevski, sued Hooters for sex discrimination after being turned down for a job as a Hooters, well, Girl. "If we lose this go around, you can next expect hairy-legged guys in the Rockettes to line up and male models in the *Sports Illustrated* swimsuit issue," complained a Hooters executive.[27] Grushevski reached a confidential settlement with Hooters later that year.

Of course, there's a difference between a chorus line dancer or swimsuit model, on the one hand, and a waitress or flight attendant, on the other: physical grace and aesthetics are indispensable parts of the chorus line and the swimsuit pictorial; waitresses and flight attendants, by contrast, perform discrete tasks that don't involve looks. No one believes Congress intended to effectively outlaw sexually titillating entertainment when it passed Title VII, nor could it do so without violating the First Amendment guarantee of freedom of expression. Like it or not, businesses are free to sell sex and use sex appeal to sell other products. But Congress did intend to prevent employers from making sex—if not sexiness—a condition of employment. Hooters discriminates against men, but the real victims of its practices are women. A few men lose out on low-wage jobs as Hooters waitstaff; by contrast, the Hooters concept threatens to promote a business culture where women—and only women—are required to use sex appeal to get mundane jobs waiting tables.

Playboy Bunnies and Hooters Girls present hard cases for civil rights laws because they combine a job for which sex is irrelevant—serving food and drinks—with a setting in which sex is everything. Most courts have used an implicit sliding scale to evaluate jobs where sex appeal is part of the business model: if sex appeal is indispensable or central to the job, sex is a BFOQ and the employer can discriminate; if sex appeal is peripheral to the job, sex is not a BFOQ and discrimination is unlawful. This is why Southwest Airlines wasn't allowed to discriminate in hiring flight attendants, who must perform a wide range of challenging and legally required tasks that have nothing to do with sex appeal. And it explains why the Playboy Clubs—more entertainment venues that happened to sell food than restaurants—were allowed to hire only women as Bunnies.

Courts have used a similar context-specific approach in evaluating sex-specific grooming standards. When image and glamour are central to a job or business model, courts are more willing to allow sex-specific grooming rules, even when they come with unequal burdens. Christine Craft and Darlene Jespersen were employed in industries that emphasize image, glamour, and appearances generally. Jespersen's sex discrimination complaint might have been stronger had she been a bartender at a dowdy airport Hilton, but her employer—Harrah's—competes in one of the most glitzy and sexualized hospitality markets in the United States. Every aspect of a typical casino is orchestrated to make the visitor forget his or her ordinary life and inhibitions: gaming floors and bars are designed without windows so visitors forget the time of day; layouts are deliberately disorienting and exits difficult to find; alluring distractions are everywhere to draw the visitor deeper into the maze of slot machines, craps tables, and roulette wheels. The implicit yet powerful message is that the casino is a glamorous fantasy world where the humdrum conventions of decorum and restraint do not apply. Of course, the casinos hope that the pervasive atmosphere of excitement and suspended inhibition will carry over from the bar and showgirl revue to the gaming tables. Every casino employee contributes to—or detracts from—this carefully planned seduction. The burlesque of the casino is only an especially conspicuous instance of the come-ons typical in the marketing, entertainment, and hospitality industries, from the chic hostess at a gourmet restaurant to the well-built, fresh-faced bellhop at a five-star hotel to the sommelier with the reassuringly urbane mannerisms and Continental accent.

Christine Craft began her career as a reporter—a job where image shouldn't matter much—but when she became an anchorperson, looks were of greater importance. Craft was held to different standards from her male counterparts, standards that were probably stricter and more detailed. That's discriminatory. But Craft was hired to fill an explicitly gendered position that called for her to "soften" KMBC's evening news program: in a sense, gendered grooming rules were necessary for her to do the job she was hired for. There's no doubt that KMBC discriminated on the basis of sex; it did so when it hired Craft in the first place. Having accepted the job, Craft had to have expected gendered standards of appearance. In fact, she tacitly acknowledged as much when she told KMBC that she didn't want to repeat her experience on "Women in Sports" but agreed to work with their image consultants. Maybe KMBC breached an implicit bargain by placing so much emphasis on Craft's image after promising not to make her relive her previous makeover experience. But it's hard to credit the claim that the grooming standards violated her civil rights simply because they involved distinctions based on sex. Craft had already acquiesced in KMBC's sex discrimination—which worked in her favor when she has hired—and only hoped to limit its scope.

The strongest arguments against gendered grooming standards don't insist that all sex-based distinctions are unlawful; they ask us to make a value judgment about which distinctions are harmful and which are innocent. In dissent in *Jespersen*, Judge Alex Kozinski points out the obvious: Harrah's "Personal Best" grooming code didn't just require *different* things of women and of men; it required *more* of women than it did of men. "Application of makeup . . . requires considerable time and care," he wrote. "Even those of us who don't wear makeup know how long it can take from the hundreds of hours we've spent over the years frantically tapping our toes and pointing to our wrists."[28]

There's no doubt that many conventional norms of grooming and dress are harder on women than on men. Even the most fastidious and fashionable man need only worry about a close shave, a sensible haircut, a clean shirt, and a well-knotted tie. Women, on the other hand, often feel the need to apply several different types of makeup, using an array of artist's brushes and surgeon's implements to curl eyelashes, pluck brows, dab on blush and eyeliner, brush on mascara, line lips, and blend in lipstick. They must contend with delicate nylons that snag and run and learn to walk in high heels that threaten twisted ankles in the short run and podiatrist's visits over the long haul. There's much to be said for using the law to loosen the grip of these grooming norms by prohibiting businesses from making them a condition of employment.

But there will probably always be differences in the ways men and women are expected to dress. Even most women who refuse on principle to wear makeup or high heels are willing to nod their pageboy haircuts to convention and wear skirts and dresses, pantsuits, women's blouses, and feminine jewelry. And of course plenty of women voluntarily endure the hassle because they enjoy feminine fashions, or they think, on balance, the positive reactions they receive make it worthwhile. Some degree of conformity to conventional gender norms is simply a part of appropriate and professional attire. It's obvious that overly provocative clothing is inappropriate for the workplace, but a woman dressed in male drag can be equally distracting: the woman who wants to be noticed for her work and not her wardrobe will avoid dressing like a tomboy as well as like a showgirl.

This may be changing: in many of America's more cosmopolitan cities, a small but growing group of transgendered people insist on deliberately androgynous dress and grooming or gender cross-dressing. But this is a very small subculture, unlikely to ever achieve the size or prominence of the gay rights movement with which it is often too casually associated. Moreover, "transgender" denotes a number of distinct and often mutually antagonistic relationships to gender: from the committed androgyne who challenges the strict bimodal male-female division to the "man trapped in a woman's body" who seeks sex-reassignment surgery and hormone therapy—hardly a repudiation of the conventional gender division but instead a bid to switch sides.

Perhaps one day a growing transgender community will make us ashamed of today's gender norms. But for now, employers are entitled to require professionalism—gender differences included. Those who oppose all such grooming policies complain that they reflect "stereotypes," but one person's sex stereotype is another's sensible distinction. Did KMBC's attempt to remake Christine Craft's makeup and wardrobe reflect "sex stereotypes" about how women should look, or a sensible decision to try to make Craft more charismatic to the viewing public? For that matter, did KMBC's decision to hire Craft in the first place to "soften" the evening news reflect sex stereotypes, or was it based on the reasonable suspicion that viewers of both sexes are more likely to warm up to a male-female team?

Deciding when gendered norms are reasonable and when they are overly burdensome or demeaning requires a subtle and context-specific inquiry. And here's the rub: in some jobs—especially those where looks are important—many reasonable gendered norms are harder on women than on men. Judge Kozinski, in his dissent in *Jespersen*, rightly takes his Ninth Circuit colleagues to task for trying to evade this problem. The *Jespersen* majority copped out: "We would have to speculate . . . [and] guess whether [Harrah's] policy creates unequal burdens for women," they demurred. But as Judge Kozinski insisted, "You don't need an expert witness to figure out that [face powder, blush, mascara, and lipstick] . . . don't grow on trees . . . [and] that application of makeup is an intricate and pains-taking process." There was no real doubt Harrah's policy burdened women more than men; the *Jespersen* court tacitly decided that the unequal burden was acceptable. That's a judgment call, based on the nature of Darlene Jespersen's job, the state of American gender rela-tions, and perhaps the judges' own reservations about how much the law can change society.

Personally, I think the *Jespersen* court made a bad call: the job of bartender isn't sufficiently image dependent to justify the un-equal burden that Harrah's policy placed on women. But the court's mistake was not in making a value judgment instead of inflexibly prohibiting any and all discrimination. The law can't rid society of sex differences or of all the differing—and at times unequal—burdens that come with them. The best it can do is to eliminate some of those burdens and control and temper those inequalities it can't eliminate. This is a delicate intervention that requires good judgment: a willingness to intervene when appropriate and forbear when necessary. That's why we need judges who are both well versed in the law and well acquainted with the subtleties of social inter-actions and the economy, judges who are both knowledgeable and wise. No rigid legal rule or unyielding moral principle ever devised or expounded on by jurists or philosophers can take the place of good judges with good judgment—or save us from bad judges with poor judgment.

Burning Down Justice

Along with astronaut, cowboy, and Jedi Knight, a job as a fire-fighter ranks close to the top of most wanted careers for five-year-old boys nationwide. For adults, a career as a firefighter retains some of its boyish charm, and, more substantively, it is typically a good-paying job with generous benefits—a rare and coveted thing in today's unforgiving economy. But modern building codes, improved wiring and gas lines, and fire-retardant building materials have left firefighters with less to do. Firefighters' jobs—long highly sought after—are now also more scarce. Like any government job, they have always been potential objects of political favoritism. In response to decades of blatant cronyism, in which privileged constituencies, often defined by ethnicity, were given control over some part of the civil service in return for loyal political support, American cities today almost universally select firefighters using some sort of objective evaluation designed to ensure that merit—not politics—determines success. Civil service reform has eliminated blatant graft and nepotism and has limited the ability of incumbent employees to handpick their successors. But it has replaced these evils with employment examinations that exclude the nuances of desirable selectivity along with the evils of favoritism.

Like many American cities, New Haven, Connecticut, changed dramatically during the 1960s and 1970s: in 1950, New Haven was 94 percent white and just under 6 percent black;[29] in 1960, it was 85 percent white and 14.5 percent black; by 2000, it was 43.5 percent white and 37.4 percent black.[30] New Haven's fire department filled its ranks from the Polish, Irish, and Italian American communities that made up much of the city's working-class population in the mid-twentieth century. But as whites left New Haven for its surrounding suburbs, they, like many suburbanites, hung on to their jobs in the city—including in the fire department. By 1973 only 3.6 percent of New Haven firefighters were black, and none were Hispanic, although the city's black population had grown to over 26 percent.[31] Black firefighters sued New Haven for race discrimination in one of the first of a wave of civil rights lawsuits against fire departments nationwide. Today, New Haven's rank-and-file firefighters are integrated, but whites still hold a disproportionate number of supervisory positions.

In 1989 black firefighters sued New Haven over discrimination in promotions; a Connecticut appellate court found that the department's promotion practices violated civil service laws. In 2004 another Connecticut court banned another promotion practice in response to another lawsuit by black firefighters, and as a result the promotions of some white firefighters were reversed. "You want to talk about a stiff workplace?" one black firefighter commented to *Slate*'s Nicole Allan and Emily Bazelon. "I don't want to remember what that was like."[32] In response to these complaints the department hired a professional consultant to develop a promotional examination that everyone could agree was fair. The consultant made a special effort to rid the exam of any hidden or inadvertent racial bias: the new test excluded personal references and supervisor evaluations, which might reflect biases or favor white applicants who were more likely to have relatives or friends in the department, and its questions were vetted for relevance to real-life firefighting skills.

But the consultant didn't have control over everything. Many professional examination experts believe that oral questioning yields more probative—and less racially skewed—results than written exams, but the firefighters' union had demanded years ago that the written portion of the exam count for 60 percent of a candidate's total score. A written exam might test a candidate's knowledge of technical information, statistics, and equipment. Anyone with a knack for exams can do well with sufficient study, and people with longer exposure to the material will have an advantage that may exaggerate their actual on-the-job competence. An oral exam might pose more open-ended questions ("Here's a picture of a building: the ground floor is on fire and a family trapped upstairs. What should you do?") and allow for follow-up depending on the candidate's answer. Another factor that the consultant couldn't control: the city's charter required that only the three highest-scoring candidates for any open position be considered for promotion. Few professional exams are fine-tuned enough to sort candidates in rank order. They are best used to set a floor for minimum competence— like the medical boards or a state bar exam—or to group candidates into rough "tiers" of qualification. Finer-textured distinctions involve more intangible factors—such as temperament and judgment—that tests can't measure.

New Haven's new promotional exam might not have been perfect, but at least it wasn't racially biased, right? Depends on whom you ask. When the results came back, no black firefighters and only one Hispanic were eligible for promotion. The New Haven Firebirds—a black firefighters group—complained that the exam and promotion rules worked together to disadvantage minority candidates. Black firefighters could make a reasonably strong case that the promotions violated Title VII, the federal civil rights law prohibiting employment discrimination. There are two ways to discriminate under Title VII. The employer can intentionally discriminate by making race a factor in employment decisions—choosing a white candidate over a black candidate because of race. An employer can also discriminate by using a selection process that has a "disparate impact" on a protected group—in other words, a process that screens out most or all members of a particular group and isn't sufficiently "job related." If the exam, rules, and decisions that made minority candidates ineligible to become lieutenants and captains—including the greater weight given to the written as opposed to the oral exam or the decision to rank candidates instead of using the exam as a floor—were not a good way to select the best candidates for the positions, they would violate the law, even if they weren't motivated by racism. A firefighter who defended the examination told a local newspaper that the exam didn't favor white firefighters per se; instead, it favored " 'fire buffs' who have spent their whole lives reading fire suppression manuals . . . Most firefighters matching that description happened to be white."[33] The legal question was whether "fire buffs" were better firefighters, or simply people who had amassed a lot of esoteric knowledge that didn't have much relevance to real-world challenges.

It wouldn't be enough for the city to prove that the *exam* was well designed. New Haven would also need to show that the rank-

ing and relative weighting of the written and oral exams—rules the
city accepted but had never evaluated itself—were a good way of
sorting the candidates. Nine black and six Hispanic candidates actually passed the exam. If the city had used the exam as a floor to
test for minimum qualification and not to rank qualified candidates, they would all have been eligible for promotion. The decision
to make the written exam worth more than the oral exam was made
under pressure from a union dominated by white firefighters. If the
oral exam had been worth 60 percent and the written exam 40
percent—closer to the norm for public safety agencies nationwide,
according to a black firefighter who later challenged the exam in
court—three black firefighters would have been eligible for promotion, even under the city's other arcane rules.

In addition to the legal liabilities, there were political perils.
New Haven's sizable black population had a tense relationship with
the predominantly white fire department. Many thought local jobs
should go to local residents rather than to whites who lived outside
New Haven. Some felt the white firefighters looked down on blacks
and on New Haven, even as they collected their city paychecks, an
impression that some black firefighters in New Haven confirmed.
Erika Bogan, a black firefighter, told *Slate*'s Allan and Bazelon that
"when black kids peek into the Howard Avenue firehouse, oohing at
the trucks . . . the suburban white guys . . . ignore the kids. She said
she has also heard them joke on the phone about 'working in the
ghetto.' 'How dare you, when you live in Madison or Guilford,
come in here and . . . take our money and talk shit about New
Haven?' "[34]

These understandable frustrations found intemperate expression
in the voice of the Reverend Boise Kimber, a black Baptist minister
and self-described kingmaker who was a member of the fire commission and a political ally of New Haven's mayor, John DeStefano.
Kimber, a powerful advocate for New Haven's black community,
wasn't above divisive race-baiting and intimidation in pursuit of his

political goals; indeed, his detractors said that these were Kimber's preferred tactics. According to the *New Haven Advocate*, Kimber "threatened a race riot during the murder trial of a black man arrested for killing [a] white Yalie . . . and call[s] whites racists who question his actions."[35] A veteran of New Haven politics claimed that in 2003, Kimber unsuccessfully tried to undermine a Latina candidate for alderperson, telling black voters that she "represented the Latino threat to blacks in New Haven."[36] In 2002, as chair of the fire commission, Kimber had insisted that the department not hire firefighters with "too many vowels in their name[s]"—an oblique reference to Italian Americans. The resulting controversy forced him to step down as chair, but he remained a member of the commission and a powerful figure in New Haven politics.

Faced with the risk of a viable civil rights lawsuit and the certainty of political upheaval, New Haven held hearings to consider whether or not to proceed with promotions based on the contested exam. New Haven's Civil Service Board heard from numerous experts who differed as to the quality of the exam and the likelihood that the city would be liable for disparate-impact discrimination. The board also heard from Kimber, who bluntly warned of political ramifications if the city accepted the exam results: "I look at this [board] tonight . . . three whites and one Hispanic and no blacks . . . I would hope that you would not put yourself in this type of position [by accepting the exam results], a political ramification that may come back upon you."[37] After a long and acrimonious public debate, New Haven's Civil Service Board voted to reject the exam results. The reason, they claimed, was in order to avoid violating Title VII.

As a result, the city was sued for violating Title VII. Frank Ricci, a white firefighter whose exam score qualified him for promotion, became the lead plaintiff in a lawsuit brought by the successful examinees. *Ricci v. DeStefano* would eventually make its way to the Supreme Court, becoming one of the most closely watched cases of 2009, and Frank Ricci would play a role in the political struggle over President Barack Obama's first selection for the high court, Sonia Sotomayor. Ricci and his cohort argued that the city discriminated on the basis of race when it scrapped the exam results: the city rejected the results because of the race of the people who scored high enough to qualify for promotion.

The claim threatened to turn civil rights law against itself. On the one hand, black firefighters argued that accepting the results would constitute disparate-impact discrimination under Title VII. On the other hand, Ricci argued that rejecting the exam results would be disparate-treatment discrimination under Title VII. The city was in what the Supreme Court justice David Souter would later call a "damned if you do, damned if you don't" situation.

A federal district court rejected Ricci's claim without a full trial, holding that the city's good-faith attempt to avoid disparate-impact discrimination under Title VII could not be disparate-treatment discrimination under the same law. The summary rejection of Ricci's claim became the source of much controversy and bitter accusations of judicial misconduct levied by the champions of Ricci's cause. But in this respect Ricci's case wasn't unusual: for better or worse, many employment discrimination claims are dismissed without trial. Intentional discrimination is very difficult to prove. Although a plaintiff doesn't have to *prove* his case in order to survive summary judgment and get to trial, he does have to present evidence that—if believed—would prove it. A plaintiff claiming intentional employment discrimination must first establish some basic evidence that makes it plausible that he was a victim of discrimination: he was fired or turned down for promotion, for example, for reasons that weren't obviously due to his own poor performance or across-the-board staff reductions. Once a plaintiff makes this showing (as Ricci did), the law requires the employer to offer a nondiscriminatory reason for the challenged decision. New Haven did this: the city claimed that it rejected the exam results in order to avoid disparate-impact discrimination against the black candidates for promotion.

At this point, the plaintiff must prove that the nondiscriminatory reason offered by the employer is a "pretext" for discrimination. It's not enough for the plaintiff to show that the employer was unwise, was unfair, or didn't have its facts straight. Basically, he has to prove that the employer's justification is really just an alibi to hide a discriminatory motive. Typically, an employer doesn't even have to prove that its nondiscriminatory justification is factually accurate; it is sufficient that the employer believed it and was motivated by it. For instance, an employer who fired a black employee based on the mistaken but sincere belief that the employee had stolen from the till would not be liable for race discrimination, even if the employee proved at trial that he did not in fact steal. Accordingly, it wouldn't be enough for Ricci to show that the exam was written by top-notch experts in the field or even that it was the best possible exam to select firefighters for promotion. Ricci would have to show that the city officials didn't really believe—even mistakenly—that promotions based on the test results would violate the law.

Ricci argued that New Haven refused to certify the exam results because of political pressure to promote blacks, citing Kimber's numerous ill-considered outbursts as evidence. But the district court held this wasn't enough to send the case to trial: Ricci offered evidence that the city might have had some bad reasons for scrapping the exam, but he hadn't offered any evidence to discredit the city's explanation or show that it was a just pretext for discrimination.

Of course, New Haven might have rejected the exam results in order to avoid disparate-impact discrimination *and* in order to placate Kimber and the city's black voters. An employer who is motivated by both legitimate reasons and race may be liable for discrimination under a distinct legal theory of "mixed motives." Ricci didn't make a mixed-motives argument, but even if he had, it probably wouldn't have made a difference. In the case that established the mixed-motives rule—*Price Waterhouse v. Hopkins*—the plaintiff, Ann Hopkins, who was passed over for promotion, easily established that sexism was a problem in her large accounting firm and for her in particular. But according to Justice Sandra Day O'Connor, it wasn't enough to show that sexism was "in the air." Hopkins won but only because she proved that *the people who made the decision* to deny her a promotion were actually motivated by sexism. Ricci's evidence suggested that, at worst, anti-white racial bias was "in the air" in New Haven. To win, he would have to show that the New Haven Civil Service Board members who rejected the exam results were actually influenced by Kimber's blustering.

A panel of the Second Circuit Court of Appeals affirmed the district court's summary judgment for New Haven, and the Second Circuit denied Ricci's petition for rehearing *en banc*. But the Supreme Court reversed in a contentious 5–4 opinion. Writing for the majority of the Court, Justice Anthony Kennedy insisted that New Haven "chose not to certify the examination results because . . . 'too many whites and not enough minorities would be promoted' . . . Whatever the City's ultimate aim—however well intentioned or benevolent it might have seemed—the City made its employment decision because of race."[38] This violated Title VII even if New Haven rejected the exam to avoid disparate-impact discrimination as defined by that very law: "Allowing employers to violate the disparate-treatment prohibition based on a mere good-faith fear of disparate-impact liability would encourage race-based action at the slightest hint of disparate impact [and] . . . amount to a *de facto* quota system."

In a sharply worded concurring opinion, Justice Samuel Alito spent several pages describing Kimber's influence in New Haven local politics and his attempts to pressure the city's Civil Service Board to drop the exam. This, for Alito, was more than enough to raise the suspicion that New Haven scrapped the exam results in order to "placate a politically important racial constituency." Alito's comments echoed the popular understanding that *Ricci* involved yet another case of racial preference. Pundits rushed to sink their teeth into the familiar comfort food of an affirmative action controversy, trotting out the same shopworn arguments for and against racial preferences that had characterized the debate since the 1970s. But the dispute did not involve affirmative action, at least as conventionally defined. New Haven had not given and never planned to give black candidates for promotion preferential treatment; even if it opted for a new exam, the city would apply the same criteria to everyone. The real issue was more obscure, though no less long-standing than the debate over affirmative action. *Ricci* was an oblique attack on the very idea of disparate-impact discrimination. The disparate-impact theory has been controversial since the Supreme Court articulated it in 1971's *Griggs v. Duke Power Company*. Unlike a claim of disparate treatment, a claim of disparate impact is proven by statistics. If an employment practice—such as the use of an exam for promotions—results in significantly fewer successful applicants of a given race, sex, religion, or national origin than random selection would, the practice has a disparate impact. The employer must then demonstrate that the practice measures skills directly related to the job in question. And even if the practice is job related, the employer is still liable for disparate-impact discrimination if there was an equally effective and less discriminatory alternative practice available.

In one sense, disparate-impact law is a logical extension of the prohibition of intentional discrimination. Intentional discrimination is difficult to establish: many plaintiffs with valid claims don't bother to bring them or can't prove their cases. Only the foolish employer announces his or her discriminatory intentions; the crafty may employ neutral rules that screen out members of disfavored groups. For instance, an employer that was biased against women might adopt a physical test of upper-body strength, knowing that it will eliminate many more women than men. Disparate-impact doctrine is designed to smoke out such discriminatory motivations by requiring the employer to defend the test. If the job in question doesn't require extraordinary upper-body strength, the test is not job related and the employer is liable.

Disparate impact also requires employers to reconsider policies adopted for legitimate reasons, but with little thought to their effect on workforce diversity. In a sense, this does require a kind of "affirmative action": the employer must take steps to ensure it selects the most inclusive workforce it can, consistent with legitimate job criteria. Conservatives object that this unduly burdens innocent employers. It involves the courts and regulatory agencies in the intricacies of businesses and enterprises with which they have little familiarity. The employer is best suited to determine whether or not a test or selection practice is job related, they complain—not judges or government bureaucrats. Free-market incentives amply punish employers who select employees irrationally. Judicial intermeddling and bureaucratic micromanaging waste the resources of employers, who must navigate a maze of regulations to defend innocent selection practices. Worst of all, the harried employer, faced with the threat of liability, may insulate itself by adopting quota hiring so as to avoid disparate impact altogether, rather than face the costly and daunting task of defending its practices. Rather than requiring employers to adopt the best test for the job, disparate-impact law would encourage them to hire less-qualified women and minorities in order to meet a de facto quota.

The conflict over disparate-impact law in *Ricci* demonstrates how vexed the notion of "discrimination" has become. Is it discriminatory to adopt a promotion exam that eliminates all the candidates of a given race when another selection process would yield a more representative workforce that's just as qualified? Or is it discriminatory to care about the racial composition of the workforce one way or the other? Practically speaking, prohibiting practices with a disparate impact might sometimes encourage quota hiring. But not doing so will perpetuate the effects of past discrimination by inertia and leave a lot of hidden discrimination undetected. Which is worse? That's a judgment call.

———

Ricci v. DeStefano became cannon fodder in the political skirmishes over the nomination to the Supreme Court of Sonia Sotomayor, who had joined a Second Circuit panel in rejecting Ricci's appeal. Her opponents characterized the Supreme Court's opinion in *Ricci* as a repudiation of Sotomayor's judgment and evidence that she was unfit to ascend to the nation's highest court. Popular opinion was with Frank Ricci—a dyslexic firefighter who took extraordinary measures to overcome his disability and score well on the promotion exam. Even liberal and left-leaning commentators questioned New Haven's decision to drop the exam: for instance, the typically liberal Ta-Nehisi Coates of *The Atlantic* wrote: "It's one thing to argue over criteria—say, should race play a role in college admissions?[39] It's another thing to argue that after we've agreed upon a criteria, we should scrap the results because we don't like how they look." More conservative commentators were even less sympathetic. John McWhorter wrote for *The New Republic* that New Haven's position—and by implication Title VII's prohibition of disparate-impact discrimination generally—was part of a long and unfortunate line of "rhetorical contortions that excuse black people from challenging examinations."[40] The vice-chair of the U.S. Commission on Civil Rights, Abigail Thernstrom, insisted in *The Wall Street Journal* that racial disparities in performance, however stark, "are not an argument for racial quotas."[41]

Some conservative pundits and legal commentators complained that the Second Circuit tried to "bury" the *Ricci* controversy for ideological reasons, by affirming the lower court's decision to dismiss the case on summary judgment without explanation in a per curiam opinion. But the district court was correct to reject Ricci's claim. As Justice Ruth Bader Ginsburg pointed out in an angry dissent, there was no evidence that the Civil Service Board that rejected the exam was motivated by racial prejudice or the desire to placate New Haven's black community. The status of the exam was hotly contested, and pressure came from all sides: some political constituencies pressed the city to accept the exam results, while others urged the city to reject them. At most there was evidence of racial favoritism "in the air" but no proof that it had hit the ground and affected the decision.

Ricci is a classic example of a case with bad facts that made bad law. It's easy to sympathize with the plaintiffs in *Ricci*, who had their hopes of promotion dashed after months of preparation culminated in impressive performance on the promotion exam. And the background of ethnic conflict and political pressure raised legitimate concerns about basic fairness. But in order to reach the intuitively fair result in an idiosyncratic case with ambiguous facts, the Court created an ill-considered new legal standard that threatens both equal opportunity and legitimate employer prerogatives. Before *Ricci*, employers had a clear mandate under Title VII to avoid practices that screen out any racial group without a good reason. Now they must worry that correcting the unjustified racial effects of their practices—as the law still requires—may be unlawful discriminatory treatment: Justice Souter's "damned if you do, damned if you don't" bind.

To find salvation, an employer that wants to change a potentially discriminatory practice must have a "strong basis in evidence" that the practice violates the law before it can do so. What this means in practice is not entirely clear. A lot may depend on timing. Once an employer has administered an exam and established a promotional process, *Ricci* makes it very hard to change course. In theory, this seems reasonable: the employer should settle on the best way to evaluate candidates and stick to it regardless of the racial mix it produces. But in practice, the ideal method of evaluation is rarely obvious, and when it is, it's often impractical. Evaluation of employees requires difficult trade-offs between efficiency and comprehensiveness and controversial judgments as to the relative importance of a host of different criteria. And many employers are not free to make these decisions based only on finding the best candidate for the job: instead, they must negotiate with current employees, unions, and, in the case of public employers, politicians and civil service laws.

New Haven faced all of these complexities and constraints when redesigning its firefighters' promotion process. Promotions in the fire department had long been a source of controversy, and the city faced pressure from all sides. Although the majority in *Ricci* focuses only on lobbying by advocates for the black community, such as the artless Reverend Kimber, white firefighters lobbied just as hard and arguably more successfully: the firefighters' union—which black firefighters complained was dominated by a white old boys' network—demanded years earlier a written exam that would count for 60 percent of the total score, even though most other public safety agencies rely more heavily on oral examination and assessment centers, which evaluate candidates in simulations of real-life situations. A written exam is cheap and easy to administer, and it eliminates the risk of outright bias. This gives a written test the charisma of objectivity, even when the skills it measures aren't the most important for the job in question. It's easy to see why New Haven—faced with tense racial and ethnic division in the fire department and in the surrounding community—would agree to rely so heavily on the written test, even if it wasn't ideal.

Title VII's prohibition of disparate-impact discrimination is designed to be a counterweight to such pressures. Ideally, New Haven would have made sure it could defend its process as job related under Title VII before administering the exam. But New Haven couldn't ensure that its process met the legal standard, because the most questionable parts of the process couldn't be changed: the union insisted that the city use a heavily weighted written exam, and the city charter required that it select from among the three top-scoring candidates for each open position. New Haven had no choice but to press ahead, under constraints that may well have violated Title VII, and hope for the best. When the exam results excluded all of the black candidates for promotion, the city knew it had a problem. It was clear that the process had a disparate impact, and as New Haven's corporation counsel, Victor Bolden, admitted, the weighting and ranking made it "hard to defend" as job related.[42]

After *Ricci*, New Haven accepted the exam results and promoted a group consisting almost entirely of white fire captains and lieutenants. Sure enough, only a few months later, a black New Haven firefighter, Michael Briscoe, filed a disparate-impact lawsuit against the city. Briscoe received the highest score of any candidate on the oral portion of the lieutenant's promotion exam. But on the written part of the test, Briscoe—like most black candidates for promotion—did comparatively badly. He wasn't eligible for promotion, because the city based 60 percent of each candidate's score on the written exam. According to Briscoe, had the city followed the more common practice of public safety agencies and given the oral part of the exam more weight, he would have been one of the top-scoring candidates, easily eligible for promotion.[43]

Justice Kennedy's opinion in *Ricci* tried to head off just this type of lawsuit: "In light of our holding today it should be clear that the City would avoid disparate-impact liability [because] . . . had it not certified the results, it would have been subject to disparate-treatment liability" for discriminating against the white test takers. But this is far from clear. In *Ricci*, the Court held that New Haven did not have sufficient evidence that the exam had an unlawful disparate impact to justify dropping it. But that doesn't mean that the evidence doesn't exist. New Haven's failure to gather that evidence can't foreclose Michael Briscoe's attempt to prove that the city discriminated against him.

New Haven may be caught in Justice Souter's "damned if you do, damned if you don't" bind despite the best of intentions. There's little evidence to suggest that New Haven sought to disadvantage white firefighters. But, as Justice Kennedy insisted, the city "chose not to certify the examination results because of the statistical disparity based on race . . . Whatever the City's ultimate aim—however well intentioned or benevolent it might have seemed—the City made its employment decision because of race." This was enough to damn New Haven.

This kind of confident and categorical condemnation should be familiar. It's what allowed Roy Den Hollander to attack ladies' night and justified a lawsuit to stop Mother's Day. It led Professor Banzhaf to treat separate men's and women's restrooms as a civil rights violation, encouraged Christine Craft to sue over gendered grooming standards in an image-conscious and implicitly gendered job, and led Darlene Jespersen to think the best reaction to a rule requiring makeup was to invest in litigation instead of lipstick. It's tempting to condemn discrimination indiscriminately because doing so promises to slice through messy and difficult political and social conflict with a razor-sharp efficiency. But too often this razor cuts off the nose to spite the face.

Many liberals and conservatives adamantly support such categorical rules against discrimination—though usually each in different contexts. And some members of both camps vociferously oppose them. For instance, many conservatives insist that a categorical antidiscrimination rule prohibits affirmative action, but many of the same people defend racial profiling based on the cold hard facts about race and crime and defend many sex-based distinctions as natural and commonsensical. There are reasonable arguments for careful and limited racial profiling, sex-specific dress codes, and sex-segregated bathrooms, but to make them, one must reject categorical rules against discrimination and turn to more fact-specific, nuanced judgments.

Many liberals insist on categorical prohibitions that apply only in the case of discrimination against "disadvantaged groups," pointing out that the reasons to abhor discrimination apply only in those cases where the group in question has faced widespread and systematic disadvantages in the market or the political process. This is a sensible argument, except that it undermines the case for a *categorical* prohibition generally. If it makes sense to limit the legal prohibition of discrimination to disadvantaged groups, that's because discrimination per se isn't really the problem—it's a symptom of the real problem: widespread prejudice and systematic disadvantage. It follows that we should prohibit discrimination *only* when it reflects or exacerbates widespread prejudice or systematic disadvantage and regardless of the identity of the victim. Ladies' nights and sex-exclusive restrooms don't reflect prejudice or further widespread disadvantage. Gendered dress codes and grooming rules can be closer calls, but it's doubtful that all such distinctions systematically undermine equality.

In this respect, Justice Alito's concurrence in *Ricci* got at the real issue in that case: the possibility that ethnic and racial politics in New Haven distorted the promotions process in the fire department, to the systematic disadvantage of whites. If New Haven dropped the exam because blacks had gained the upper hand in local politics and could systematically disadvantage whites, Frank Ricci deserved to win his civil rights lawsuit for discrimination. Because the lower courts never fully evaluated this claim, it would have been best to send the case back to the district court for further proceedings, as Justice Ginsburg suggested in her dissent. Instead, the Court sidestepped what should have been the central question in the case, and settled on a categorical condemnation of discrimination that defies common sense and perverts the spirit of civil rights.

Congress understood that it's necessary to consider race in order to avoid and reverse the effects of racism. Because people rarely announce their illegal motives, and because seemingly innocent practices can lock in the effects of past discrimination, often the only way to spot inequality of opportunity is to look for lopsided results. That's why the law allows discrimination plaintiffs to prove their cases with statistics. If a workforce has a far smaller proportion of women or minorities than the qualified labor pool, we might infer a pattern of discrimination, even if the plaintiff can't prove every specific case of discriminatory intent. And if a practice screens out a disproportionate number of women or minorities and the employer can't show that it's job related, we're entitled to suspect that the practice needlessly perpetuates historical biases and disadvantages. Both of these well-established legal standards require courts and employers to consider sex and race. That doesn't mean that the employer must adopt a quota. Because job qualifications, interest level, and diligence may differ across social groups, statistical lopsidedness isn't a civil rights issue in and of itself. But it may be a symptom of discrimination, suggesting that a more thorough examination is in order.

After *Ricci* an employer must build a Title VII disparate-impact case against itself before reexamining and changing possibly discriminatory practices. To do so is risky: because the legal standards are ambiguous and fact specific, an employer can rarely be certain that it has a "strong basis in evidence" that a questionable practice is discriminatory. If the employer drops the practice, it may be liable for disparate treatment under *Ricci*. If it follows through on the practice, it will have helped to build the factual record for a plaintiff in a disparate-impact lawsuit.

Some of the *Ricci* opinion's language suggests that the holding is limited to cases in which an employer tosses out the results of a test *after* it has been administered. But that's not clear: the logic of *Ricci* would seem to apply more broadly. If it's discriminatory to discard the results of an employment exam in order to avoid a racial imbalance, isn't it also discriminatory to choose one exam over another in order to avoid such a racial imbalance in the first place? If an employer chooses Exam A instead of Exam B because Exam A is more likely to increase the number of successful minority applicants, the members of the disfavored racial groups may well have a reverse-discrimination case similar to Frank Ricci's. Employers now must walk a knife's edge between contradictory mandates under civil rights laws. To keep their balance, many will be forced to spend more than ever on "validation" consultants and experts to establish an evidentiary record validating tests before they adopt them, or invalidating tests before they reject them.

Because the Supreme Court typically interprets Title VII's prohibition of race discrimination to match the Fourteenth Amendment's similar prohibition of racial classifications and vice versa, *Ricci* puts a wide range of race-conscious policies under a legal cloud.

Consider, for instance, the vaunted "Texas 10 percent" admission policy, developed to replace the University of Texas's affirmative action policy after it was held unconstitutional. The university now admits any student in the top 10 percent of his or her public high school class, and because so many of the public schools in Texas are racially segregated, this guarantees a racially diverse student body. Opponents of race-conscious affirmative action have pointed to this policy as an example of a viable, race-neutral alternative. But no one denies that a motivation for dropping the traditional admissions criteria in favor of the 10 percent plan is to achieve a better racial mix. If we extend the logic of *Ricci*, this looks like impermissible race discrimination against the students who would have been admitted under the old criteria, just as dropping the firefighter promotion exam was impermissible race discrimination against the white firefighters who would have been promoted. And why stop there? Even recruitment efforts aimed at underrepresented minorities are designed to increase the representation of those groups in workforces and entering classes with a limited number of openings. If these outreach efforts are successful, some minorities will necessarily displace some whites who would otherwise have been hired or admitted. Are those efforts discriminatory, too?

One could say that any effort to combat racial inequality is itself race conscious and therefore discriminatory. Opponents of gay rights have made just such an argument, attacking laws that prohibit discrimination on the basis of sexual orientation as "special rights." In 1996, in *Romer v. Evans*, the Supreme Court invalidated a state constitutional amendment in Colorado that eliminated civil rights for homosexuals statewide. Justice Scalia, in dissent, described the amendment as "merely prohibiting . . . special protections" and insisted that the basic civil rights banned by the amendment gave gay men, lesbians, and bisexuals "favored status because of their homosexual conduct."[44]

Of course, for the gay person looking for a job or an apartment and facing bias at every turn, basic protection against discrimination doesn't seem like favoritism. But taken out of their social and historical contexts, all civil rights can be made to look like special privileges. Civil rights laws aren't just applications of abstract principles of justice; they also reflect policy decisions about how to best direct the scarce resources that must be dedicated to the enforcement of the law and the litigation of disputes. Federal law doesn't demand that employers treat all of their employees fairly in every respect; it prohibits only unfairness that's based on race, color, sex, religion, national origin, age, and disability. (I hope we'll add sexual orientation to this list soon.) No one doubts that civil rights laws were intended to, and do in fact, disproportionately benefit those groups most likely to suffer from the prohibited types of discrimination: racial minorities, women, religious minorities, the elderly, the disabled.

So is it discriminatory to prohibit discrimination? Of course not. This country has a long and ugly history of specific types of discrimination, such as discrimination on the basis of race. Although things have changed for the better, racism isn't a thing of the past yet. And the continuing effects of past racism still limit opportunities for many racial minorities today. Addressing these injustices isn't doing anyone a special favor; it's simply doing justice. The majority in *Ricci* ignored more than three decades of judicial precedent and the explicit endorsement of Congress, which wrote disparate-impact law into Title VII in 1991, but worse yet, it ignored the social and historical context that define and must guide civil rights law. Without attention to context, the civil rights ideal of nondiscrimination is self-consuming: one must discriminate to decide what types of discrimination to prohibit. Stripped of the human experiences that give them meaning and moral weight, civil rights can easily turn against themselves and against social justice. The logic that condemned New Haven's awkward but defensible attempt to avoid the discriminatory effects of its promotion exam can be extended to condemn any attempt to prevent any form of discrimination. It will take only a sympathetic plaintiff, a hapless defendant, some bad facts, and some clever lawyers to make even the most well-established civil right look like a special privilege.

For Judgment

I've argued for a socially responsible, commonsense approach to legal rights. The common person should use common sense when asserting his or her rights and eschew extreme, antisocial, or trivial claims. Judges should use good judgment guided by appropriate social goals and a subtle evaluation of the limits of the law, and reject ill-advised, perverse, or selfish claims of right, separating deserved entitlements from rights gone wrong. Each of these ideas rejects a rigid, rule-like approach to the civil rights tradition in favor of a more supple approach that acknowledges the necessity of trade-offs and requires the discretion of decision makers.

This may strike suspicious minds as a bad idea: If rights are supposed to protect us from the biases of the powerful, how can we allow the powerful to define rights? It's a valid concern: sometimes it can be hard to tell the difference between common sense and common prejudice. It was common sense in the 1950s that the best jobs and neighborhoods should be explicitly reserved for whites. Until recently, it was common sense that women were the weaker sex and needed to be cloistered in the suburban home, away from the rigors of the market economy. It's still common sense among too many people that homosexuality is a sin against God and nature. Legitimate worries about what passes for common sense lead many people to put their faith in rigid rules and absolutes that can ensure that justice isn't subject to the whim of the powerful or the majority.

But rights can't rescue us from our own biases and ignorance. In fact, legal rights—even those guaranteed by the Constitution—rarely change or thwart public opinion; they almost always follow it. For instance, racial attitudes in the United States didn't change because of *Brown v. Board of Education* or other legal victories: the legal victories were possible because of changed attitudes. American racial attitudes improved in the mid-twentieth century as a result of the experience of World War II, while national politics began to shift toward racial justice in response to geopolitical pressures.

Most Americans saw World War II as a war against Nazi racism. And yet when black soldiers returned from war, they often reported receiving better treatment at the hands of the enemy in Vichy France or Mussolini's Italy than in their home country. In 1946 a Georgia mob shot and killed George Dorsey—a GI recently returned home after five years of service—along with his wife and two companions in what can only be called an execution. Racist lynchings were, tragically, not uncommon in the mid-century American South. But Dorsey's case sparked an extraordinary public outcry. Letters and telegrams of protest flooded into the Department of Justice. National newspapers decried the incident. The California senator William Knowland read a denunciation of the event into the *Congressional Record*. "Such things must not continue in the United States of America," he insisted. Something in American race relations—and something in American common sense—had begun to change.

Even in the recalcitrant South, public opinion was already turning against Jim Crow segregation by the time *Brown v. Board of Education* was decided. As the legal historian Michael Klarman points out, "By the early 1950s, many southern cities had relaxed Jim Crow in public transportation, police department employment, athletic competition, and voter registration."[45] Meanwhile, Jim Crow racism had become a serious liability for the national image overseas. As the leader of the free world, the United States promoted its traditions, values, and institutions, contrasting them to the totalitarianism of communist governments. But racism was a conspicuous blemish on the face the government wished to present to the world. Nonwhite foreign dignitaries faced discrimination when visiting the United States. Foreign newspapers covered incidents of American racism. The Soviet Union highlighted American racism in its efforts to convince the third world to embrace communism and reject the West. A 1948 *New York Times* article noted that the United States was "the most powerful spokesman for the democratic way of life, as opposed to the principles of a totalitarian state. It is unpleasant to have the Russians publicize our . . . lynchings, our Jim Crow statues and customs . . . but is it undeserved?"[46]

Common sense began to change as a result of these events. And legal rights changed in direct response to the evolution of popular opinion. Without these changes, the civil rights movement would not have enjoyed the success it did in the following decades. The civil rights movement nurtured and capitalized on these changed attitudes. The genius of Martin Luther King Jr. was that he understood and tapped into the change in common sense that led Americans to protest, rather than celebrate or quietly accept, the murder of George Dorsey. By leading hundreds of dignified, well-dressed, determined, and peaceful blacks on marches and in sit-ins, King appealed to the better angels—and the better judgment—of the American people.

It would be preferable, of course, if we didn't have to rely on common sense. When "common sense" is really common prejudice, it can be slow to change. Rights seem to offer an escape from the caprice of ordinary human judgment. It's oddly comforting to insist that slavery and Jim Crow violated the rights of blacks all along, even if it took the courts centuries to recognize it. It seems to follow that close enough attentiveness to rights will help us to avoid injustices today. But this has the relationship between rights and social consciousness exactly backward. Rights don't help us to identify injustices that we otherwise would not have; instead, we identify the injustice and *then* conclude that it violates rights. At best, rights are a way of talking about and bearing in mind the commitments that we already hold *for other reasons*. The legal scholar Patricia Williams writes that "rights are to law what conscious commitments are to the psyche."[47] But that's a bit too strong. Rights are really no more than a *symbol* of our commitments: the right to "equal protection of the laws" symbolizes our rejection of wrongful social hierarchy in the same way that a string tied around a finger symbolizes my promise to buy coffee and milk on the way home from work.

Robert Post, now the dean of Yale Law School, makes this point nicely in the context of legal rights against discrimination:

> Antidiscrimination law is itself a social practice, which regulates other social practices, because the latter have become for one reason or another controversial. It is because the meaning of categories like race [and] gender . . . have become contested that we seek to use antidiscrimination law to reshape them . . .[48]

Moral and ethical commitments do not follow from rights; commitments come first, and rights follow. And every successful application of our civil rights tradition depends on good judgment. Judges—and ideally potential litigants as well—must decide when the commitments underlying a legal right demand change and when they suggest restraint. It's rare that this is a matter of mechanical application of a simple rule to a set of facts.

Even though judges must use judgment, they don't just make up the law as they go along. A judge applying a legal right—even when it's as vague a guarantee as "equal protection"—is constrained by previous interpretations of the same legal right and by a tradition of interpretation that is reasonably well understood by his or her peers. Just as there are sound and convincing interpretations of literature as well as frivolous or incompetent readings, there are also skilled and inept interpretations of legal rights. Sound legal practice is not primarily a matter of mechanical rule application; instead, it requires the exercise of sound judgment, studied expertise, and common sense in interpreting and applying the law. Inept applications of the law will typically be reversed on appeal or roundly criticized by others in the legal community. The prestige of the courts depends on their reputation for evenhanded and competent jurisprudence: no judge—not even a Supreme Court justice—can afford to write too many opinions that are too far outside the accepted judicial practice. But this doesn't mean there's always one clear right answer. There are often several plausible interpretations of the same legal rule or principle. Again, the judge must exercise his or her own judgment in order to apply the law well.

Too many people, misled by simplistic metaphors likening judges to umpires and the law to a rule book in a game, seem to think that a judge can just apply the law to the facts without her own wisdom and judgment playing a role. The charge of "judicial activism" is sure to follow any public statement that acknowledges the centrality of human moral, ethical, or practical evaluation in adjudication. For instance, when the Supreme Court justice Sonia Sotomayor endured the extended public hazing that now passes for the confirmation process before the U.S. Senate, she was repeatedly asked to repudiate President Obama's suggestion that a justice of the Supreme Court should have empathy. Sounding the same absurd and tired theme that they have for decades, Republicans accused Sotomayor of endorsing "judicial activism" when she said, in a public lecture, that federal court judges "make policy." She prudently repudiated the statement, as the theater of the moment required. But it's perfectly clear that any judge charged with the interpretation of intentionally vague and ambiguous statutes and constitutional provisions articulated at the highest possible level of generality must "make policy." Because the judge's opinion will serve as precedent in future similar disputes, she must think through the more general consequences of the legal rule she articulates in the specific case, much in the way a policy maker must think through the general consequences of a new piece of legislation. And it's equally clear that a good judge must empathize with the litigants that come before her. In fact, policy making and empathy are the two bookends of sound judicial practice: a judge must consider the broader policy implications of the case before her, but she must also not lose sight of its immediate human stakes for the people immediately involved.

The importance of value judgment and good sense frightens many people, who worry that judges will simply decide cases according to their personal political preferences—that we will have the rule of men instead of the rule of law. In 1962 the legal scholar Alexander Bickel, writing about *Brown v. Board of Education*, worried that "when the Supreme Court declares unconstitutional a legislative act or the action of an elected executive, it thwarts the will of representatives of the . . . people . . . ; it exercises control, not on behalf of the prevailing majority, but against it. That, without mystic overtones, is what actually happens . . . And it is the reason the charge can be made that judicial review is undemocratic."[49] Bickel's concern is a valid one, which still haunts constitutional law today: there are plenty of examples of both liberal and conservative judges who have abused their authority. This explains the appeal of the idea that judges vindicating rights should instead simply apply strict and unambiguous rules, like an umpire in a baseball game.

The soft constraints of interpretive custom and the sanction of one's peers seem insecure compared with the ideal of the strict letter of the law. But the alternative—a judge who mechanically applies strict rules without nuance, common sense, or empathy for those affected—is much worse. Consider Shylock's rigid demand for a pound of Antonio's flesh in *The Merchant of Venice* and the judge's equally formalistic reply that Shylock is entitled to the pound of flesh, but may not spill a drop of blood. Of course there is a type of poetic justice in this verdict: he who insists on the letter of the law must conform to its letter. But isn't this really an example of the law at its worst? An inhuman system of rules applied without common decency (in the case of Shylock's monstrous but formally justified demand for a pound of Antonio's flesh) or common sense (in the case of the judge's decree that Shylock take the pound of flesh but not a drop of blood). Shylock could, in a more sensible legal system, justly insist that the contract for a pound of flesh necessarily implies the spilling of blood; Portia, on Antonio's behalf, could insist that Shylock's inhumane contract violates equitable principles, yet he seeks equitable relief from the strict terms of his own poorly drafted agreement—*he who seeks equity must do equity.*

Let's consider a realistic defense of a judicial role, without "mystic overtones," as Professor Bickel would have it. The *purpose* of judicial review is to allow well-educated and (hopefully) civic-minded elites who are relatively insulated from short-term politics to overrule the popular branches on occasion. Through constitutional review of legislative and executive action, the federal courts occasionally temper the excesses of representative government and more occasionally jump-start needed but stalled political reform. Antidemocratic? Perhaps, but republican in the best Madisonian tradition. Similarly, when courts interpret rights created by an act of legislation, their role is to take the necessarily vague and general prescriptions of the legislature and apply them in specific cases, using their own judgment and good sense to ensure that the results balance individual fairness and the public good. The Supreme Court justice John Paul Stevens described this cooperative relationship between legislatures and courts to *The New Yorker*'s Jeffrey Toobin: "[As a lawyer for the House Judiciary Committee] I remember explaining one of the tricky problems in the statute to one of the members of the committee . . . He said, 'Well, you know, let's let the judges figure that one out' . . . The legislature really works with the judges—contrary to the suggestion that the statute is a statute all by itself."[50]

At their best, judges are not like umpires, because the law is not a game with a few strict rules and petty stakes. The law must grapple with the full range and complexity of human conflict, where stakes are usually high and sometimes dire and the impractical ideal is often the enemy of the attainable good. The law trades in tragic compromises and the lesser of evils. The challenges of the judge mirror not the prim precision of a strike zone but the wrenching conflicts of a triage ward. There is no such thing as law without human reason (and, unavoidably, human error) or judging without human judgment.

3

The Unintended Consequences of the Law

Over the course of five decades, the civil rights movement has come to enjoy the prestige of a national epic: its leaders are revered as heroes and as saints; its pivotal moments have become the stuff of legend and myth; its accomplishments, canonized; its guiding principles have acquired the status of scripture. Law is, of course, at the very center of the civil *rights* movement, and the defining legal text of the civil rights movement is the opinion of the Supreme Court in *Brown v. Board of Education*. If Martin Luther King Jr.'s "I Have a Dream" speech is the movement's Sermon on the Mount, the Court's taut opinion in *Brown* is its Golden Rule.

In 2004, the nation celebrated the fiftieth anniversary of *Brown v. Board of Education*. Most reasonably well-educated Americans knew that racial segregation in public schools ended when the Supreme Court decided *Brown* in 1954. Even for those who did not pore over every line of celebratory text in the scores of books, editorials, blogs, magazines, newspapers, academic journals, and law reviews—even for those who did not sit glued to their televisions and radios, basking in the glow of patriotic self-congratulation—it

would have been hard not to notice *how far we've come as a nation*.
Even for those people cloistered in convents without access to media or holed up inside log cabins and tin shacks in remote locations,
it would have been difficult to avoid the contagious swelling of
pride and sense of goodwill. And for this remarkable progress in
social justice, this unprecedented moral achievement, we have to
thank our singular, wise, and time-honored tradition of constitutional rights, guided by the careful, learned, and even hand of the
Supreme Court. Before *Brown* ours was a racially segregated nation
in which public education reinforced racial hierarchy and undermined the dignity of black students. Since *Brown* we have become
a racially integrated society in which, as the Court in *Brown* had
hoped, public education is "a principal instrument in awakening the
child to cultural values, in preparing him for later professional
training, and in helping him to adjust . . . to his environment."[1]

But there were a few naysayers and malcontents spoiling *Brown*'s
fiftieth-birthday party. Some people *had* to focus on the empty half
of the glass, as the Harvard Civil Rights Project did when it pointed
out that "a substantial group of American schools . . . are virtually
all non-white . . . These schools educate . . . one-fourth of black
students in the Northeast and Midwest."[2] Critics complained that
in the decades since *Brown* the courts had slowly but steadily
backpedaled, weakening *Brown*'s integrationist mandate. Others
groused that far from awakening children to healthy cultural values
and preparing them for professional training, many public schools—
especially those that served poor blacks—introduced their pupils to
dysfunctional values and even crime while failing to teach such ru-
dimentary skills as reading, writing, and arithmetic. According to
such detractors, many students left school with a first-rate education in vice and unable to write a simple sentence. Marring *Brown*'s
fiftieth-birthday celebration like a preacher at a stag party, the law
professor and veteran civil rights lawyer Derrick Bell went so far
as to suggest that the nation's minority children might have been
better off if the plaintiffs in *Brown* had lost and the nation had

committed itself to fulfilling the breached promise of segregation: separate *but equal*. He lamented that "*Brown* [is] a magnificent mirage . . . to which all aspire without any serious thought that it will ever be attained."[3]

What *Brown* accomplished was and is important. But its accomplishments are more modest, the progress toward racial justice it inspired more halting, and the meaning of *Brown* both more limited and more mixed than the typical triumphal account suggests. *Brown* did not integrate public education with the strike of a gavel: in fact, in 2006, more than fifty years after *Brown*, two of every five black and Latino public school students attended a school that was over 90 percent nonwhite.[4] *Brown* provided the civil rights movement with renewed energy and sharper focus, but it also helped to divert the attention of the movement away from the economic injustices affecting working-class black people and toward the social and psychological preoccupations of black elites. *Brown* did not undo Jim Crow segregation; in fact, *Brown* may actually have strengthened Jim Crow by inspiring a backlash among Southern whites, many of whom were turning against racial segregation before the *Brown* litigation. *Brown v. Board of Education*—perhaps the most celebrated victory of the American civil rights movement—is not an unimpeachable example of the virtues of legal rights. In many ways it is a cautionary tale of the limitations and hazards of legal rights, a story of rights gone wrong. Indeed, the malcontents were more completely vindicated than they could have imagined possible, three years after *Brown*'s fiftieth anniversary. In 2007 the Supreme Court held that the legal precedent of *Brown v. Board of Education*—which in 1954 had required the end of segregation— prohibited policies that advanced racial *integration*.

When *Brown* was decided in 1954, many people attacked the Court's decision for all-too-predictable reasons: they opposed racial mixing and resented the inevitable demise of Jim Crow, of which *Brown* was a conspicuous symbol, if not an indispensable cause. But others criticized *Brown* for more surprising and more respectable reasons. The most famous of the respectable critics was the eminent Columbia Law School professor and labor rights lawyer Herbert Wechsler. Wechsler was one of the nation's most formidable legal minds: an expert in constitutional law, criminal law, and the federal courts and a technical adviser to the judges in the Nuremberg trials. He would go on to win one of the century's most important cases involving freedom of expression, *New York Times v. Sullivan,* and to write the American Law Institute's Model Penal Code, which fulfilled the ambition that its name suggests and prompted criminal law reform in dozens of states.

In 1959, Wechsler delivered an address at Harvard Law School. In it he attacked the now-familiar idea that "racial segregation is . . . a denial of equality" and quoted approvingly from *Plessy v. Ferguson,* which had established the doctrine of "separate but equal" that *Brown* had overturned. "Is there not a [valid] point in *Plessy,*" Wechsler asked, "that if 'enforced separation stamps the colored race with a badge of inferiority' it is solely because its members choose 'to put that construction upon it'?" Wechsler questioned the reasoning in *Brown,* attacking the psychologist Kenneth Clark's contention—central to the Court's holding in *Brown*—that segregation was psychologically damaging to black children. He queried:

> Was he [Clark] comparing the position of the Negro child in a segregated school with his position in an integrated school where he was happily accepted and regarded by the whites; or was he comparing his position under separation with that under integration where the whites were hostile to his presence and found ways to make their feelings known? And if the harm that segregation worked was relevant, what of the benefits that it entailed: sense of security, the absence of hostility? . . . Suppose that more Negroes in a community preferred separation than opposed it? Would that

be relevant to whether they were hurt or aided by segregation as opposed to integration?[5]

Wechsler insisted that the strongest case against segregation wasn't that it denied blacks equality—equal resources could be provided in segregated schools—it was that it curtailed the freedom of association guaranteed by the First Amendment. But this rationale had its problems too, Wechsler cautioned:

> If the freedom of association is denied by segregation, integration forces an association upon those for whom it is unpleasant or repugnant. Is this not the heart of the issue involved . . . ? Given a situation where the state must practically choose between denying the association to those individuals who wish it or imposing it on those who would avoid it, is there a basis in neutral principles for holding that the Constitution demands that the claims for association should prevail? I should like to think there is, but I confess that I have not yet written the opinion.[6]

Future generations have not been kind to Wechsler's critique of *Brown*: the more charitable treat it as the work of a great intellect with sadly limited vision; the less charitable, as an apologia for bigotry. Because of the Harvard speech, published in the *Harvard Law Review* under the title "Toward Neutral Principles of Constitutional Law," Wechsler—despite his many impressive accomplishments—is probably best known today as a man on the wrong side of history. But in the decades since *Brown*, many of Wechsler's concerns have been proven valid.

For instance, many psychologists today would question the *Brown* Court's confidence that segregated schools were in and of themselves psychologically damaging to black children.[7] It was the entire social structure of the Jim Crow South and indeed of mid-century America generally—the pervasive racial stereotypes, the contempt of whites in positions of power and influence, and the daily humiliations, of which segregated schools were hardly the most severe—that undermined the self-esteem of black children, as it did of blacks generally. Moreover, *Brown*'s focus on psychological injury was a symptom of a new and questionable shift for the racial justice struggle, away from a long-standing commitment to economic justice and in pursuit of the less tangible goals of personal dignity and that elusive grail of pop psychotherapy, self-esteem. In the decades that followed, as pop psychotherapy gave the veneer of science to the preoccupations of the newly affluent Me Generation, self-esteem became a major preoccupation of the American mainstream. The obsession with self-esteem and psychotherapy grew to feed not only a significant cadre of medical professionals but also a multimillion-dollar semipro industry of 12-step programs, TV talk show confessionals, encounter groups, self-actualization clinics, lecture circuit gurus, and uncredentialed self-help experts. The culture of therapy nurtured and exploited the idea that self-esteem was a natural entitlement. The ruling in *Brown* made it into a civil right, giving it the moral authority of the racial justice struggle and the imprimatur of law.

The legal historian Risa Goluboff points out that civil rights litigation before *Brown* had emphasized "the economic harms that segregation entailed: less work, worse work, inadequate salaries, and economic insecurity and lack of advancement."[8] Civil rights lawyers in the early twentieth century saw the exclusion of blacks from the labor market as the greatest evil of Jim Crow segregation. The "right to work" in the face of whites-only labor unions and racially stratified workplaces was the paradigmatic civil rights goal. Given the nature of American racism, the centrality of labor rights was inevitable and appropriate. Labor, beginning with slavery, defined the black experience. After emancipation and the brief period of Reconstruction, Southern farmers and Southern state governments joined forces to keep blacks on plantations in conditions that mirrored slavery. Sharecropping replaced slavery as the involuntary labor regime of American agriculture. In theory, a sharecropper freely agreed to work for a farmer on mutually acceptable terms. But in practice, sharecropping was a trap: farmers "advanced" sharecroppers their meager wages at usurious rates of interest, sold them supplies and the necessities of life at drastically inflated prices on credit, and insisted that the sharecropper was obligated to work until his debts had been paid. Because the sharecropper would need to buy more goods on credit in order to keep working, each additional day on the job could actually put him deeper into debt. The sharecropping system relied on laws in place throughout the American South that made it illegal to leave a job before working off an advance from one's employer. The legal fiction justifying these laws—which effectively enforced indentured servitude—was that an employee who accepted an advance from an employer and quit without repaying it must have intended to defraud the employer from the outset. Once convicted of criminal fraud, the hapless worker would be forced back into the unpaid labor force on a prison chain gang. Despite such ingenious rationalizations, many employers dispensed with legal contrivances and simply held black laborers by force.

When World War II created labor shortages throughout the United States, Southern blacks moved north in droves to find employment in wartime industries. Southern states responded with beefed-up enforcement of nineteenth-century vagrancy laws and new wartime "work or fight" laws that empowered police to arrest able-bodied people who appeared to be unemployed and forcibly put them to work.[9] Civil rights lawyers, both in government and in nonprofit civil rights organizations such as the NAACP, attacked these practices with a variety of political and legal tools. Mobility and access to jobs were crucial civil rights issues: if blacks were to escape slave-like conditions as agricultural laborers, they would have to find work as wage laborers in the industries of the North. The NAACP Legal Defense Fund sued racially exclusive unions under federal and state laws, arguing that the federal laws that allowed them to organize and represent workers in collective bargaining obliged them not to discriminate on the basis of race.[10] But shortly after

World War II, civil rights organizations soured on labor-focused litigation. The NAACP became politically allied with organized labor and was anxious to demonstrate that it was not antiunion. At the same time, organized labor was losing its former clout: as a result, the right to join a closed shop was worth less than it once had been. And some historians speculate, perhaps uncharitably, that the relatively privileged NAACP lawyers simply began to find the concerns of working people less compelling than the kinds of injuries to dignity and status that professional blacks like themselves suffered under Jim Crow in racially segregated bathrooms, public transportation, restaurants, and schools.

As civil rights lawyers moved away from the focus on equal access to jobs, their bête noire became the 1896 case *Plessy v. Ferguson*, which upheld the racial segregation of Louisiana railroads under the doctrine of "separate but equal."[11] Infamously, the Court in *Plessy* opined that in the absence of objective differences between black and white facilities, segregation stigmatized blacks only because "the colored race chooses to put that construction upon it." Earlier challenges to Jim Crow had accepted *Plessy* and attacked the objective inferiority of segregated black facilities. But in *Brown v. Board of Education*, the NAACP Legal Defense Fund lawyers wanted to demonstrate that segregation *by its very nature* harmed blacks. The growing prestige of social science—and of psychology in particular—offered civil rights lawyers a battery of evidence that was unavailable to Homer Plessy.

Today popular psychotherapy is so commonplace as to be background noise, but in the mid-twentieth century psychotherapy was new and fashionable. The rigors and deprivations of World War II had forced Americans to focus on the needs of the body, but in the postwar years Americans had the leisure and the resources to devote to the health of the mind. The American Psychiatric Association began work on the first *Diagnostic and Statistical Manual: Mental Disorders* in 1948 and published it in 1952. The number of licensed psychiatrists in the United States doubled in the 1950s, and the therapist's couch became a regular staple of popular culture. Psychotherapy grew from a somewhat suspect indulgence to an accepted part of bourgeois hygiene. The psychotherapy zeitgeist inspired public policy: Congress created the National Institute of Mental Health in 1946. A 1950 White House conference promoted "a healthy personality for every child."

The Supreme Court was primed to treat psychological evidence that segregation caused mental injury as hard scientific fact. In the 1930s and 1940s the psychologists Kenneth and Mamie Clark had gathered just such evidence. They conducted a series of heartbreaking experiments with black children in the South. They presented the children with two dolls, one black and one white. When asked which doll was the nice doll and which he or she would like to play with, the typical child chose the white doll. When asked which doll was the bad doll, the child chose the black doll. When asked which doll was most like her, she chose the black doll. The Clarks concluded that segregation undermined the self-esteem of black children, warping their personalities and damaging their ability to learn.

The Clarks' psychological studies provided the previously missing link between segregation and tangible inequality: segregation harmed the self-esteem of black children, which in turn harmed their ability to learn, thereby depriving them of equal educational opportunities. Because they stigmatized black children, segregated schools necessarily offered them an inferior education.

Brown established the idea that such psychological injury was the defining evil of Jim Crow segregation—and by extension of racism generally. Echoes of the earlier civil rights emphasis on employment remained audible in the historic 1963 March on Washington for *Jobs* and Freedom, and Martin Luther King's attempt to help lead the Poor People's Campaign in the late 1960s was arguably a return to these concerns. But the post-*Brown* civil rights movement shifted away from this focus on economic inequality born of the specific historical practices of American racism and set its sights on more abstract targets: the psychology of racism, the mental state of the bigot, and the stigma that results from racial discrimination. This new approach was dramatically successful at first, but it proved costly in the long run. By downplaying economic justice, civil rights lawyers escaped being vilified as communists—a charge segregationists had made persistently—and successfully won over the courts and eventually the American mainstream. But they left some of the most severe racial injustices unaddressed. And because their choices shaped civil rights law—and, for many Americans, defined racial justice—they may have also made it harder for future generations to confront those injustices.

The Civil Rights Act of 1964 prohibits discrimination in employment and housing, addressing these economic considerations—but only to a limited extent. The Civil Rights Act was organized around the post-*Brown* idea that racial injustice was a matter of stigmatizing animus and stereotypes. Its effectiveness hinged on elusive and conceptual evidentiary questions. How could a plaintiff establish the prohibited mental state when an employer or landlord declined to announce it? Did unexplained racial segregation or exclusion imply discriminatory animus? Was discrimination unlawful because it was motivated by animus or because of its effects, or was it objectionable per se? Such conceptual ambiguities continue to limit the effectiveness of the Civil Rights Act today.

Civil rights inspired by psychotherapy evolved in a very different— and less useful—way than they might have, had the movement remained focused on economic justice and the tangible evils of the American racial hierarchy. Stigmatic injury, stereotypes, and subjective emotional harm acquired a centrality in civil rights law they never enjoyed in other areas of law and that they did not merit. Today the influence of psychology is felt in age discrimination law, where "stereotypes" define the legally actionable discrimination instead of tangible injury; in sex harassment doctrine, where emotional harm due to sexual expression outweighs objective impediments to women's advancement; and in disability law, where legal intervention responds less to social injustice than to the extent a disability limits self-actualization.

The courts heard challenges to segregated schools against a political backdrop of intensive resistance and desperate hope—and one in which the always-fragile legitimacy of the federal courts was at stake. Overreaching might lead the courts into administrative complexities that they could not manage and that other governmental officials would refuse to take on; it could even lead to outright defiance and a crisis of authority for the courts. On the other hand, retreat would encourage recalcitrance, again undermining the authority of the courts.

As a result, the courts adopted a series of aggressive half measures that managed to infuriate whites, disappoint civil rights advocates, and do little to address inequalities in education or segregation of the races. *Brown*'s bold pronouncement that separate schools were inherently unequal and offended the constitutional guarantee of equal protection was quickly limited as a practical matter by the Court's holding one year later that desegregation should proceed with "all deliberate speed"—a statement that sounded assertive but was in fact a calculated retreat that allowed schools to remain segregated for years to come. This did not mollify Southern bigots, who threatened "massive resistance" to integration. In 1957, Governor Orval Faubus of Arkansas called out the National Guard to prevent the menace to public order and decency threatened by nine black students who were set to attend the all-white Little Rock Central High School. A federal court ordered the National Guard to stand down, but an angry mob took their place for several weeks until President Dwight Eisenhower, fearing for America's public image overseas, sent in the 101st Airborne Division to enforce desegregation.

In 1968 the Court began to answer the most important question posed by *Brown*: Did the Constitution require racially integrated schools, or did it simply forbid explicit, state-enforced segregation? New Kent County in eastern Virginia was a perfect place to pose this question. Roughly half black and half white, New Kent County had only two public schools, each of which combined elementary and high school. Before *Brown*, one—the New Kent School—had been reserved for whites and the other—Watkins—for blacks. Virginia had required racial segregation in public schools until *Brown* was decided in 1954 and continued to encourage segregation in resistance to *Brown*. As of 1964 no black student had ever attended the New Kent School, and no white student had ever attended Watkins.

The NAACP Legal Defense Fund sued the New Kent County School Board, which responded by adopting a new "freedom of choice" plan. Students in the first through eighth grades were required to choose a school; high school students would attend the school they had previously attended unless they requested a transfer. No whites requested to attend Watkins, and only 15 percent of blacks requested New Kent: the county still ran an exclusively black school and an overwhelmingly white one.

In *Green v. County School Board of New Kent County*, the Supreme Court invalidated this plan. The Court held that under *Brown* public schools had an "affirmative duty to take whatever steps might be necessary to convert to a unitary system in which racial discrimination would be eliminated root and branch."[12] For the first time the Court explicitly required schools to do more than eliminate formal race-based exclusion; it also required the schools to counteract the racial patterns that decades of segregation had put in place.

Ironically, the Court found support for this more aggressive desegregation requirement in the "all deliberate speed" language, which allowed school districts to desegregate gradually instead of ending race discrimination immediately. Under "all deliberate speed," instead of ordering immediate desegregation, the federal courts were to "consider problems related to administration, arising from the physical condition of the school plant, the school transportation system, personnel, revision of school districts and attendance areas . . . and revision of local laws and regulations . . . to effectuate a transition to a racially nondiscriminatory school system."[13] The federal courts had to evaluate the details of the more gradual desegregation efforts to assess their compliance with the "all deliberate speed" mandate. They discovered numerous and varied attempts to delay or skirt *Brown*'s mandate and avoid desegregation. Unsurprisingly, such foot-dragging and recalcitrance often relied on private intimidation and inertia to keep segregation in place as a matter of fact, even as it was slowly abolished as a matter of law. For instance, assigning students to the school they had previously attended wasn't *explicitly* discriminatory, but there was no doubt that it would— and was intended to—keep the schools racially segregated.

In order to fulfill *Brown*'s promise to eliminate segregation, the courts had to do more than outlaw explicit racial classifications. Because the courts couldn't evaluate the policies on form alone, they had to look to their likely effects and reject policies that would predictably maintain racial segregation. Practically speaking, this came close to requiring integration.

It came closer still in 1971 when the Supreme Court considered the pupil assignment policies of North Carolina's Charlotte-Mecklenburg Board of Education. The city of Charlotte merged its public schools with those of the surrounding Mecklenburg County in 1961 to create one of the nation's largest school districts. The district served 71 percent white and 29 percent black students in 1968. In response to earlier legal challenges, the district assigned students to neighborhood schools without regard to race. But almost all of the district's black students lived in the city of Charlotte, most in a single section of the city; as a result, two-thirds of the district's black students attended schools that were 99 to 100 percent black.

The federal district court that first heard the challenge to the Charlotte-Mecklenburg district's school assignment policy considered several desegregation plans. The school board proposed a relatively modest plan that divided the district into pie-shaped zones that joined the heavily black inner city with white neighborhoods in suburban Mecklenburg County. This plan would have desegregated the district's ten high schools, but more than half of black elementary school students would attend schools that were over 85 percent black, and half of white students would attend schools that were over 85 percent white. More ambitious plans combined rezoning with long-distance busing from inner-city schools to suburban schools to achieve between 9 percent and 38 percent black enrollment at every school in the district. The district court required the board to choose between three more aggressive plans, all of which required busing. The Court of Appeals for the Fourth Circuit worried that the long-distance busing was too burdensome and sent the case back to the district court for reconsideration. But the Supreme Court stepped in and affirmed the district court's order in full in *Swann v. Charlotte-Mecklenburg Board of Education*.[14]

Was this a logical extension of *Brown*? The Court in *Green* had invalidated New Kent County's race-neutral "freedom of choice" plan because it perpetuated past racial segregation. One could say the same of the Charlotte-Mecklenburg school assignment policy: given the residential segregation of the county, well-known to school officials, neighborhood schools would inevitably be racially homogeneous schools. Moreover, the district court found that past federal, state, and local policies had contributed to that residential segregation. The school board's race-neutral assignment policies worked hand in glove with the segregated housing patterns put in place by government: "Locating schools in Negro residential areas and fixing the size of the schools to accommodate the needs of immediate neighborhoods, resulted in segregated education."[15]

But the freedom-of-choice plan invalidated in *Green* seemed designed to facilitate private racial intimidation and anxiety. By contrast, the Charlotte-Mecklenburg schools had adopted a commonplace policy of assigning pupils to schools in their neighborhoods—precisely the kind of policy one would expect a color-blind school district to adopt. Indeed, one commonly voiced objection to segregation was that students were required to attend geographically distant schools, often walking past more convenient schools in their neighborhoods that were reserved for another race.

Swann was only a mild extension of the Court's logic in *Green*, but it required a dramatic extension of the intervention of the federal courts as a practical matter. Because racial discrimination had been widespread and severe, especially in the South, one could plausibly attribute almost any racial disparity to past governmental action. Did the Court's admonishment in *Green* to eliminate discrimination "root and branch" entail eliminating all racial imbalances? The Supreme Court offered only obscure guidance: it insisted that "the constitutional command to desegregate schools does not mean that every school . . . must always reflect the racial composition of the school system as a whole" but also opined that "the racial composition of the whole school system is likely to be a useful starting point in shaping a remedy to correct past constitutional violations."

As civil rights litigators pressed for integration after *Brown*, black parents reluctantly but consistently voiced concerns that echoed those of Wechsler. Following *Swann*, the civil rights lawyers who sued recalcitrant school districts across the United States insisted that *Brown* guaranteed nothing less than complete racial integration of the public schools. In most cities, integration would require packing black kids onto buses and driving them long distances to schools in white neighborhoods. In some school districts, integration required busing black children out of town to lily-white suburbs.

The time, inconvenience, and expense involved in mass busing were not the greatest prices to be paid for integration. Whites in many schools were hostile and often violent: the black children who integrated schools in the South after *Brown* faced angry and violent white mobs on their way to school. Once inside the classrooms, they were taunted and often attacked by their white classmates.[16] The legal historian Michael Klarman makes a convincing case that

Brown breathed new life into a dying segregationism. *Brown*, seen by many white Southerners as a new form of Yankee carpetbag interference, inspired resentment and drove moderate politicians into the segregationist camp or out of politics.[17] In the early 1950s, many Southern cities and states had relaxed or eliminated Jim Crow laws involving public transportation, sports, higher education, and voter registration, either voluntarily or without great resistance, in response to court orders; after *Brown*, voters and politicians reimposed strict segregation and intensified discriminatory practices. The Ku Klux Klan, which was slouching toward extinction before *Brown*, "reappeared in states such as South Carolina, Florida, and Alabama, where it had rarely been observed in recent years."[18]

White hostility to racial integration was hardly exclusive to the South. In fact, some of the worst cases were in the heart of liberal New England. In South Boston, some whites boycotted the public schools in response to desegregation, and white mobs threw stones at school buses carrying children from the predominately black Roxbury district. Protesters planned to overturn and burn school buses carrying black students, a plan that was foiled only because an anonymous tip warned black community leaders, who arranged for the black children to spend the school day elsewhere.[19] Similar incidents occurred in the Charlestown section of Boston.

According to the law professor Derrick Bell, who consulted with Boston's black community groups at the time, many black parents were wary of ambitious busing plans: "They did not wish to back away [from] . . . efforts to desegregate Boston's schools, but they wished to place greater emphasis on upgrading the school's educational quality . . . and to minimize busing to the poorest and most violent white districts."[20] Yet civil rights lawyers, convinced that *Brown* required integration at all costs, pressed for a plan that required extensive busing.

Similarly, in Atlanta, the local NAACP hammered out a compromise with the school board that called for full desegregation of faculty and employees and an increased number of blacks in top administrative positions but only partial desegregation of students. Local black leaders and school board members supported the plan for pragmatic reasons. But the national NAACP and Legal Defense Fund lawyers saw the compromise as a betrayal of civil rights principles. They fired the Atlanta-branch NAACP president, who had supported the compromise, and filed an appeal to block it.

Black parents, teachers, and students were often ambivalent about desegregation for sensible, practical reasons. Black schools, even when they suffered from lack of funds, often offered black students intangible benefits that integrated schools did not. Black faculty and administrators were positive role models for black students, and all-black schools gave black students a safe haven from white racism and its debilitating effects on self-esteem. Ironically, although desegregation was premised on the belief that school segregation hurt the self-esteem of black students, Kenneth and Mamie Clark's studies cited in *Brown* actually showed that the self-esteem of black children in segregated schools was typically *higher* than that of black children who attended integrated schools in the North.[21] It was not segregation in and of itself that damaged the hearts and minds of black students, but rather the racism that underlay it. Black students who could escape that racism while in school had healthier self-esteem than those who were constantly exposed to it.

After desegregation, it was almost always the underfunded black schools that were closed, and the black faculty and administrators often lost their jobs. In many cases, the black community bitterly complained about the loss of a neighborhood school in which they took great pride. For instance, former students of the black Second Ward High School in Charlotte remembered "nurturing in the classroom without the strife of racial overtones." When the school closed, one graduate recalls, "it was heartbreaking." Another insisted, "We thought that it was the utmost in betrayal." A teacher recalled, "When we made the transition from Second Ward to West Charlotte, you had . . . trauma. I still kept contact with those kids from Second Ward, and they would call and sometimes cry." A former student from Tampa, Florida, complained, "It was bad. It was terrible . . . What we thought is that they would improve our school and bus in some white kids." A former teacher at a Florida high school insists, "Blacks were seeking for equality of facilities, equipment and on and on. I know they never asked for their schools to be closed."[22]

Desegregation also faced practical impediments. White flight to surrounding suburbs in the years since *Brown* had drastically changed the demographics of many American cities, making integration more costly and less effective: for instance, in 1952 the Atlanta school district was 32 percent black; by 1974, when the desegregation compromise was proposed, it was 82 percent black. The Detroit school district was over 70 percent black in the early 1970s when civil rights lawyers pressed for desegregation there. Economic and technological changes were pushing people out of the cities and into the suburbs across the country. Encouraged by recently built highways and inexpensive real estate, both the middle class and industry left the inner city to relocate in roomier and less costly digs in the suburbs. Integration was unworkable in such cities given the small number of whites, and potentially counterproductive given the ease of white flight to neighboring suburbs.

The unusual facts of 1971's *Swann* case had allowed the Court to avoid the widespread problem of white flight and racially homogeneous school districts. The Charlotte-Mecklenburg school district was the result of the consolidation of the formerly separate Charlotte and Mecklenburg County school districts in 1961. The new, merged district combined the overwhelmingly white suburbs of Mecklenburg County with the racially mixed city of Charlotte. But for the consolidation, any desegregation plan would almost certainly have been limited to Charlotte alone—eliminating many of the white schools included in the Charlotte-Mecklenburg district, without which meaningful integration would have been impossible.

This made *Swann* somewhat misleading as precedent: the fortuity of a recently consolidated district that combined a heavily black city and heavily white suburban and rural communities made a roughly 70 percent white to 30 percent black mix mathematically possible within a single district. But in cities such as Atlanta and Detroit, the urban school districts had not been consolidated with their surrounding suburbs.

Civil rights lawyers convinced a federal district court that because "relief of segregation in the public schools of the City of Detroit cannot be accomplished within the corporate geographical limits of the city," the law required a desegregation plan that included suburban school districts in the Detroit metro area. The federal Court of Appeals for the Sixth Circuit agreed, noting that "if we [were to] hold that school district boundaries are absolute barriers to a Detroit school desegregation plan, we would be opening a way to nullify *Brown v. Board of Education*."[23]

Apparently unafraid of blazing this trail, the Supreme Court reversed, in *Milliken v. Bradley*, holding that federal courts could not require a district that had never discriminated to participate in a desegregation plan. In his dissenting opinion, Justice Thurgood Marshall lamented, "In *Brown v. Board of Education*, this Court held that segregation of children in public schools on the basis of race deprives minority group children of equal educational opportunities . . . After 20 years of small, often difficult steps toward [equality], the Court today takes a giant step backwards."

By the mid-1970s the Supreme Court was already in retreat from its earlier commitment to widespread integration. Most American public schools remained both separate and unequal. A cruel irony of the Court's conflicted desegregation jurisprudence is that while it ended legally mandated segregation, it also may have sped the process of white and middle-class flight from many cities, making matters worse for those left behind. Civil rights required aggressive desegregation measures such as long-distance busing in districts that had been segregated by force of law, but not in suburban school districts that had not used the law to enforce segregation. As a result, desegregation was effectively stymied in metropolitan areas marked by the familiar "chocolate city, vanilla suburb" pattern. The people responsible for de jure segregation in the urban districts had, in many cases, decamped for the suburbs, in part in order to avoid desegregation, leaving the *victims* of segregation behind to face the lawsuits and clean up the mess.

Consequently, busing integrated only schools attended by the relatively poor whites who lived in inner cities; wealthier suburban whites continued to attend virtually all-white schools. This created the impression that racial integration was another of the many indignities and inconveniences that the rich could afford to avoid. Region-wide integration would have brought busing to the wealthier neighborhoods, possibly improving its prestige. And practically speaking, it would have reduced the effect of busing on urban schools by dramatically increasing the number of white students in the pool of students to be integrated. The combination of aggressive desegregation within urban districts and exemption for suburban districts created a powerful incentive to leave the inner city. Perhaps worst of all, the Supreme Court's desegregation jurisprudence encouraged the nation to prematurely celebrate victory over racial inequality: because racial justice had been defined in terms of formal civil rights and desegregation, unequal resources in the nation's still effectively segregated schools looked like a secondary consideration.

This may have been the most the courts could do. Busing was unpopular and cumbersome even when limited to a single school district; it could easily become unmanageable if extended to several districts or an entire metropolitan region. Students would be forced to travel greater distances, white resentment might be even greater, and inner-city black students would almost certainly feel even more out of place in leafy all-white suburbs than in white urban neighborhoods. Evaluating these complex policies and their likely consequences would have required detailed sociological study. Courts faced with live controversies have neither the time nor the resources for such analyses, and conventional civil rights analysis does not easily accommodate such considerations. Given these daunting conditions in the trenches, the courts beat a face-saving retreat from *Brown*'s more ambitious implications. In the heady and optimistic days of the 1950s and 1960s, the Warren Court promised unequivocal victory over racial injustice. By the mid-1970s, a chastened Burger Court was ready to accept a thinly disguised defeat, the judiciary's iteration of peace with honor.

Some had hoped for a more pragmatic approach. Judge J. Braxton Craven was appointed by President John F. Kennedy to the federal District Court for the Western District of North Carolina and had heard one of the cases that led up to the *Swann* litigation. Judge Craven suggested that the Civil Rights Act of 1964, which enforced *Brown*'s mandate by withholding federal funding from segregated school districts, offered a chance to take desegregation out of the courts and place it in the hands of "administrators, especially if they have some competence and experience in school administration[, who] can likely work out . . . the problems of pupil and teacher assignment in the best interests of all concerned better than can any District Judge operating within the adversary system. The question before this court . . . is not what is best for all concerned but simply what are plaintiffs entitled to have as a matter of constitutional law."[24] After over fifty years of frustrating struggle, resulting in controversial and often ineffectual judicial remediation, this suggestion seems apt. An administrative approach may not have done as much as quickly as the courts did. But administrators might have accomplished more profound and more durable change in the long run by encouraging compromise and skirting backlash.

In 2007 the Supreme Court of the United States, inspired by the legacy of *Brown v. Board of Education*, invalidated the racial school assignment policies of two school districts—one in Seattle, Washington, and one on the edge of the Old South, in Louisville, Kentucky. Both districts had been sued for racial segregation, and both had developed integrationist policies in response. In Louisville the school district did so under court order; in Seattle, to settle a civil rights lawsuit. Over time, both districts abandoned aggressive desegregation policies such as busing in favor of milder policies. In Seattle, the school board tried to combine individual choice with racial integration by allowing incoming high school students to choose from among any of the district's high schools, ranking them in order of preference. For the most popular schools, places in the entering class would be filled using a series of tiebreakers: the district gave preference to students with a sibling attending the school, to students who lived nearby, and to students who would contribute to the racial diversity of the student body. In Louisville, the district adopted a desegregation plan of its own design after a court order imposing busing was lifted in 2001. Like the Seattle plan, it considered student preferences, residential proximity to the school, and racial integration in making school assignments and approving transfers. These desegregation policies were weak tea compared with the strong medicine of mandatory busing that they replaced. And their effect was correspondingly mild: according to Chief Justice John Roberts, in the 2000–2001 school year only fifty-two Seattle students were assigned to a school they hadn't chosen because of the district's mild attempt to promote integration. Similarly, only about 3 percent of school assignments in Louisville were affected by the district's racial integration plan.

Like Chief Justice Earl Warren more than fifty years earlier, Chief Justice John Roberts offered a ringing endorsement of racial equality in condemning these policies. He quoted the plaintiffs in *Brown v. Board of Education*, the landmark case that brought an end to school segregation, at length. But *Parents Involved in Community Schools v. Seattle School District No. 1* wasn't the typical civil rights case. This time the school districts were under attack for promoting racial *integration*. The problem, according to a majority of the Supreme Court, wasn't that the districts hadn't done enough to integrate the schools; it was that they had done too much. Using the arguments developed in *Brown*, Roberts insisted that " 'the Fourteenth Amendment prevents states from according differential treatment to American children on the basis of their color or race.' " Using the legacy of the civil rights movement as its guide, the Supreme Court held that the Constitution of the United States prohibits racial integration.

After John Roberts had been nominated to lead the high court by President George W. Bush and confirmed by the Senate, liberals and civil rights lawyers held their breath. During his confirmation hearings, Roberts came across as the exemplary jurist: humble, self-effacing, mild mannered. In a comment that would become famous, he compared the role of a Supreme Court justice to that of an umpire: "Umpires don't make the rules; they apply them . . . [This] is a limited role. Nobody ever went to a ball game to see the umpire." But the umpire had come out swinging for the bleachers, attacking long-standing liberal precedents and establishing new conservative ones with a vigor that was well captured by the word "active"—if not "activist." With *Parents Involved*, Roberts had stolen home base, turning the most cherished liberal Supreme Court precedent against liberals. With the definitiveness of an umpire declaring a pitch outside the strike zone, he insisted that "the way to stop discrimination on the basis of race is to stop discriminating on the basis of race."[25] Roberts also quoted directly from the historic argument of the plaintiffs' lawyers in *Brown*: " 'We have one fundamental contention which we will seek to develop in the course of this argument, and that contention is that no State has any authority under the equal-protection clause of the Fourteenth Amendment to use race as a factor in affording educational opportunities among its citizens.' "[26]

The segregated schools at issue in *Brown* classified students by race in order to keep the races separate; the Seattle schools in *Parents Involved* classified students by race in order to bring the races together. Yet according to the Supreme Court, both uses of race are unconstitutional. Justice Roberts warned against unwarranted "confidence in [the] ability to distinguish good from harmful . . . uses of racial criteria."[27] Justice Clarence Thomas's concurring opinion drove the point home: "Can we really be sure that the racial theories that motivated *Dred Scott* and *Plessy* [notorious opinions that reinforced slavery and Jim Crow segregation] are a relic of the past or that future theories will be nothing but beneficent and progressive? That is a gamble I am unwilling to take, and it is one the Constitution does not allow."[28]

Is it really so hard to tell the difference between defensible and pernicious uses of race? When *Brown* was decided, everyone understood that the holding called for an end to a specific practice: segregation. Segregation was a brute and tangible fact of life, and the reason for prohibiting it was obvious: it was inspired by racial contempt and was a crucial medium of such contempt. "Racial classification," by contrast, is a lawyer's construction that covers a host of very different policies: de jure segregation and affirmative action, racial profiling by police, and the use of race in the census. It's not at all obvious that we should categorically condemn "racial classification." Race discrimination was demeaning and hurtful in the context of a social system that was *designed* to demean and injure. Race discrimination is objectionable because of the history of slavery, Jim Crow segregation, and widespread invidious prejudice. Civil rights, at their best, are a response to such concrete injustices, not a mechanical application of an abstract principle. In the social context surrounding *Brown* it's clear that segregation—not racial classification generally—was the problem: the Court in *Brown* explicitly noted that "the policy of *separating* the races is usually interpreted as denoting the inferiority of the Negro group."[29] *Brown v. Board of Education*, read in its proper historical context, is inconsistent with Justice Roberts's bloodless interpretation of "equal protection of the laws" as prohibiting segregation and integration alike, equally hostile to the poison and its antidote.

After *Brown*, federal courts struggled to devise desegregation plans that local communities would accept. They often failed, but eventually some cities like Seattle and Louisville authored desegregation plans of their own. The local democratic process yielded proposals that most people supported, and local administration promised a smoother and more efficient implementation than any court order could. These plans are just what one would hope a mature civil rights tradition would produce: local communities embracing their constitutional obligations, taking desegregation out of the courts and, as Judge Craven suggested over thirty years earlier, handing it off to "administrators . . . [with] some competence and experience in school administration [who] can likely work out . . . the problems of pupil and teacher assignment in the best interests of all concerned better than can any . . . Judge operating within the adversary system." But tragically, civil rights have often required cumbersome, unworkable, and counterproductive judicially imposed mandates, and today they prohibit the egalitarian policies developed and blessed by the people through the democratic process.

Civil rights litigation has never been the main engine of social justice in the United States; at most, it has occasionally jump-started a stalled political process or boosted sluggish change in social attitudes. But judges and lawyers have taken credit for the accomplishments of social activists who struggled against racism and of average Americans who struggled against their worst prejudices and nurtured their best instincts. And because civil rights have become synonymous with social justice, the courts, by virtue of their legal authority, have also asserted authority over the cultural meaning of social justice itself. When Justice Roberts insisted that the true meaning of *Brown v. Board of Education* was to prohibit racial classifications—including those that would advance racial integration—he opined not only on a question of constitutional law but also on the meaning of decades of historical struggle against racism. As a result, men and women who spent much of their lives suffering through and resisting the evils of segregation can be told that in fact they struggled to prohibit integration.

The civil rights movement is heroic and profound because of its specifics: the struggle against Jim Crow, the lunch counter sit-in, the freedom ride, and the public demonstration, all of which required personal sacrifice and entailed ever-present danger. The constitutional guarantee of equal protection of the laws would mean something very different—and something much less profound—but for the struggles and triumphs of the civil rights movement. If the struggle for racial justice relied on rights and the courts for its victories, today rights and the courts rely on the racial justice movement for their prestige and their legitimacy. Yet, with alarming frequency, civil rights and courts now bite the hand that feeds them, undermining racial justice and equality. When civil rights deprive long-oppressed groups of their still young and meager victories, they have gone very badly wrong.

Sex as a Weapon

When Lois Robinson started working as a welder at Jacksonville Shipyards in September 1977, she was one of a tiny vanguard of women working in such a position there—or anywhere. In 1980 she was one of two women in "skilled crafts" in a place where 958 men were employed. Despite the challenges of breaking through the gender line, Robinson was a success: she was promoted twice, attaining the status of first-class welder while at Jacksonville Shipyards.

But being a woman in what her co-workers described as a "man's world" wasn't always easy. At Jacksonville Shipyards, as at many predominantly male workplaces, the etiquette of the locker room prevailed. Pornography was the decoration of choice: "pictures of nude and partially nude women appear[ed] throughout the . . . workplace," including "two plaques of naked women," lovingly glued to a wood backing and varnished for long-term durability. As if the monthly centerfold weren't sufficient, many of Jacksonville Shipyards' business partners supplied the shop with advertising calendars that featured naked women striking sexually suggestive poses while holding various power tools, valves, gauges, and other equipment. Robinson was treated to daily demonstrations of her co-workers' refined appreciation of the female nude, such as a photograph of a woman with the words "USDA Choice" stamped on her naked chest and a picture of a woman with a meat spatula pressed against her crotch. Her co-workers' artistic evaluation of this dime-store erotica was no less subtle than the images themselves, including observations such as "I'd like to get in bed with that" and "I'd like to have some of that."

One day when Robinson was on the job, a co-worker jovially passed around a photograph of a woman with long blond hair wearing high heels and holding a whip: Robinson had long blond hair and regularly worked with a welding tool known as a whip. Another co-worker extended Robinson this friendly invitation: "Hey, pussycat, come here and give me a whiff." Another shared his wish that Robinson's shirt would blow over her head so he could admire her unadorned form, and yet another remarked that for similar reasons, he wished her shirt were tighter. Robinson's co-workers and supervisors also reserved distinctive endearments just for her, such as "honey," "dear," "baby," "sugar," and "momma."

When Robinson told them that she found the pet names, ribald witticisms, and ubiquitous porn offensive, her co-workers responded to her concerns immediately. They put up *more* pornographic images, making sure to leave them in Robinson's workstation and on her toolbox. One ambitious co-worker found a photograph of a nude woman with a welding shield, remarking, "Lois would really like this." Robinson complained to management and the union; both ignored her. Finally, she sued Jacksonville Shipyards for sex discrimination. In 1991, a federal court agreed with Robinson that Jacksonville Shipyards was a discriminatory, hostile environment for women and ordered the company to clean up its act—and its workplace.

Robinson v. Jacksonville Shipyards was a significant victory for feminists, who had agitated for a more aggressive response to sex harassment for years.[30] Although the law had acknowledged that a hostile environment could be a distinctive form of discrimination for over a decade, many courts had required plaintiffs to prove tangible injury or show that they had been subject to explicit sexual overtures or targeted intimidation. Some courts opined that the open display of pornography was a form of constitutionally protected free expression and therefore beyond the reach of the law. *Jacksonville Shipyards* seemed to vindicated the feminist contention that pornography could be, in and of itself, harmful to women.

In this, *Jacksonville Shipyards* indirectly furthered a more ambitious feminist agenda that targeted pornography wherever it appeared, whether in the workplace or outside it. Feminists had lobbied against the porn industry for years, working to close down peep shows and topless clubs, shutter theaters that specialized in blue movies, and stymie the sale of girlie magazines. They argued that porn led to sexual assault, citing studies that found that sexual predators were disproportionate consumers of pornography. (Skeptics questioned the relationship of cause and effect: maybe sexual predators were more likely to read porn because they were generally obsessed with sex. Some argued that porn might actually provide a release for urges that would lead to rape if left unsatisfied.) They argued that the average smutty movie or *Playboy* centerfold was on a moral continuum with the "snuff film," in which an actual sexual assault that climaxed in the murder of the female victim was captured on celluloid (skeptics doubt that any such snuff films exist or have ever existed).

For these antiporn feminists, suppressing pornography was a civil rights issue. The law professor Catharine MacKinnon authored local ordinances that would have virtually banned pornography in Minneapolis; two such ordinances were passed by the city council, but the mayor vetoed both. In Indianapolis, a similar law was enacted with the support of an odd coalition of feminists and religious conservatives. The "antipornography civil rights ordinance" made it illegal to "traffic in . . . produce, sell, exhibit or distribute pornography." A federal court, predictably, invalidated the Indianapolis ordinance as a violation of the First Amendment, taking the air out of the antiporn movement (at least in the United States: the Supreme Court of Canada accepted feminist antiporn arguments and upheld the obscenity conviction of a pornography distributor in 1992). *Jacksonville Shipyards* gave the antiporn movement new momentum: if pornography could not be outlawed outright, at least it could be punished as sex harassment.

Many feminists advanced the idea that sexually suggestive or erotic expression is distinctively harmful for women and should be banned from the workplace. For instance, the law professor and former Democratic Party adviser Susan Estrich insisted that sexual conduct is "more offensive, more debilitating, and more dehumanizing . . . precisely [because] it is *sexual*" and argued in favor of "rules which prohibited men and women from sexual relations in the workplace" whether or not both parties wanted the relationship.[31]

Two years after Lois Robinson won her discrimination lawsuit against Jacksonville Shipyards, Jerold Mackenzie lost his job after nineteen years at the Miller Brewing Company. Mackenzie started down the road to unemployment when he turned on his television on March 18, 1993, and sat down to watch the situation comedy *Seinfeld*. The sexually suggestive episode shocked Mackenzie, and the next day he took another step closer to a pink slip when he decided to discuss the *Seinfeld* show with his co-worker Patricia Best. Mackenzie was surprised that the racy episode had made it past the network censors and asked whether Best shared his opinion. Best said she hadn't seen the show, so Mackenzie filled her in: Jerry Seinfeld has forgotten the name of his latest date. He can remember only that her name rhymes with a part of the female anatomy. Eventually, the woman begins to suspect that Jerry can't remember her name and demands that he repeat it. Jerry makes several desperate guesses—"Gipple?" "Mulva?" As the woman storms out in disgust, vowing never to see him again, Jerry calls after her: *"Dolores!"*

Best said she didn't get the joke. Then Mackenzie took the final unwitting leap into joblessness when he copied a dictionary page with the entry "clitoris" and gave it to Best. Best complained to her supervisor, who suggested she confront Mackenzie directly. She did so and he apologized, but also remarked that because Best herself frequently used vulgar language at work, he had assumed she wouldn't be offended. The half apology didn't satisfy Best, who complained again. This time Best's supervisor reported the incident to the personnel department. Before Mackenzie had any inkling that his job was in jeopardy, the personnel department had discussed the incident with Miller's in-house counsel, its CEO, and a private employment law firm. The next day Mackenzie was summoned to a meeting with a personnel manager and two lawyers. After an hour he was fired and shown to the front door of the building.

Mackenzie sued and convinced a jury that he was treated unfairly and deserved a total of over $26 million. But Miller appealed the verdict, arguing that Mackenzie was an employee "at will," which means that Miller wasn't legally required to be fair to him: it was legally entitled to fire him for a good reason, a bad reason, or no reason at all. An appeals court reversed the judgment for Mackenzie, and the Wisconsin Supreme Court affirmed the reversal. Mackenzie wound up with nothing.

Mackenzie v. Miller Brewing Company was the tip of an iceberg, visible only because Mackenzie sued his employer rather than quietly accept a severance package. Below the choppy surface of a volatile labor market, the threat of sex harassment litigation inspired thousands of employers to crack down on off-color jokes, racy art-work, and office romances. In the fearful minds of employers, civil rights law no longer simply prohibited sex discrimination; it had become a general civility code that potentially outlawed any expression with sexual or erotic content. One commentator de-scribed Mackenzie's case as an example of "the inconsistency be-tween the anything goes freedom of expression that reigns in the media and the sexually neutral atmosphere that [the] law requires employers to enforce in the workplace . . . the law's insistence on sexual neutrality in the workplace has reached an absurd and un-workable limit. Certainly it seems unfair for a man to lose his job for saying in an office in Wisconsin what Jerry Seinfeld can say on national television."[32] This fear was confirmed by a common slip-page in nomenclature: what was originally called *sex* harassment had come to be known, in popular and in legal parlance, as *sexual* harassment. This small difference was telling: *sex* harassment sug-gests that the legal wrong is harassing a woman because of her *sex*. By contrast, *sexual* harassment suggests that it's the sexual content of the harassment that makes it unlawful.

Emphasizing the threat of expensive and embarrassing lawsuits, human resources consultants advised a "zero tolerance" approach to sexual expression and fraternization in the workplace. The pru-dent employer would prohibit dirty jokes, racy gossip, sexy pic-tures, any physical contact more intimate than a handshake, and unchaperoned social contact between male and female employees after hours. Office doors were to be kept open when two members of the opposite sex met, and if possible a third party would be pres-ent to ensure that no one felt uncomfortable (and to provide a wit-ness to events in case of possible litigation).

If employers didn't forbid office romances outright, lawyers and consultants recommended that the lovers sign "love contracts," which would explicitly spell out the terms of the relationship—and clarify what would happen if Cupid's spell wore off. For example, an employment law firm advises its clients to draft letters based on this template:

> *Dear [Name of object of affection]:*
>   *As we discussed, I know that this may seem silly or unnecessary to you, but I really want you to give serious consideration to the matter as it is very important to me.* [Add other material as appropriate.]
>   *It is very important to me that our relationship be on an equal footing and that you be fully comfortable that our relationship is at all times fully voluntary and welcome. I want to assure you that under no circumstances will I allow our relationship or, should it happen, the end of our relationship, to impact on your job or our working relationship. Though I know you have received a copy of [our company's] sexual harassment policy, I am enclosing a copy* [Add specific reference to policy as appropriate] *so that you can read and review it again. Once you have done so, I would greatly appreciate your signing this letter below, if you are in agreement with me.*
>   [Add personal closing.]
>   *Very truly yours,*
>   [Name]
>
>
>   *I have read this letter and the accompanying sexual harassment policy, and I understand and agree [that] . . . my relationship with [Name] has been (and is) voluntary, consensual and welcome. I also understand that I am free to end this relationship at any time and, in doing so, it will not adversely impact on my job.*
>   [Signature of object of affection][33]

Love contracts should have surprised no one. They arrived, on cue, a few years after colleges and universities began to regulate sexual intimacy between students and professors and, in some cases, between students and other students. The most notorious of the many collegiate sexual regulations was Antioch College's Sexual Offense Policy. A student group known as the Womyn of Antioch agitated for and drafted the policy, which required explicit, verbal consent to any and all intimate contact. Like any good legal document, the policy was drafted to deal with a dynamic relationship between the parties: new and unanticipated hazards lurked behind every whispered endearment and affectionate coo. The policy hence required renewed consent with "each new level" of sexual activity: explicit, verbal consent to kiss on the lips did not imply acquiescence to use of the tongue; heavy petting did not imply agreement to unbutton garments; fellatio did not—contrary to the almost unanimous advice of sex therapists—suggest a reciprocal desire for cunnilingus. Nor could the universal language of lovers take the place of unambiguous and literal verbiage. "Body movements and non-verbal responses such as moans are not consent," the policy warned. As students emerged from the protective jurisdiction of campus sexual codes such as Antioch's, many expected, and some demanded, similar regulation in the work world.

Sex harassment law developed in response to blatant sexism: bullying and intimidation designed to drive women out of the workforce and sexually predatory behavior, such as demands for sexual favors backed by blunt threats of retaliation. The law also addressed variations on these ugly themes: amorous supervisors who hinted at career advantages or impediments they could bestow or impose, sexual taunts used as a way of maintaining male dominance. But as sex harassment evolved into *sexual* harassment, the target of litigation was no longer just sex discrimination or male chauvinism; it was sexuality generally. *Sexual* harassment law didn't just treat sexuality as a *means* to the prohibited *end* of sex discrimination; it insisted that the offending jokes and images were demeaning and dehumanizing *because they were sexual*. This reformulation made any sexually charged encounter, image, or statement a target of legal prohibition, whether it reinforced male privilege and sex segregation or not.

This was a direct reaction against the sexual revolution that took hold of the nation in the Roaring Twenties and reached its apotheosis with the free love of the youth counterculture in the 1960s. Some feminists insisted that sexuality was a dangerous force that had to be kept in check with strict rules and attacked modern sexual freedom as little more than a ruse by unscrupulous men out for an easy lay. This attempt to repress *sexuality* in general was one of the most successful feminist agendas because it, unlike much of modern feminism, was extremely familiar. The religious right tilted at the windmill of the modern sexual revolution for most of the twentieth century, but it was radical feminists, armed with the lance of civil rights, who did real damage to modern sexual licentiousness. If conservative sexual repression tried to toss tepid water on the sexuality of other people, antisex feminists volunteered to take the cold shower themselves as they hosed down their peers.

Feminists could not maintain a monopoly on—or control over— the idea that sexual expression was a violation of civil rights. Prudish men used sex harassment law to attack women who made crude sexual jokes in predominantly female workplaces, proving that turnabout is, if not fair play, then inevitable. Effeminate men sued for sex harassment when they were made the butt of locker room jokes. Straight men who were propositioned by gay supervisors or overheard the raunchy sexual conversations of their gay co-workers made a federal case of their injured—and quite likely homophobic—sensibilities. Indeed, a legal regime that punished unwelcome sexual expression regardless of its objective effects predictably fell most heavily on unconventional forms of sexual expression, such as those typically exhibited by minority groups, gay men, and lesbians. As Harvard law professor Janet Halley put it, "Sexual harassment law has become . . . sexuality harassment."[34] None of this bothered committed antisex feminists; in fact, some argued that these claims were really claims for *women's* rights because anyone who suffered unwelcome sexual advances or expression was "feminized" by the unwelcome encounter.

But some claims of sexual victimization were in direct conflict with feminism.

Part of Yale College's extraordinary prestige owes to its unique extracurricular traditions. Yale's Skull and Bones society, an exclusive club for undergraduates, is shrouded in intrigue and mystery. Since the 1970s its membership has been a secret, although very high-ranking military officers, heads of the CIA, CEOs of Fortune 100 firms, and American presidents are said to be members. Its members are sworn to secrecy and are reportedly instructed to make sure no one sees them enter or leave the club's well-known windowless clubhouse, or "tomb"—in its many years of existence few students have seen anyone do so (giving rise to further rumors that the building is served by subterranean entrances, or that it is an unused decoy, left vacant to fool the uninitiated masses). Skull and Bones does not accept applications: members are "tapped" in a selection process as secretive as the society itself.

But Yale does not leave the less conspiratorial or less well connected adrift in the chilly New Haven social climate. Every Yale undergraduate is assigned a residential college and resides there for his freshman and sophomore years. The residential colleges are more than dormitories: each college has a distinctive collective personality, and students retain a relationship with their college throughout their undergraduate years and beyond. Each of the twelve colleges has its own dean, lectures, tea parties—even its own endowment (some of which are larger than those of entire universities). The residential colleges are a big part of the distinctive Yale experience, a proudly and jealously guarded tradition. When the university admitted its first female undergraduates in 1969, it also integrated the residential colleges, assigning the handful of female students randomly, just as it had long done with the male students.

Traditionalists worried that Yale would suffer a decline in the esprit de corps that made it the envy of the Ivy League. It didn't, but the change did sow the seeds of a threat to Yale's residential colleges, which came to fruition almost thirty years later.

Because of the residential colleges' centrality to the carefully cultivated Yale experience, affiliation with one is not optional. But in 1996 five admitted students refused to live in their assigned colleges. Their complaint: Yale's coed residential colleges were a Sodom and Gomorrah of sexual temptation. According to the Yale Five, as they came to be known, the erotically charged and permissive atmosphere of coed living offended their religious sensibilities and was therefore a form of antireligious discrimination. Conservative commentators quickly championed the cause of the Yale Five. The noted antifeminist Phyllis Schlafly praised the Yale Five's "courage to challenge the rule that requires students to live in coed dormitories, where many engage in casual sex without shame and most use coed showers and toilets."[35] In fact, Yale's residential colleges had not only single-sex bathrooms but single-sex *floors* available for students who wanted them. One suspects that the real cause of the Yale Five's distress was not a university policy forcing them into intimate contact with the opposite sex, but rather the reaction of their classmates: in the heady atmosphere of sexual opportunity that saturated the colleges, their religious commitments to modesty and chastity would provoke ridicule and social isolation—or, worse, those commitments would yield to the daily onslaught of carnal temptation. The Yale Five made a federal case of that universal tribulation of adolescence: peer pressure.

When Yale admitted its first female students, sex integration was a civil rights imperative. Now it was a civil rights violation. Religious conservatives turned the idea of a sexually hostile environment, first advanced by feminists, against a fundamental commitment of feminism. But religious conservatives hadn't distorted the feminist antisexuality agenda; they had simply taken it to its logical conclusion. If erotically charged situations were dangerous because of their sexual electricity, then wasn't the sexual polarity—and mutual attraction—of male and female the underlying cause of the hazard? If so, then the solution was obvious: keep the sexes safely insulated. If this happened to coincide with a long-standing and independent conservative position on appropriate gender roles, well, that was just a happy coincidence.

The Yale Five were just the beginning. Across the nation, evangelical Christians, fundamentalist Muslims, and ultra-Orthodox Jews sued their employers to avoid working with women in jobs that required shared sleeping arrangements or changing rooms, such as fire stations, emergency room quarters, and trucking dormitories. Such claims—often inspired by ambiguous religious admonishments to avoid "temptation"—effectively discourage employers from hiring women in jobs where gains in sex equality have been recent and hard-won.

Of course, such claims were only a small part of a larger agenda of sexual repression—an agenda that consistently disadvantaged women. For instance, religious and political leaders have suggested that pharmacists with religious objections should have a right to refuse to fill prescriptions for contraception. Devout police officers have argued that religious liberty entitles them to refuse to protect abortion clinics. And psychological counselors have argued that offering relationship counseling to gay and lesbian couples offends their religious convictions, turning the right to religious freedom into a right to discriminate, in direct conflict with the laws of many states that guarantee equal opportunity for gay men and lesbians. Title VII has always required employers to accommodate the religious practices of their employees, but typically this has entailed things like reorganizing work schedules to allow religious employees to observe a holy day or prayer break. These new claims were more aggressive, expanding on the idea—borrowed from sex harassment law—that offended sensibilities in and of themselves could constitute a civil rights violation.

When *sex* harassment law morphed into *sexual* harassment law, with the implication that the enemy was sexuality in general and not just male chauvinism, employers responded by implementing rules that prohibited any and all erotic expression or activity, real or perceived. As the Yale Law School professor Vicki Schultz has observed: "Sex harassment policies now provide an added incentive and an increased legitimacy for management to control and discipline relatively harmless sexual behavior without even inquiring into whether that behavior undermines gender equality on the job."[36]

Because most such activity involves male-female relations, these rules scrutinized and regulated sex-integrated interactions much more severely than same-sex interactions. In workplaces and professions where men held most of the positions of influence and authority—in other words, in most workplaces and most professions—this reinforced the existing inclination of many powerful men to prefer other men as their protégés and co-workers. Professional women reported being unable to have private, job-related conversations with their male superiors because of "open door" policies that required male-female interactions to be conducted in public in order to avoid the appearance of sexual impropriety. Because male supervisors worried about inadvertently offending their female employees—and thereby violating increasingly strict workplace rules against sexual misconduct—conversations between male supervisors and female subordinates were often stilted and tense, and comfortable working relationships took longer to develop, if they developed at all. Cautious employers hesitated to send a male and a female on out-of-town business travel together, for fear of what might happen after a long night in a strange city. Because the more senior members of the potential teams were most often men, it was usually women who lost out on valuable work opportunities. Strictly speaking, all of this was sex discrimination, and therefore unlawful. But proving that a mentoring relationship was cool and distant or that a plum assignment went to someone else because of sex is hard. Proving that a boss made a racy joke or that an out-of-town trip mixed business and pleasure is relatively easy. Employers correctly assumed that the risk of sexual harassment litigation was greater than the risk of being sued for subtle sex discrimination.

When the law that protected women from harassment because of their sex morphed into the idea that anything *sexual* must be harassment, a legal theory that was designed to help women get ahead in the workforce wound up restricting their chances to interact with men as equals. Civil rights law began with a modern, enlightened demand for respect and fairness, but wound up reinforcing the old, chauvinistic idea that women are frail hothouse flowers that require delicate handling and protective isolation from the hardscrabble working world. This perverse metamorphosis of sex harassment law into sexual harassment law—butterfly into worm—is a case of rights gone wrong.

There's an argument to be made for most of the decisions I've discussed and criticized in this chapter. Mandatory busing was the only way to achieve meaningful integration, and perhaps the objective costs and widespread resentment that came with it could have been managed. Race-conscious public policies, like those invalidated in *Parents Involved*, strike many people as unfair, even when their effects are mild, and sometimes they do more harm than good to race relations, reinforcing racial divisions. Sexual expression is offensive to many people of both sexes, and it is often used to belittle and threaten women: maybe, on balance, a virtual ban on racy talk and romantic overtures on the job makes sense.

But the advocates of these changes didn't have to make the arguments in these practical terms, which would have required detailed study of the social context and likely effects of the policies in question. Instead, they bypassed the discussion any sensible person would want to have before making a sweeping policy change and argued their cases in terms of abstract rights and rigid rules: public schools must be integrated as quickly as possible, regardless of the costs to everyone involved or the possibility of mutually preferable

compromises; the government may not make "racial classifications," regardless of the benefits in terms of social justice; romantic
overtures and crude jokes are presumptively discriminatory, even if
both parties directly involved sought out the interaction.

A more pragmatic approach to these problems might have been
more effective and less costly. School desegregation could have employed a range of tools and remedies: integration when feasible,
supplemented with better funding for the best predominantly black
schools and improved job opportunities for black teachers and administrators in integrated schools. Instead of a sharp distinction
between districts that once practiced formal segregation and those
that did not, which unreasonably put inner-city schools under strict
desegregation orders while leaving nearby suburbs free from any obligation to integrate, administrators could have developed a range
of remedies that took local demographics and local preferences into
account. Such a practical approach to civil rights would be the an-
tithesis of the simplistic idea that the law forbids "racial classifications" regardless of their effects or the motivations underlying
them. And had schools gradually integrated on terms more people
would accept, the backlash against integration that inspired reverse-
discrimination lawsuits might have been less severe. Likewise, a
civil rights approach that focused on a practical goal of improving
women's access to jobs would not have been so easily captured by
an antisex moralism. Any viable approach to women's equality
must confront and punish sex harassment like that in *Jacksonville
Shipyards*, but more ambiguous cases involving hurt feelings, offended sensibilities, and consensual relationships are probably better
left to the normal forces of the market, informal social pressure,
compromise, common decency, and common sense.

At their best, civil rights guarantee both individual and collective
justice, ensuring that every citizen gets a fair shake and reversing the
effects of widespread bigotry and entrenched social hierarchies.
When asserted and interpreted with sensitivity to social context
and guided by responsible policy goals, rights improve democratic

politics and markets by correcting unexamined biases and unjustified prejudices. But rights go wrong when abstractions take precedence over real-life experience and conceptualism wins out over common sense.

Like cloistered medieval theologians who derive their worldview from the intangibles of ancient scripture rather than from empirical observation, judges and lawyers at their worst allow legalistic conceptualism to blind them to both practical constraints and logical consequences. As a result, rights to racial justice now prohibit some of the most promising means of achieving it, and rights to women's equality reinforce chauvinistic condescension and women's isolation.

4

Civil Rights Activism as Therapy

Civil rights aren't just the tools of courts and lawyers. Popular social movements have used the language of civil rights to raise awareness of injustice, rally a complacent public to action, and press for concrete change from government and businesses. Rights aren't just the language of lawyers and the jargon of jurists; they are also a popular patois used to name moral wrongs and shame those who caused them. Ideally, such popular rights could redeem legal rights, bringing the pragmatism of the concrete streets to the chilly conceptualism of the marble courtroom and the ivory tower. Alas, the reverse is often the case. Popular civil rights activism is often as immoderate as the most aggressive lawsuit, as inflexible as the most rigid rule, and as impractical as the most scholastic rumination.

By the time the Jena Six scandal came to a head in the autumn of 2007, civil rights activists had spent decades trying to bring the moral authority and social momentum of the civil rights movement to bear on more complex and impersonal social evils. Hard-core "race" men and women would turn out for activists such as the Reverend Al Sharpton and his less famous counterparts in other cities to protest the latest racial outrage, whether real or concocted. For the most part, sympathetic people of all races would nod in agreement, furrow their brows in concern, and then go on with their business. But occasionally someone or something would strike a chord that reverberated with thousands of people nationwide.

Despite Sharpton's bold claim that the Jena Six protests marked the beginning of the twenty-first century's civil rights movement, in many ways they echoed Louis Farrakhan's brash and insistent call, in 1995, for the Million Man March. It was an unlikely occasion for a civil-rights-style demonstration because there was *no* occasion for such a demonstration. There was no specific racial injustice to be brought to the attention of a complacent public, no landmark racial justice legislation to be pressed in the halls of Congress. There was only the familiar set of social problems that had plagued inner-city black communities for decades: crime, joblessness, broken homes, failing schools. Nor did the Million Man March call for a renewed public commitment to racial justice: there was no demand for more aggressive civil rights laws, no impassioned plea for investment in inner-city neighborhoods, no emotional reminder of the nation's unfulfilled commitment to integration.

Instead, the Million Man March was to be a "day of atonement" and "reaffirmation" for black men. Black men were to atone for the reckless and destructive behavior that was destroying black families and neighborhoods—drugs, gang violence, promiscuous sex—and reaffirm their commitment to their families and communities. This was a message that had been central to the ethics of the black community since the era of Booker T. Washington, the founder of the Tuskegee Institute, and it was a message that people of all races and political dispositions could support: personal responsibility, self-reliance, moral discipline, the straight and narrow.

But self-reliance didn't require a march on Washington. The Million Man March was awkward because it tried to combine the two great warring ideals of black uplift: Booker T. Washington's strategy of industrious self-help and the political activism that found its most erudite advocate in W.E.B. Du Bois—a founder of the NAACP—and reached its apotheosis in the lunch counter sit-ins and freedom rides of the 1960s. The result was an assembly whose substance was in direct opposition to its form: a group rally for individual self-reliance; a mass protest in service of personal atonement. It was the form of the Million Man March that was responsible for much of its appeal: like the march on Jena, Louisiana, it was buoyed by nostalgia for the civil rights movement, for the moral certainty of an unambiguously noble cause, for the courage and heroism of speaking truth to power, for the nurturing solidarity of a community united in resistance to a common oppressor.

Substantively, however, the Million Man March had neither courage, nor solidarity, nor certainty. The central message of personal atonement and the primacy of the family echoed the prevailing neoconservative ethos of the time; far from a courageous challenge to the status quo, it harmonized with a growing popular exasperation with racial politics, hostility to social welfare policies, and celebration of a narrowly defined conventional family. Had the spokesperson for this idea been a less notorious figure than Louis Farrakhan, the Million Man March might have inspired the admiration of the ideological right; as it was, prominent conservatives expressed their support for many of the ideas underlying the march, even as they condemned its demagogic leader.

Meanwhile, the deliberate and explicit exclusion of women exacerbated these reactionary tendencies and guaranteed that the march would breed resentment and division rather than solidarity. The speakers at the march admonished black men to show more respect for women and take responsibility for their offspring. Farrakhan added an unmistakably patriarchal gloss to the theme of responsibility: "We wanted to call our men to Washington to make a statement that we are ready to accept the responsibility of being the heads of our households, the providers, the maintainers and the protectors of our women and children."[1] The subtext—made palpable by the exclusion of women from the march itself—was that black men had allowed overbearing black women to control their families, to the ruin of all concerned, and that men must reassert their dominance.

Because of such unabashed male chauvinism and the unrepentant racial bigotry and anti-Semitism of its spokesman, Louis Farrakhan (despite the theme of atonement, Farrakhan refused to atone for his well-publicized and oft-repeated slur that Jews were "bloodsuckers"), the march split the black community. Prominent black women condemned the march. The former Black Panther and UC Santa Cruz professor Angela Davis complained, "No march movement or agenda that defines manhood in the narrowest terms and seeks to make women lesser partners . . . can be considered a positive step."[2] Mary Frances Berry, then chair of the U.S. Commission on Civil Rights, remarked: "I do not trust Louis Farrakhan . . . to lead us to the Promised Land." Congressman John Lewis, a veteran of the civil rights movement, did not march; General Colin Powell begged off, citing a conflict with his book tour, but when pressed, he admitted to being "concerned my presence on the stage with Farrakhan would give him a level of credibility I would not like to have seen."[3]

As for moral certainty, even many of those who marched were ambivalent. For instance, Mayor Kurt Schmoke of Baltimore insisted, "I don't accept hate-filled, anti-white, anti-Semitic language coming from anybody," but he joined the march "because I think it is an important event [that] will probably *be seen* as significant in the history of African Americans."[4] Schmoke's response was telling: he referred not to the actual ideals, goals, or likely achievements of the march but rather to how the march would be perceived. The march was valuable because other people valued it. Like the student who enthused that the Jena Six protest was his generation's "chance to experience" the civil rights movement, Schmoke marched because the march itself was an event.

In another context one might have argued that individual personalities were unimportant compared with the gravity of the injustice or the importance of the cause the march was to draw attention to. But the Million Man March did not highlight any discrete injustice or advance any specific cause. This made the individual personalities involved of central importance, a fact that did not escape the notice of Louis Farrakhan, who, in his remarks to the crowd, did his best to eliminate the option of embracing the message but shunning the messenger: "Although the call was made through me, many have tried to distance the beauty of this idea from the person through whom the idea and the call was made . . . You can't separate Newton from the law that Newton discovered, nor can you separate Einstein from the theory of relativity. It would be silly to try to separate Moses from the Torah or Jesus from the Gospel or Muhammad from the Koran . . . So today, whether you like it or not, God brought the idea through me . . . If my heart were that dark, how is the message . . . so clear, the response so magnificent?"[5]

Even as the dutiful employees of the National Park Service cleaned up and the hundreds of thousands of black men piled into cars, trains, Greyhounds, and chartered coaches to head for home, the Million Man March had inspired others. The Promise Keepers, a men's fundamentalist Christian organization, planned their own gathering and day of atonement on the mall. Like Elvis to the Million Man March's Junior Wells, the Promise Keepers sang the same tunes to a larger audience. "Stand in the Gap: A Sacred Assembly of Men" was the largest gathering ever at the National Mall. Like the Million Man March, Stand in the Gap sought not a political revolution but a personal one. Like the Million Man March, the Promise Keepers traced many social ills to the decline of the traditional, male-dominated family and admonished men to seize control of their households from potentially recalcitrant wives. The Promise Keeper Tony Evans insisted: "I am not suggesting that you *ask* for your role back, I am urging you to *take* it back. There can be no compromise here."[6] Meanwhile, at a sister rally, ambiguously named "Chosen Women," a female speaker told the faithful throng: "Our job is to submit to our [husbands as our] teachers and our Professors . . . even if we know they are wrong. It is then in God's hands."[7]

The similarity between the Million Man March and the Promise Keepers was neither coincidental nor the result of simple mimicry. Both movements grafted the style of the civil rights movement onto what was basically an encounter group, staged on a scale undreamed of by the practitioners of est and Gestalt therapy. The goal—other than that of aggrandizing the movement leaders, which, as Farrakhan's speech made clear, was always primary—was to disguise group therapy in the macho garb of political activism: "solidarity" was bonding on steroids; "empowerment" was a macho synonym for self-actualization; "speaking truth to power" was the talking cure with a Y chromosome; "pride" was a tough guy's self-esteem; and the call for "atonement" was a fist-pumping way of saying, *The first step to recovery is to admit you have a problem*. As in any therapy session, the experience was all: although there was vague talk of economic investment in black communities and voter registration, this was an afterthought. Any practical goal, political agenda, or policy objective would only impede the gestalt—as counterproductive as asking an analyst how you'll know when you're no longer neurotic.

The biggest irony was that both the Million Man March and the Promise Keepers—for all of their patriarchal muscle flexing and boys' club exclusivity—had lifted this blend of the personal and the political directly from 1970s feminism. Both were consciousness-raising on a grand scale, politics turned inward; even the targets of social critique—the home, the family, and the individual trapped in an oppressive domestic relationship—were those first identified by feminists. Feminists had good reason to politicize the intimate and the private. The home, family, and intimate relations were (and are) mechanisms of women's inequality, and women have been conditioned from their earliest years of life to accept—even crave—that inequality. So for feminists, the centrality of consciousness-raising made sense. But men weren't trapped in this distinctive cultural iron cage, except to the extent that the male social role is the necessary complement to that of the female. Male consciousness-raising— whatever its racial cast—took on all of the worst aspects of feminism—narcissism, myopic self-pity, ressentiment—but left behind feminism's redeeming potential for liberating insight. Thirty years after Betty Friedan wrote *The Feminine Mystique*, men were using the syntax of feminism to bemoan the loss of male authority and prestige and deploying the tools of the women's movement to keep women in their place.

The rickety fit between the style of political protest and the substance of navel-gazing group psychotherapy led to some stark contradictions. For instance, a central theme of the Million Man March was that black men should make greater efforts to be industrious, responsible providers for their families. The leaders of the march asked those who could not march to stay home from work as part of a national "day of absence." This was an oblique reference to Douglas Turner Ward's 1965 play depicting the mysterious and sudden disappearance of all black people from a small town in the Jim Crow South. Tellingly, when Ward's play was staged again almost thirty years later, the *New York Times* critic remarked that it was "direly in need of an excuse in 1993."[8] The same thing could be said of the Million Man March itself. A stated goal of the march was to encourage responsible behavior, but sacrificing at least a day's wages and perhaps the goodwill of one's employer for the sake of a symbolic gesture is not the action of a responsible provider. The march's leaders claimed that they hoped to improve the public's perception of black men, but they encouraged their disciples to skive off from work, effectively reinforcing one of the worst racial stereotypes: the shiftless Negro.

The activism of the 1960s had its share of self-indulgence and self-destructiveness, but it was redeemed by a focus on a handful of unquestionably profound social issues: racism, war, feminism, environmentalism. But today the aesthetics of mass protest meet the micro politics of the blog, and every hobby, pastime, and personal preference is a potential inspiration for righteous indignation. Nowhere is this truer than in San Francisco, the epicenter of the counterculture and of digital culture, where lifestyle is inseparable from ideology and the personal isn't just political but a matter of civil rights.

San Francisco is home to some of the most crowded streets in the United States. Only the hyper-urban borough of Manhattan puts New York City ahead of San Francisco in terms of the ratio of human bodies to square feet of real estate. With its crowds come the vibrant street life, energetic public culture, avant-garde arts scene, and gritty subculture that San Francisco is famous for. And with those crowds comes a more mundane day-to-day local culture of frayed nerves, raised elbows, and bruised ribs: a daily push and shove that continually threatens to transform the city's lonely crowd into a violent mob.

San Francisco was a pioneer in resisting freeway construction in the 1970s, and local politicians and activists convinced state officials to demolish rather than retrofit two of the city's remaining freeways after the Loma Prieta earthquake in 1989. The fruits of their efforts: a red-hot real estate market in the neighborhoods formerly blighted by freeway overpasses and some of the worst traffic in North America. Gridlock in the Bay Area rivals that of Los Angeles and metropolitan Atlanta for the worst in the nation. Road rage is a widespread local affliction: the *San Francisco Chronicle* reported that a group of professional anger-management counselors vowed never to return to the city by the bay after suffering the ire of clients who were livid about the lack of parking near their therapy meetings.

San Francisco's pedestrians seize the right-of-way whether they are entitled to it or not, strolling into rush-hour traffic mid-block, purposefully oblivious to oncoming traffic. They are, all too often, proven dead right: the city's hilly streets are now marked with white chalk outlines, symbolizing the bodies of pedestrians struck dead by cars. The outlines are a form of protest–cum–public art painted by an anonymous provocateur whose motives remain unknown: they serve to warn motorist and pedestrian alike to slow down and take care.

And then there are the cyclists. San Francisco bicyclists aspire to the status of their counterparts in Amsterdam, where bicycles are the preferred and dominant mode of transportation. Like a classic cocktail, cycling culture combines in equal measure three potent California characteristics: physical fitness, environmentalism, and the counterculture's self-righteousness. Cyclists are a small but growing fellowship bound together by a sense of moral superiority born of their commitment to transportation with a human, rather than carbon, footprint. And what thanks do they get for reducing global warming, air pollution, and dependence on foreign fossil fuels? They are regularly run off the road, cut off at intersections, and bullied into the gutter by callous motorists.

Cyclists began to fight back against the hegemony of the horseless carriage, forming the San Francisco Bicycle Coalition, which has successfully lobbied the city to convert street parking and traffic lanes into designated bicycle lanes, with the stated goal of making all of San Francisco's roadways "bike friendly." They also fought back by driving as aggressively as the worst motorists: professional and weekend warrior alike adopted the bike messenger's daredevil maneuvers, darting in and out of traffic, sailing through stop signs and red lights, jumping curbs, bullying pedestrians off sidewalks, and heaping abuse—verbal and physical—on drivers who get in their way. Most notorious of all, the bicyclists fought back by forming a monthly mob scene known as Critical Mass, in which hundreds of cyclists with axes to grind or time to kill ride through the city's major thoroughfares in a parade so dense as to block motorist, pedestrian, and chicken alike from crossing the road. These unauthorized events often stretch for miles and tie up traffic for blocks in every direction. Most motorists and pedestrians wait resignedly, if impatiently, for the parade to pass by. A few do not. Pedestrians who dare to breach the column find themselves quickly run down; numerous injuries have resulted, and police—powerless to stop the events—warn both motorists and pedestrians to steer clear. Motorists have occasionally tried to nose their way across the parade or have inadvertently steered into it (because Critical Mass is not authorized, its route is neither publicized nor marked). Those who have have been made to regret it: in April 2007 a mother and her two children visiting from a nearby suburb made the mistake of steering their car onto a Japantown street that had been commandeered by Critical Mass. Cyclists surrounded their car and pummeled it with fists, feet, tire pumps, and bicycle frames, breaking windows and causing over $5,000 in damage. Critical Mass participants were unrepentant: they claimed that the driver sped through the crowd of cyclists, knocking one off his bike, and then tried to drive away. Police later concluded that she may have inadvertently tapped a cyclist's tire while trying to maneuver amid the dense crowd of cyclists.

If Critical Mass was supposed to inspire public sympathy for cyclists, it has achieved precisely the opposite. Public opinion in liberal San Francisco is overwhelmingly negative, even among many cyclists. When a San Francisco blogger wrote a sympathetic piece about Critical Mass, comments were almost unanimously critical of the mass cycling event. Here's a sample: "A ban can't come soon enough. Critical Mass isn't a recreational activity, it is an invitation to thuggery and vandalism. Prior to the first Critical Mass, I actually had a lot of respect for cyclists. Not anymore." "No other organization routinely breaks traffic laws, impedes other road users and, in general, acts like a bunch of 3-year-olds on a playground. As a bike rider, I'd love to see Critical mAss shut down." "Critical Mass is a Critical Mistake. I can't believe they have been allowed to terrorize the City this long. Would they even stop long enough to allow an ambulance to get through? I don't think so."[9]

Organized mass protest was central to the black civil rights movement, as it had been to the women's suffrage movement before it, and as it would be to the antiwar movement, the gay rights movement, and countless other social causes. At its best, mass protest is a powerful tool of political opposition: a bold and striking reflection of society's most serious frustrations and noblest ambitions. But increasingly, mass protest has become self-centered and civil disobedience has become safe and predictable. Organized pressure groups of every political perspective clamor on an almost weekly basis for an overstimulated and inured public's attention. Mass protests on college campuses are a rite of spring and a yearly initiation into the world of higher learning as conventional as the tailgate party or the dorm room one-night stand. As a result of this explosion of activism and outrage, serious injustices must compete with superficial gripes, the profoundly aggrieved share space with narcissistic attention seekers, and well-considered propositions are drowned out by unreasonable demands and half-baked proposals.

It's hard to avoid the conclusion that much of today's social protest is motivated by the self-image of those protesting more than the urgency of the cause. Like a Che Guevara T-shirt or a Palestinian kaffiyeh scarf bought at Urban Outfitters, social activism has become a fashion statement for impressionable young people searching for a personal style and for older folks who really ought to find more age-appropriate attire. The demonstration in Jena, Louisiana, offered a cathartic fantasy of moral absolutes and heroic struggle to a generation that confronts frustrating moral ambiguity and the tedium of protracted negotiation and piecemeal reform. The Million Man March was ultimately an excuse for a big get-together—a group hug that was palmed off as a demonstration. Such aimless activism cheapens the legacy of the civil rights struggle and demeans the real risks and sacrifices of those for whom civil disobedience was a matter of moral and practical urgency.

Worse yet, as civil disobedience bleeds into a kind of extended public therapy, it loses its capacity to inspire. The faceless corporations and governments, the implacable bureaucrats, and the complacent bourgeoisie are supposed to sit up and take notice of the rage and indignation spontaneously bursting forth in the form of a mass demonstration, their comfortable daily routines disrupted and their fragile illusion of stability and control shattered. But social protest is now an expected part of life in every postindustrial mass democracy on the planet. Social protest no longer challenges the status quo; it *is* the status quo. Governments are resigned to mass protest: cities issue permits for political demonstrations, assign extra police (who appreciate the inevitable overtime pay), and prescribe planned gathering sites and march routes to maximize exposure and minimize inconvenience. The bourgeois-capitalist-white-supremacist patriarchal state may even welcome such domesticated mass demonstrations as a useful safety valve for frustrations that, if pent up, might lead to more serious unrest. Corporate managers, ensconced in the high towers of capital, coolly calculate which losses occasioned by boycotts and strikes are manageable and which must be appeased with some symbolic gesture or acceptable sacrifice; meanwhile, they compensate for any losses by taking advantage of the boycotts and strikes their competitors will inevitably face and by marketing the accoutrements of radical chic to an all-too-receptive buying public. Bureaucrats study mass demonstrations as a social phenomenon, taking photographs, gathering data, making calculations, comparing incidents. And the bourgeoisie sniff in annoyance when *yet another demonstration* threatens to delay happy hour or picking up the kids from day care, but of course everyone understands—*it was announced on the news, after all*—the day care will waive the late-pickup fee, the martinis will be just as cold a half hour later, everyone has a contingency plan in place because we all know this is just part of living in a big city, and after all I did it when I was a bit younger and more naive or idealistic. What did Churchill say: *If you're not a radical at twenty, you have no heart* . . . Hell, maybe I'll just pull over and join them . . . What are they protesting *this* time, anyway?

Obama and Racial Justice in the Twenty-first Century

"I'd like to cut his nuts off." That's what the Reverend Jesse Jackson—civil rights veteran, former presidential candidate, and man of God—said of the first black nominee of a major political party. Unbeknownst to him, Jackson's microphone was still live as he whispered his disdain for Obama to a fellow guest on Fox News on July 6, 2008. And Fox News—no doubt after a great deal of agonizing and soul-searching—decided to run the footage. *They had a duty to the public,* the Fox anchor Bill O'Reilly explained: *Who was he to keep this important news from the American people?*

And why did Jesse Jackson want to castrate the man who was likely to become the first black president of the United States? "He's talking down to black people . . . telling niggers how to behave," Jackson had whispered on the candid footage. Obama had just given a speech to the NAACP in which he stressed the need for an emphasis on education, personal responsibility, and dedicated parenting in the black community. There was nothing especially controversial or surprising in Obama's speech; it had been expertly crafted to offend no one. It was neither overtly liberal nor overtly conservative, but it touched on themes that might appeal to either ideological camp: it made no radical policy proposal; it broke no new ground. Indeed, the Republican Party nominee John McCain's address to the same group, marked by all of the hallmarks of a colonial magistrate's careful, diplomatic salutation to a foreign and potentially hostile tribe, was in its own way more daring, with its suggestion that vouchers might help to improve the quality of public education in black schools—a slightly risky attempt to press one of the few conservative pet policies that might appeal to blacks.

What was it about Obama's speech that pushed Jackson's buttons? Why did Jackson think that Obama was "talking down" to his audience? It wasn't the substance of Obama's comments, which echoed themes that both Obama and Jackson himself had sounded many times in the past. Jackson's bitter aside reflected a much deeper and more long-standing animosity, unexpressed but never far beneath the surface of his public endorsements. Obama had been making Jackson and many other black community leaders nervous for quite some time. Some complained that Obama had few, if any, blacks in the most important decision-making positions in his campaign. Others were distressed by what they saw as Obama's betrayal of Trinity United Church of Christ's Reverend Jeremiah Wright—and with him, all of black liberation theology. But these specifics were little more than excuses. No one of them, nor all of them in combination, could explain the unease and tentativeness that black opinion leaders like Jackson felt about what should have been an unambiguous cause for celebration—a black man with a real chance of becoming president.

"Barack Is the New Black," read the bumper stickers displayed proudly on bright red Mini Coopers, on sleek and sedate silver BMWs, on pimped-out Cadillac Escalades, on rusted "vintage" VWs, on Vespa scooters, stuck right next to Union Jacks or those red, white, and blue target emblems popularized by the mods in the 1960s, and on bicycles that raced through the financial districts of major cities or across college campuses. This slogan had not been approved by Barack Obama, Obama for America, or the Democratic Party. But by the middle of 2008 it had become the unofficial theme of an informal subcommittee of Obama supporters. Obama was a new kind of black politician. He had consciously and conspicuously avoided the style—and much of the substance—of black politicians of Jackson's generation. Jackson was a brash, belligerent, speak-truth-to-power race man in the Black Power tradition, a somewhat more respectable Stokely Carmichael, a cleaner-cut Al Sharpton but still unmistakably a product of the long hot summers, a field marshal in the culture wars of the 1960s and 1970s.

Obama wasn't angry or belligerent; he was poised, confident, and unflappable. The older generation of black activists—and this included many who in fact held public office—tried to pressure *other people* to take action on their behalf. They lectured white liberals and railed against conservatives. The basic model was oppositional, and the tools used—mau-mauing, dramatic confrontation, public embarrassment, the guilt trip—were the tools of the weak. Obama didn't raise the roof about social injustice, hoping that those in control would take some notice; he had every expectation that *he* would be in control. Obama and the black politicians of his new generation didn't speak truth to power; they *were* power. And as such, they used the language and tools of the powerful: moderation and compromise, backed up by the proverbial big stick.

Obama was leaving Jackson and his breed of angrier race politics behind, and that cast a shadow of doubt on his racial loyalties. In February 2008, when the black television and radio host Tavis Smiley held the annual "State of Black America" conference in New Orleans, the presidential hopeful Hillary Clinton made the obligatory appearance, but Obama politely declined, citing a prior commitment in Springfield, Illinois. The Princeton University professor and prominent race relations commentator Cornel West attacked Obama, suggesting to the largely black audience that his absence cast doubt on Obama's commitment to the black community: "The problem is . . . him going to Springfield the same day Brother Tavis has set this up for a *whole year* . . . is not fundamentally about us. It's about somebody else. He's got large numbers of white brothers and sisters who have fears and anxieties, and he's got to speak to them in such a way that he holds *us* at arm's length . . . [but] you can't take black people for granted just because you're black . . . he's got to be accountable, and starting off in Springfield, Illinois, is not impressive to me."[10]

Earlier, when Jackson and Al Sharpton led the civil-rights-style march to Jena, Louisiana, Obama steered well clear of the controversy. Jackson commented to the press that he thought Obama had been wrong not to speak out about the Jena Six. "If I were Obama, I'd be all over Jena," Jackson chided. But Obama was poised to become the Democratic Party nominee for president in part because he wasn't "all over" every racial scandal that offered a photo op.

Obama was judicious and measured rather than righteous and opinionated; he avoided controversy, while Jackson and Sharpton chased it. Obama was a viable candidate for president because he *wasn't* Jesse Jackson. Obama's critics and ambivalent supporters among black opinion leaders understood this fact. But they also resented it, and they resented Obama for his willingness to distance himself from the symbolic issues that had historically defined black political activism.

Obama pulled together an unlikely coalition of college students, hard-core progressives, and political independents and raised millions of dollars from small individual donations. Obama, with his Ivy League pedigree and inspiring but nuanced rhetorical style, reminded some of a black Adlai Stevenson: he might appeal to latte-sipping intellectuals and idealistic liberals, but racism, they predicted, would stop Obama cold in the vast, conservative, and backward American heartland. Yet some of Obama's most impressive victories were among politically moderate white voters in Midwestern and Western "red" states such as Iowa and Nebraska, corn farmers and cattle ranchers who had never seen the inside of a Starbucks.

Obama was not alone in his new, less confrontational style of politics. He was part of a cohort of new black politicians who have won office not by appealing to narrow racial solidarities but by drawing broad support from voters of all races, and in some unlikely locations. Mayor Cory Booker of Newark has made reform of that city's notoriously corrupt racial politics one of the hallmarks of his tenure as mayor. He ran against a corrupt black mayor, Sharpe James, who beat Booker in 2002 by slandering him, according to an account in *Esquire* magazine, as "a white, gay, Jewish Republican funded by the KKK."[11] Booker returned to so thoroughly trounce James in 2006 that the incumbent mayor threw in the towel before Election Day. Governor Deval Patrick of Massachusetts ran an Obama-style campaign in 2006 (or one might say that Obama ran a Patrick-style campaign in 2008) and became the commonwealth's first black governor. Mayor Michael Nutter of Philadelphia won election in 2007 as a pragmatic reformer who combined such liberal positions as smoking bans and support for gay rights with more conservative policies such as mandatory curfews and warrantless police searches in high-crime areas. This cohort of younger politicians have rewritten the playbook by which blacks can win election. Their success suggests that white racism is no longer the insuperable barrier to black success that it has been for all of American history and that the old style of black politics, which relied heavily on racial bloc voting and influence peddling within the black community, may be obsolete.

Part of Obama's appeal was that he implicitly promised to bring America's long, ugly racial struggle to a heroic conclusion: the charismatic black president would heal the nation's racial wounds just as he promised to bridge its ideological chasm. But some had begun to suggest that if dust-bowl aggies and high-plains cowboys were ready for a black president, the nation had *already* gotten beyond race. Obama's surprising success suggested that the nation was already *post-racist*.

This fueled the nagging concerns and resentments of old-school black opinion and political leaders. At least some of Obama's considerable support among white voters was the result of an implicit promise: that if America could elect a black president, this would prove that the nation had finally overcome the long-lived evil of racism. Voting for Obama was like reparations on the cheap. Obama hadn't encouraged this kind of thinking. But as a savvy politician he had to have understood it was at work, and he hadn't discouraged it. Obama's success might actually make it harder for traditional civil rights activists to get attention and sympathy for their causes. And while many hoped that the nation's first black president would aggressively address the racial injustices that still mired the nation's inner cities in poverty and despair, what mandate would Obama have to confront racial injustice when his candidacy had implicitly promised a "post-racial" America?

Meanwhile, some began to ask whether race wasn't actually an *advantage* for Obama (and, by implication, for other blacks as well). In a *New York Times* op-ed, the noted feminist Gloria Steinem had suggested that Obama's race might be a political asset: "Racism stereotyped black men as more 'masculine' for so long that some white men find their presence to be masculinity-affirming."[12] Walter Mondale's 1984 running mate, Geraldine Ferraro, went even further, suggesting that Obama was, effectively, the beneficiary of a kind of electoral affirmative action. "If Obama was a white man, he would not be in this position," she insisted. "He happens to be very lucky to be who he is."[13]

Lucky? Had black skin—what W.E.B. Du Bois called a badge of insult—become a sign of privilege? The idea that black race could be an advantage wasn't new: the decades-old opposition to affirmative action was driven in large part by resentment that blacks had turned past oppression and white liberal guilt into a present-day advantage. The 1986 movie *Soul Man*—a postmodern inversion of John Howard Griffin's classic work of investigative journalism *Black Like Me*—took the idea that black skin could give you a leg up to its reductio ad absurdum. The protagonist, an ambitious white college student who hopes to attend Harvard Law School, resorts to megadoses of tanning pills and an Afro wig to pass as black and qualify for a minority scholarship. He attends Harvard as a black man and has a series of unexpectedly difficult (and comical) encounters with militant black students, white sexual fetishists, and pervasive racism before he eventually repents his deception.

The film reflected the changing racial climate and increasingly competitive economy of the 1980s. Despite still tense and often hostile race relations, overt racism was rare, and businesses and government were, at least formally, committed to racial equality. At the same time, blacks were heavily represented among popular musicians and professional athletes—those rare individuals who personified sexiness and cool in the popular culture. As a result, naive whites could imagine that being black might be kind of fun. *Soul Man* perceptively tapped into an inchoate fantasy of temporary metamorphosis: *What if I woke up, not as a cockroach, but as a black guy? I could get into a great college on affirmative action, get lucky with all of those girls with jungle fever . . . and then go back to being white when it's time to land that job on Wall Street.* The temporary nature of the transformation was, of course, critical: no one in 1986 really believed that the meager advantages of race-based scholarships and admissions preferences outweighed the day-to-day injuries of racial prejudice. But had this changed in the twenty-odd years that separated *Soul Man* from the candidacy of Barack Obama? Had America become post-racist, as many in the media began to argue when Obama became a viable candidate for the presidency?

In reaction to such millenarian suggestions, some insisted that Obama's success said little about the demise of racism because Obama wasn't really black. Obama, the son of a Kenyan father and a white mother, was one of a growing number of Americans of mixed racial parentage, and part of his compelling personal autobiography, *Dreams from My Father*, involved his struggle to come to terms with this atypical racial identity. For most people, Obama, like so many Americans of mixed parentage before him, was simply black. But for others, Obama personified a crisis—whether welcomed or feared—for the meaning of race itself. Even as Obama's political successes gave currency to the notion of a society that was post-*racist*, some insisted that Obama himself—his biography, perhaps even the very core of his DNA—was racially enigmatic, post-*racial*.

Obama inadvertently helped to promote such unconventional ideas about race, but they predated his rise to prominence. For instance, the novelist, Nobel laureate, and esteemed commentator on American race relations Toni Morrison asserted in a 1998 *New Yorker* article that Bill Clinton was "our first black President." She insisted that the fair-haired and pink-cheeked Clinton was "blacker than any actual black person who could ever be elected in our children's lifetime."[14] Ten years later, in 2008, Obama—someone most people would instinctively call an "actual black person"—was on the verge of being elected. As the contest for the Democratic nomination heated up in heavily black South Carolina, the civil rights veteran and Hillary Clinton supporter Andrew Young picked up Morrison's line, arguing, "Hillary Clinton . . . has Bill behind her and Bill is every bit as black as Barack."[15]

Young wasn't the first to question Obama's racial bona fides. Obama's former opponent for the Illinois senatorial race, the black conservative Alan Keyes, had complained that Obama wrongly "claims an African-American heritage." Contrasting Obama's presumptuous claim to blackness to his own valid one, Keyes channeled the spirit of left-liberal multiculturalism to perfection: "My ancestors toiled in slavery in this country . . . My consciousness, who I am as a person, has been shaped by my struggle, deeply emotional and deeply painful, with the reality of that heritage."[16] Later, the columnist Debra Dickerson echoed this opinion, writing for *Salon* magazine: "Obama isn't black . . . 'Black,' in our political and social reality, means those descended from West African slaves. Voluntary immigrants of African descent (even those descended from West Indian slaves) are just that, voluntary immigrants . . . It can't be assumed that a Nigerian cabdriver and a third-generation Harlemite have more in common than the fact a cop won't bother to make the distinction. They're both 'black' as a matter of skin color and DNA, but only the Harlemite, for better or worse, is politically and culturally black."[17]

Obama's detractors have made much of the fact that he is the son of an African immigrant and not the descendant of American slaves. This makes him unlike most American blacks, including almost everyone in the civil rights establishment, but it also joins him to an increasingly prominent segment of the black middle class and elite—immigrants from Africa and the Caribbean—who, for many reasons, have been disproportionately successful among Americans of African descent. In 2004, when Obama was still campaigning for election to the Senate, the Harvard professors Henry Louis Gates Jr. and Lani Guinier worried publicly that a growing percentage of "black" students admitted to Harvard were the children of African or Caribbean immigrants rather than descendants of American slaves.[18] In this sense Obama represented a crisis in black identity precipitated by recent waves of immigration from Africa and the Caribbean—people who were undeniably black in terms of phenotype and ancestry, but who did not share the experience, culture, or oppositional politics of American blacks.

But while some have argued that Obama—with his mixed parentage, international upbringing, and Ivy League pedigree—isn't representative of most American blacks, in a sense their real worry is that he's all too representative. Obama is a symbol of a change in American race relations, from a black community unified by common neighborhoods, experiences, culture, and grievances, to a black community increasingly *divided* by all of the above.

Obama is successful, well educated, and cosmopolitan. He seems free from the counterproductive rage, alienation, and self-doubt that are often a toxic by-product of the American black experience. But he is not atypical: there are millions of successful blacks who share these characteristics with Obama. They represent a large and growing share of the black students I teach at Stanford Law School; they are an even larger share of the black undergraduate students that I encounter at Stanford, and, I suspect, an even larger share of the black grade school students nationwide who are likely to attend college in the future.

This is a generational divide, but more than that it is a socioeconomic divide. Many of the parents of these students are learning from their children. As Obama was about to have his first debate with John McCain at Ole Miss, I had drinks with a black man who attended that bastion of the Old South in the racially tense 1970s.

He wore a blue oxford shirt, tweed jacket, bow tie, and gold-rimmed glasses—the standard uniform of the East Coast cultural elite. And he spoke—in the accent of a Beltway Brahmin—with unbridled astonishment of the changes that have taken place at his alma mater, where the Confederate flag was once proudly flown at school football games, waving in the thick Mississippi air to the sound of "Dixie"—the school's de facto fight song. He remarked that for his son, who attends prep school in New England, race isn't much of an issue. The civil rights leaders who have greeted Obama's success with chilly apprehension are worried that a new generation of Americans will undermine the struggle for civil rights by prematurely declaring themselves, and their society, post-racist. But for this black alumnus of Ole Miss, a certain kind of post-racism is the ripe fruit of the civil rights struggle.

American racism is in steady decline as aging white supremacists influenced by *The Birth of a Nation* and Father Charles Coughlin are replaced by a generation raised on *The Cosby Show* and Oprah Winfrey. Legally enforced segregation is a thing of the past: today the law prohibits race discrimination by government, employers, and landlords. Elite employers and selective universities aggressively seek out minority-race applicants in order to achieve racial diversity. For well-educated blacks, acculturated to the norms of the prosperous American mainstream, racism is rarely a serious impediment to success, esteem, and well-being. Yes, there are still the vexations caused by petty insults and slights, but for many blacks the once-ubiquitous iron law of white supremacy is now an occasional and petty hindrance; the once arrogant and terrifying bigot is little more than a pathetic annoyance; the menacing Jim Crow has been reduced to an irritating gnat.

But many of America's cities are as racially divided as they were during the era of Jim Crow segregation, racial discrimination in employment and housing stubbornly persists, racial stereotypes are a staple of popular culture, and hardly a month goes by without a new race scandal to occupy the intensive if fleeting attention of the mass media. Racist cops, prejudiced employers, and bigoted land-lords seem to have little trouble knowing whom to discriminate against. In these and many other respects, racism and race seem as blatant and implacable as ever.

Today's race relations are a good-news, bad-news story. The good news: since the civil rights legislation of the 1960s life has got-ten much, much better for blacks with the resources, skills, and socialization necessary to enter the American mainstream. Racism has consistently and steadily declined, and opportunities for well-educated blacks have grown even more quickly than a rapidly grow-ing economy. The bad news: things got worse for those without such advantages. The exodus of the more successful blacks left poor blacks without economic capital and positive role models. A changing economy shed many of the once plentiful good-paying blue-collar jobs. The War on Poverty morphed into a war on the poor: social welfare programs yielded to a "tough love" that slashed benefits and pushed millions into homelessness and abjection, and a zero-tolerance approach to law enforcement led to the incarceration of unprecedented numbers of black men.

Today "racism" does not describe a single attitude or phenome-non, but rather a number of distinct and often unrelated social prob-lems. The joblessness, isolation, and despair that afflict poor blacks in inner-city ghettos are different in kind—not simply in degree—from the subtle bigotry, ambiguous slights, and "soft" exclusion that wealthier and professional blacks complain of.

The success of the more fortunate blacks who can tell the good-news story does not suggest any improvement in the dire circum-stances of the blacks who must live out the bad-news story, nor are the benefits of policy reforms designed to help the former group likely to trickle down to the latter group. The very idea of *a* black community is an anachronism. Today there are, effectively, at least two black communities: an increasingly prosperous and well-educated professional class, and an increasingly isolated, poorly socialized, and demoralized underclass. These two black communities are joined by a shared history but increasingly divided by lifestyle, values, norms of behavior, and life prospects.

"Let me tell you something about niggers," begins an article published in the November 2006 issue of *Esquire* magazine. "Always down. Always out. Always complaining that they can't catch a break . . . Constantly in need of a leader but unable to follow in any direction that's navigated by hard work, self-reliance. And though they spliff and drink and procreate their way onto welfare doles and WIC lines, niggers will tell you their state of being is no fault of their own."[19]

"The Manifesto of Ascendancy for the Modern American Nigger" was not a racist screed penned by a white supremacist, although it occasionally read like one. It was a tendentious yet often nuanced polemic written by an African American writer and film producer, John Ridley. It relied on a distinction popularized by the comedian Chris Rock between "niggers"—the down-and-out, impoverished, and culturally dysfunctional underclass—and those blacks who are "undeniable in their individuality and exemplary in their levels of achievement." Its prescription was a stark repudiation of the racial solidarity that has been a common theme of almost all serious black social thought since Reconstruction. "It's time for ascended blacks to wish niggers good luck. Just as whites may be concerned with the good of all citizens but don't travel their days worrying specifically about the well-being of hillbillies from Appalachia, we need to send niggers on their way."

This was a shocking inversion of W.E.B. Du Bois's notion of the talented tenth. The talented tenth were the most successful blacks who, by their efforts and by their example, were to improve the welfare of their race. As late as 1995 the Harvard professors Henry Louis Gates Jr. and Cornel West cited the idea of a talented tenth, asking how they and their students could make good on Du Bois's promise. But since then, some prominent members of the talented tenth have publicly gone on strike. Bill Cosby, civil rights activist and longtime goodwill ambassador between the races, lamented at the Rainbow PUSH Coalition annual conference in 2004, "People marched and were hit in the face with rocks to get an education, and now . . . the lower economic people are not holding up their end in this deal . . . They think they're hip. They can't read. They can't write. They're laughing and giggling, and they're going nowhere." Cosby struck back at Afrocentrists who celebrate black cultural distinctiveness, making a pointed demand for assimilation: "With names like Shaniqua, Taliqua and Mohammed and all that crap, and all of them are in jail . . . They're standing on the corner and they can't speak English." He lambasted black parents who failed to raise their children well, and attacked the culture of ostentatious consumption so prominent in many poor black neighborhoods: "These people are not parenting. They are buying things for kids. Five-hundred-dollar sneakers for what? And they won't spend $200 for *Hooked on Phonics.*"

"Giving back to the community" has long been a deeply felt obligation—and a loudly voiced admonishment—for successful blacks. "Giving back" was not only a moral obligation but also a matter of self-preservation: successful blacks owed their own comfort to the efforts of past generations. Courageous struggles against slavery, post-Reconstruction backlash, Jim Crow segregation, and subtle but pervasive institutional racism had paved the way: *We all stand on the shoulders of giants.* And at the same time, white racism tied the fates of all blacks together: the bourgeois Negro who thought he could ignore the plight of poor blacks was a selfish fool; his position was more precarious than he knew, and the same racism that held his less fortunate brethren down would also bring him low soon enough.

But increasingly, the racism suffered by more successful blacks was different in *kind*—not just in degree—from the racism that plagued the underclass. And the responses to that racism also diverged. Middle-class blacks worried about an increasingly subtle bias that denied them professional networking opportunities, business contacts, and effective mentoring and inspired chilly receptions in predominantly white neighborhoods and social settings. But traditional civil rights agitation and legislation could not change such subtle and elusive attitudes: in fact, to the extent it reinforces the stereotype of the black militant, civil rights activism might even contribute to the problem. Middle-class blacks hoped to change subtle bias with the technocratic tools of management science: sensitivity training and diversity consultants became almost as common a fixture in corporate and professional America as pinstripes and wing tips.

By contrast, the underclass had to contend with failing schools, violent crime, abusive law enforcement, and a pervasive ethos of nihilism, recklessness, and despair. Traditional civil rights legislation didn't address these problems either, so a new, increasingly angry, confrontational, and scandal-driven style of activism filled the gap. Watchdog groups monitored police and were quick to condemn any hint of bias or abuse. Religious leaders, poverty services professionals, and civil rights lawyers adopted an attitude of permanent umbrage. Community leaders became adept at organizing mass demonstrations on short notice. Rage became not only acceptable but almost obligatory—and occasionally erupted into uncontrolled and aimless violence.

This oppositional and often belligerent political stance has been a central part of black identity since the civil rights and Black Power movements. But for the significant cohort of blacks who enjoyed the fruits of those movements, blatant white racism was less and less common. And their own successes suggested that racism was not simply more subtle but also less severe than in the past. Some began to wonder whether it was injury due to *racism* that they shared with an increasingly dysfunctional and antisocial black underclass or simply race—and an outdated sense of solidarity. Against the harmony of civil rights solidarism—*There but for the*

grace of God go I—a discordant refrain, voicing a kind of seces-
sionist impulse, was just barely audible: *We need to send niggers on
their way.*

While Obama's mixed parentage and cosmopolitan upbringing
led some to question his racial authenticity, this was a tempest in a
teapot: the perfect storm that threatened racial solidarity was the
split—in lifestyle and language, norms and neighborhoods—between
successful American blacks and the black underclass.

In the 1970s the sociologist Nathan Glazer argued that the black
experience was best understood in comparison to the experiences
of other distinctive ethnic groups in American society, such as the
Irish, Italians, or Jews.[20] Like blacks, these groups were the targets
of pervasive and invidious discrimination, and yet they eventually
assimilated into the prosperous mainstream of American society
and had, by and large, shed the stigma they bore in the past. With
the benefit of civil rights legislation, blacks too would take their
place in this nation of minorities, and the distinctive stigma of black
race—W.E.B. Du Bois's badge of insult—would fade to insignifi-
cance. Time has not been kind to this hypothesis: indeed, two decades later Glazer repudiated his own earlier position, admitting,
"Even after taking account of substantial progress and change, it is
borne upon us how continuous, rooted, and substantial the differences between African Americans and other Americans remain."[21]

But to many, the election of Barack Obama suggests that
Glazer's prediction of successful black assimilation might have been,
not wrong, but simply premature. Obama's election signals a new
type of racial consciousness among Americans. It suggests that whites
are beginning to make distinctions between those blacks whom they
associate with negative racial stereotypes and those whom they see,
increasingly, as an ethnic group—people with slightly different ac-
cents, culinary styles, and traditions, but otherwise assimilated to

mainstream norms of behavior. It's the difference between associating a black face with gangbangers, crack addicts, and panhandlers and associating that face with jazz, soul food, and Kwanzaa.

The emphasis in the 1980s on multiculturalism may have sped this development. Multiculturalism emphasized the *cultural* difference between racial groups, implicitly, if unintentionally, analogizing racial difference with ethnic difference. Consider this example:

> At least since the American civil rights movement, many people have become more aware of the harm suffered by ethnic or cultural minorities laboring under discriminatory practices or inequities . . . The conditions of the American black and the American Indian, the Canadian Inuit, the New Zealand Maori, and the Australian Aborigine have been the subject of various administrative and legislative initiatives. And the political claims of the Basques in Spain, the French Canadians in Canada, and the Tamils in Sri Lanka have been gaining wider prominence.[22]

The author implies that blacks are analogously situated to Spanish Basques and Quebecois, groups distinguished not by race but rather by ethnicity. It's not a big leap from this analysis to Glazer's, which analogized blacks with Irish and Italian Americans. And the tendency to treat race as a type of cultural difference was also reinforced by the diversity idea of racial difference, ensconced by the Supreme Court as, practically speaking, the only legally acceptable rationale for affirmative action in higher education. Under the Supreme Court's diversity jurisprudence, racial minorities would provide a distinctive cultural perspective that would enhance classroom and extracurricular conversation in colleges and universities. This encouraged applicants to selective schools and the schools themselves to emphasize the cultural aspects of racial difference. Multiculturalism and the diversity rationale for affirmative action both reinforced the idea that racial difference was a kind of cultural or ethnic difference. College students of all races received the message that race was primarily a matter of relatively innocuous cultural difference: among the elite, the stigma of race began to morph into a stylish ethnicity.

The promise of finally shedding the unique stigma of race—still tantalizingly just out of reach—underlies the disparate set of opinions, arguments, manifestos, screeds, and jeremiads that lament the continuing dysfunctional culture of the underclass and suggest that they bear some of the blame for their own dire circumstances. The frustration of these successful blacks isn't just a twenty-first-century iteration of the distaste and desire for social distance from poor blacks exhibited by E. Franklin Frazier's *Black Bourgeoisie*.[23] For Frazier's black bourgeoisie, disdain for poor blacks was born of insecurity and self-contempt: the black bourgeoisie occupied a precarious social position that depended on the sufferance of whites; poor blacks threatened to undermine the delicate and meager esteem that the black middle class clung to in their relations with white society. But the new generation of "ascended" blacks weren't clinging to an only slightly and precariously improved second-class status. They were close to achieving meaningful social equality with whites, and in some cases they had in fact done so. And while Frazier's black bourgeoisie were simply embarrassed by poor blacks, who threatened to reinforce racial stereotypes and sully the bourgeoisie by association, Ridley's ascended blacks felt not embarrassment so much as *betrayal*.

For example, in his Rainbow PUSH Coalition speech Cosby complained that "the lower economic people *are not holding up their end in this deal*." That deal was not only—or even primarily—between blacks and whites; it was a bond among blacks, forged in the Freedom Summers: *We will make our stand against a weakened but still powerful white supremacy together, and we will reach the promised land together.* This pact underlay the long-standing admonishment that successful blacks give back to their communities, both their time and their resources, by a continued political solidarity (hence the widespread accusation of "sellout" or "Uncle Tom") and by serving as positive role models (which required both continued expressions of solidarity and exemplary behavior and achievement).

But some of the successful blacks who had adhered to the terms of this implicit bargain (or had suffered the condemnation and contempt of their peers when they failed to do so) started to ask whether the weaker members of the community bore some corresponding obligations. *To whom much is given, much will be required,* but wasn't *something* required even of those to whom little was given? Cosby's notable expression of betrayal reflected the frustrations of a man who had dedicated his career to improving the image of blacks and who had been remarkably successful in doing so. Yet for every black child who aspired to the respectability and prestige of the college-educated and college-bound Huxtables, there seemed to be two or three who preferred the tawdry bling-bling of the gangster rapper and the momentary highs of drugs and promiscuous sex.

Obama's cool style of politics, his political moderation, and his Ivy League affect all suggest a post-racial politics. If Barack becomes the new black, perhaps whites will come to associate black race with the elite characteristics of Obama. But it's more likely that Americans will learn—as Obama's election proves that they are already learning—to distinguish between elite, Obama-like blacks, whom they will treat like an ethnic group, and the underclass, whom they will continue to treat as a despised and inferior race. It's plausible that more successful blacks could eventually escape racial stigma, but only by breaking solidarity with the underclass—by *sending the niggers on their way.*

Obama has kept his own views on racial politics close to his belt: even his famous speech on race, delivered in response to the Jeremiah Wright scandal, was remarkable for its lack of specifics and for its ideological ambiguity. This reticence is understandable as a matter of political expediency, but it naturally fuels speculation and anxiety about what Obama's success will mean for race

relations. Obama's visibility will undermine stereotypes and improve the public perception of blacks. This will be to the advantage
of many blacks—especially those who are well positioned to improve their social and economic status by moving into good-paying
jobs and into better neighborhoods. But if they do so by emphasizing the class distinctions *among* blacks, this latest improvement in
race relations may come at the expense of precisely those blacks
who were least able to take advantage of the last great improvement
in race relations: the civil rights reforms of the 1960s. It's hard to
fault the more advantaged members of the black community for
trying to build on their successes, but it's also hard to think of this
potential development as an unequivocal improvement in social justice. In this context, the misgivings of such left-liberal black politicians and activists as Andrew Young, Cornel West, Tavis Smiley, and
Jesse Jackson—while sometimes artlessly expressed—are understandable. It was unclear whether the Obama phenomenon would
mark the renewal of civil rights or the repudiation of its historical
commitment to the most disadvantaged.

The civil rights movement of the twenty-first century will need
to confront and exploit the social changes that Obama's presidency
symbolizes. As the black community splits along lines of income,
skills, and socialization, it's less and less valid to treat all racial inequities as the result of a single cause: racism. Blacks may slowly
begin to occupy the status of an ethnic group in some contexts; for
instance, Justice Alito's concurrence in *Ricci* suggests that blacks in
cities such as New Haven have become a privileged ethnic constituency, as many white ethnic groups have been in the past. Justice
Alito probably exaggerates the power of New Haven's black community, but there's little doubt that black influence in economic
markets and popular politics is greater now than ever before, and
racist aversion to that influence is waning. As blacks become influential in business and politics, as older racial stereotypes become
less widely accepted, and as people of all races become less bigoted,
the civil-rights-style confrontation is no longer the only option:

more constructive and cooperative approaches to furthering racial equality are available. Just as the Reverend Boise Kimber's confrontational approach backfired in New Haven, civil rights activism often misses its mark in a society of greater racial complexity and ambiguity. While Jesse Jackson castigated Obama for refusing to march in Jena as part of the civil rights movement of the twenty-first century, Obama's successes—and those of many others like him—may show the way to achieve social justice without the excesses and theatrics of movement politics.

Civil rights activism today suffers from a debilitating combination of nostalgia, narcissism, and false solidarity. Nostalgia leads civil rights activists to analyze and attack contemporary racial problems—of which there remain many—with the tactics of the past. But today's most severe racial problems are different from those of the past, even if they are continuous with historical injustices. The disintegration of the inner-city black family today is not like the deliberate division of families during slavery, even if the latter contributed in complex ways to the former. The incarceration of young black men is not a new Jim Crow, even if some of the prejudices of the latter have contributed to the former. Without a discrete and conspicuous target, much of today's civil rights protest comes off as both shrill and aimless, in stark contrast to the heroic struggles of the mid-twentieth century, where civil rights activism was resolute and focused.

Narcissism poisons civil rights activism by elevating drama and spectacle over practical results. Many of the solutions to today's social injustices will require wonkish policy intervention, frustrating compromises, and tedious negotiations with government, businesses, and other organizations. Instead of the high drama of the Freedom Summers (as seen through the sepia-filtered lens of a Ken Burns film, from the relative safety of the twenty-first century), we face a long, slow winter of institutional reform. The real legatees of the civil rights movement will learn to wield power rather than fight it; cooperate with businesses more often than boycott or sue them; run for office rather than march on the Capitol. Sustained institutional change offers few resounding victories and fewer opportunities for conspicuous heroism. One must be satisfied with the steady accumulation of modest improvements.

False solidarity obscures the real stakes of social conflicts and allows opportunists with weak moral claims to ride the coattails of the truly deserving. Racists may not make fine distinctions within racial groups, but many of the most debilitating racial disadvantages do. The acculturated and the privileged can avoid much of the toxic legacy of past discrimination. The racial disadvantage faced by the privileged is different in kind—not just in degree—from that faced by the poor, who must struggle against social isolation, dysfunctional public institutions, counterproductive socialization, high crime, and the resulting psychological despair. Police and prosecutorial bias falls, with few exceptions, on those who have committed *some* crime, however petty; the poor live in environments where petty crime is commonplace and the gray-market economy often the only obvious means of daily support. Job discrimination is based more on affectations, grooming, and dialect than on skin color alone, and those with a good education can more easily shrug off their encounters with discrimination and find employment elsewhere; the poor are both more likely to exhibit the characteristics that trigger bias and less likely to have the resources to recover from it. The false solidarity that fixates on an imagined common enemy even as actual menaces become more and more diverse has preempted genuine solidarity based on a shared history and humane compassion. True solidarity requires confronting problems that are *unlike* one's own; it requires empathy, not identification. Not coincidentally, we need a similar empathy among citizens, regardless of race, in order to address our most persistent social injustices.

5

Righting Rights

Wal-Mart, famous for its everyday low prices and notorious for its everyday low wages, epitomizes many of the twenty-first century's defining social controversies. To its many detractors, it is the predatory big-box chain store that drives small businesses under and exacerbates suburban sprawl; the mass retailer that encourages a soulless and ecologically destructive habitual consumption of disposable products; the avaricious multinational corporation that exploits the land and the labor of developing nations; and the skinflint employer that pays its workforce a poverty wage. In this last respect, Wal-Mart's influence has been profound: Wal-Mart is the largest employer in the United States; with 1.4 million employees, it sends paychecks—such as they are—to more people than live in any one of ten American states.

Sam Walton was opening his first stores in Arkansas at just the time mechanization was replacing agricultural labor across the Ozarks. Walton stepped into the role of straw boss, offering unemployed former farmhands the jobs of the future at fifty cents an hour.

According to the historian Nelson Lichtenstein, when Congress extended the minimum wage to retail employers in 1965, Walton responded with the ingenuity that would make Wal-Mart a market leader: the minimum wage law applied only to businesses with $250,000 or more in annual revenues, so Walton divided his business into smaller corporations that would fall under the statutory threshold. A federal court saw through the scheme and ordered Walton to compensate his employees retroactively. Walton had no choice but to pay up, but he also dug in with the tenacity that employees and suppliers alike would come to know and fear; he delivered a warning along with the back pay: "I'll fire anyone who cashes the check."[1]

Wal-Mart's Southern roots, scofflaw tendencies, and plantation-style labor practices seem a recipe for rampant discrimination. Indeed, Wal-Mart has faced more than its share of complaints. For instance, in 2009 the Equal Employment Opportunity Commission (EEOC) settled a discrimination suit brought by black applicants for jobs as truck drivers for $17.5 million, and in 2010 African employees of a Colorado Wal-Mart complained that a manager remarked, "Wow, there are a lot of Africans . . . I don't like some of the faces I see here. There are people in Eagle County who need work."[2]

Wal-Mart's early efforts to improve its image were largely cosmetic and backfired badly. The company hired the former Atlanta mayor and U.S. ambassador to the United Nations, Andrew Young, as a spokesman for the company's community service programs. After six months on the job as goodwill ambassador, Young told a reporter for the *Los Angeles Sentinel*, one of the nation's oldest and largest black-owned newspapers, that Wal-Mart was performing a community service by displacing local grocers: "[Wal-Mart] ran the 'mom-and-pop' stores out of my neighborhood . . . Those are the people who have been overcharging us—selling us stale bread, and bad meat and wilted vegetables . . . I think they've ripped off our communities enough. First it was Jews, then it was Koreans and now it's Arabs."[3] In a single sentence the former diplomat managed to offend three distinct ethnic groups *and* confirm Wal-Mart's image as a predatory mass retailer bent on destroying its smaller competitors. More recently, Wal-Mart has made greater efforts to increase minority hiring and mentoring and to use women- and minority-owned suppliers; as a result, Wal-Mart has begun to change its image as a postmodern plantation employer.

But Wal-Mart's most serious civil rights problem is sexism. Wal-Mart appears to have had little success in changing widespread patriarchal attitudes among its managers. According to the *American Prospect* editor and *Washington Post* columnist Harold Meyerson, "The Southern traditionalism of Walton and his lieutenants dictated that the stores' managers would be men and its salesclerks women."[4] Because over 90 percent of Wal-Mart's cashiers are women, sexism would affect far more people than other forms of discrimination, even if it was no more pervasive or severe in degree. Not surprisingly, then, sexism has become a serious financial liability for Wal-Mart, as the company has faced numerous discrimination lawsuits. In one of the more recent, the EEOC sued Wal-Mart, claiming that the company's London, Kentucky, distribution center systematically excluded women from warehouse jobs. On March 1, 2010, Wal-Mart agreed to pay $11.7 million to settle the suit out of court.

That's small change compared with what Wal-Mart might have paid if Betty Dukes had had her way. Dukes worked for Wal-Mart in Pittsburg, California, a working-class city about thirty miles east of San Francisco. She had been on the job for seven years and sought promotions that, she claimed, went to less-qualified men. Dukes claimed that women were routinely assigned to stereotypically feminine departments, such as baby clothing, and excluded from masculine departments, such as hardware. "I can mix a can of paint," she complained. "I want a chance to do it."[5] According to Dukes, openings for managerial positions were never announced and were filled by men before she could apply. In 2001, Dukes, along with six other women, sued Wal-Mart in a class action lawsuit filed on behalf of every woman who worked for the company since 1998—roughly 1.5 million women. Had it been allowed to proceed, this would have been the largest class action lawsuit in American history and could have cost Wal-Mart billions of dollars; Wal-Mart's 2009 annual report to shareholders deadpanned that "the Company cannot reasonably estimate the possible loss or range of loss that may arise from the litigation."[6]

Class action litigation is the bête noire of critics of American litigiousness. The class action lawsuit allows the ambitious attorney to sue on behalf of hundreds, thousands, or—as in the case of *Dukes v. Wal-Mart Stores, Inc.*—*millions* of people without ever meeting most of them, much less consulting them or getting their agreement. You've almost certainly been involved in such a lawsuit, whether you wanted to be or not. You probably didn't even find out about it until after the litigation had ended or had been settled, when you received a cryptic letter in the mail, informing you of the good news that several million dollars had been obtained on behalf of you and other people like you. Hopefully, you didn't rush out and buy that Ferrari before reading the fine print: your share after attorneys' fees had been deducted was probably a coupon good for $10 or $15 worth of the defendant's products. Here's an example of a settlement notification for a case brought on my behalf:

> If you purchased an uncoated Apple First Generation iPod nano, you could be entitled to benefits under a class action settlement . . . To qualify, you must have purchased . . . a new . . . iPod nano and experienced scratching of your iPod nano that impaired your use or enjoyment of your iPod nano . . .
>
> Apple denies all allegations in the Lawsuit . . . [but] is entering into this settlement to avoid burdensome and costly litigation . . .
>
> Apple has agreed to provide a total cash settlement fund of $22.5 million . . . After payment of all notice and administration costs, Plaintiffs' counsel's attorneys' fees and expenses . . . payments of $15 will be distributed to Settlement Class Members.[7]

Like a lawsuit over a scratched iPod, almost any mishap or slight can wind up in litigation. Class action lawsuits have been filed on behalf of almost every imaginable injured party: victims of tainted food, substandard pharmaceuticals, misleading advertising, faulty products, dishonest lending practices, and, of course, civil rights violations. Once a class action is filed, the plaintiff class must be approved or "certified" by the court. Under rule 23 of the Federal Rules of Civil Procedure, a valid class must satisfy four criteria: (1) the class must be so large that it's impractical to include all of the class members as named plaintiffs in a joint lawsuit; (2) all of the class members must have similar legal claims or claims that turn on common factual questions; (3) the claims of the named plaintiffs must be typical of those of the rest of the class members; and (4) the named plaintiffs must be trustworthy to represent and protect the interests of the class as a whole. As the scratched-iPod lawsuit suggests, many class actions seem designed to benefit plaintiffs' lawyers, who collect handsome fees for themselves, more than class members, who wind up with minuscule cash settlements or coupons good for more of the defendant's presumably shoddy products. But even in these cases, class action litigation can have social benefits: the threat of litigation encourages businesses to make safer and more reliable products and frightens them into treating their employees fairly.

Class actions have long been one of the most important civil rights enforcement tools. Class actions are a natural fit for civil rights litigation because the deterrent effects of any antidiscrimination case benefit everyone who might suffer the type of discrimination involved. In the 1960s and 1970s, federal courts opined that "racial discrimination is by definition a class discrimination."[8] When the Civil Rights Act was in its infancy, many large employers had widespread discriminatory practices that affected numerous employees. Some had only recently eliminated formal segregation, overt racial exclusion, and separate pay scales in response to Title VII; in practice, these policies continued, and the attitudes responsible for them still influenced decision making. The civil rights plaintiff acted as a "private attorney general" enforcing the law for everyone who shared his or her social status.

Is the Wal-Mart of the new millennium like the discriminatory employers of the sixties and seventies? Betty Dukes and her co-plaintiffs claimed that Wal-Mart systematically discriminated against women in pay and promotions. They pointed out that almost three-fourths of Wal-Mart's hourly wage sales employees are women; by contrast, only about a third of its managers are. They argued that Wal-Mart's executives in Bentonville, Arkansas, set the tone for all of the thirty-four hundred stores in the United States—the same tone of traditional Southern chauvinism and contempt for civil rights laws that Sam Walton exhibited in the 1960s. They gathered declarations by 120 women who said that they were victims of sex discrimination at Wal-Mart. And they enlisted the sociologist William Bielby, who claimed that Wal-Mart's employment practices are especially vulnerable to the influence of sex stereotypes because they leave personnel decisions to local store managers, who use subjective criteria of evaluation such as "teamwork, ethics, integrity, and the ability to get along with others."

Not surprisingly, Wal-Mart denied all of this. "We don't have policies and practices in place that promote discrimination of any kind," Wal-Mart's spokesman Bill Wertz insisted.[9] Wal-Mart and its supporters insisted that the *Dukes* plaintiffs couldn't point to any specific discriminatory company-wide policies or practices; instead, they cited isolated and "widely divergent" anecdotes and a vague hypothesis of a monolithic corporate culture to conjure up the specter of a common pattern of discrimination.[10] According to one observer, the plaintiffs' claims amounted to little more than "accusations by women that supervisors, including female supervisors, made disparaging remarks about women workers—something entirely possible in a company of more than 1 million employees . . . There is nothing in this collection of anecdotes that amounts to a company-wide pattern of discrimination."[11]

Wal-Mart insisted that the *Dukes* class should not be certified.

The class members had nothing in common other than their gender and their employment at Wal-Mart. Even if the anecdotal claims of the class representatives were true, they didn't establish that the women had been victims of a *common* policy; instead, they showed, at most, that they had been victims of different, isolated acts of discrimination, for which each injured woman could bring a separate lawsuit. Betty Dukes complained that she was demoted in retaliation for earlier complaints of discrimination; another plaintiff, Patricia Surgeson, claimed that she was sexually harassed; another, Cleo Page, was quickly promoted to manager but denied subsequent promotions and paid less than a man with less seniority; another was fired after being accused of "stealing time" and claimed retaliation for earlier complaints of discrimination.[12] These claims involved different theories of liability and different contested facts and were susceptible to different defenses.

If Wal-Mart had exercised tight centralized control over personnel decisions, any gender imbalance could have been attributed to systematic bias among the upper management in Bentonville, Arkansas. If it had promulgated detailed objective rules for personnel decisions, perhaps the rules themselves could have been attacked as discriminatory in effect. Either of these scenarios might have justified a class action attacking practices or rules that affected all Wal-Mart employees nationwide. But Wal-Mart did not control personnel decisions centrally: it left them to the discretion of local managers, who, like many managers in the service industries, employed vague and subjective criteria such as "integrity" and "team spirit." Such decentralized management is less susceptible to a firm-wide class action because each store arguably operates under its own decision-making regime. Even if many Wal-Mart employees suffered sex discrimination, if each individual store has its own distinctive personnel practices, there are no questions of law and fact common to *all* of the victims.

The plaintiffs struggled to make the square peg of Wal-Mart's decentralized and subjective personnel decision-making process fit the round hole of a class action with an injury common to all class members. They insisted that Wal-Mart had a centralized corporate culture—if not a centralized decision-making process—that affected all 1.5 million women who had worked at Wal-Mart since 1998. And how did Bentonville's ethos of sexism make its way to Wal-Marts from Maine to Modesto? Through *decentralization* of control over personnel decisions that left them "vulnerable" to the influence of sex stereotypes. The plaintiffs wanted to have their centralization and eat it too: on the one hand, Wal-Mart was so centralized that a monolithic corporate culture affected decisions nationwide; on the other, it was so decentralized that individual managers could do whatever they pleased. One commentator complained of a "contradiction in describing a corporate system as both excessively subjective and at the same time centralized" and worried that under the plaintiffs' legal theory "decentralization in management, which has been one of the core productivity-boosting principles of American business in the last two decades, becomes something that companies must avoid or limit."[13]

But the core of the plaintiffs' discrimination case was statistical. Wal-Mart draws most of its managers from its hourly wage employees, of which 72 percent are women. But only one-third of Wal-Mart's managers are women, and "even this figure overstates the proportion of female managers [because it] . . . includes traditionally 'female' positions, such as assistant managers . . . the lowest level of managers . . . Women comprise less than 10% of all Store Managers and approximately 4% of all District Managers . . . There is only one woman among the 20 executive officers of the company."[14] By contrast, "among [Wal-Mart's] 20 top competitors, women comprise over 56% of management . . . In fact, female representation among managers at Wal-Mart is at a substantially lower level today than [it was] among Wal-Mart's competitors in 1975."[15]

The *Dukes* class action would have severed the question of Wal-Mart's blameworthiness from the question of any individual woman's right to compensation. According to the trial plan established by the district court:

> Plaintiffs would attempt to prove that Wal-Mart engaged in a pattern and practice of discrimination . . . [Then] . . . a formula would be used to calculate the "lump sum" . . . that Wal-Mart owes to the class . . . A separate procedure would then be used to distribute those lump sums to those class members entitled to share in them—a stage in which Wal-Mart would no longer have an interest.[16]

The district court sensibly concluded that although it might be able to determine whether or not Wal-Mart is guilty of discrimination, it would not be able to determine which women were victims of discrimination and which were not. The class action would allow the court to order Wal-Mart to change discriminatory practices and to impose monetary damages in order to deter potential future discrimination by Wal-Mart and other employers.

But Wal-Mart complained that the class action mechanism was unfair to individual women. Opponents of the trial plan argued that this process "virtually guarantees non-victims will share in a monetary damage award along with those truly harmed by Wal-Mart's alleged discrimination."[17] As the Ninth Circuit judge Andrew Kleinfeld—who voted to stop the lawsuit from going forward—argued:

> Women employed by Wal-Mart who have suffered sex discrimination stand to lose a lot if this sex discrimination class action goes forward. All the members of the class will be bound by the judgment . . . Women who have suffered great loss because of sex discrimination will have to share the punitive damages award with many women who did not . . . Women who have left Wal-Mart will

get injunctive and declaratory relief of no value to them, while new female Wal-Mart employees will benefit from the injustice done to other women.[18]

Wal-Mart also argued that a class action would deprive it of many of its defenses under federal civil rights law. For instance, in an individual case, Wal-Mart could avoid paying money damages by showing that a decision that was influenced by sexism would have been the same even without the sexism. In the sex harassment context, Wal-mart could defend itself by showing that it had an internal process in place to deal with sex harassment complaints and the plaintiff unreasonably failed to use it. The class action plan didn't allow for such individual defenses.

But such individualized defenses are irrelevant in a case argued largely on the basis of statistics. Despite the *Dukes* plaintiffs' anecdotal evidence of discrimination, theory of a centralized and sexist corporate culture, and sociological evidence that Wal-Mart's organizational structure is "vulnerable" to influence by stereotypes, the case would stand or fall on the statistical evidence. It's fair to infer discrimination from an inexplicably lopsided workforce. Of course, if Wal-Mart could offer a convincing alternative explanation, it would avoid liability; if it could offer evidence that partially explains the disparity, its liability would be reduced accordingly.

In a sense, *Dukes v. Wal-Mart* was a back-to-the-future civil rights case, using a now-disfavored type of litigation and an older conception of what civil rights litigation should accomplish in order to confront a very contemporary social problem. Shortly after the Civil Rights Act was passed in 1964, the class action was one of the most important types of discrimination litigation. Legal challenges to a pattern and practice of discrimination—a collective injury—have been at the center of civil rights litigation since the early 1970s. The law against disparate impact—widely considered one of the most important parts of employment discrimination law for years after it was established in 1971—addresses a group-based injury. As late as

1978, legal commentators considered the individual civil rights case a relatively minor part of civil rights enforcement. Early civil rights cases saw individual rights as a means to the end of equal opportunity for everyone: the individual plaintiff was considered a "private attorney general" who basically reinforced collective efforts.[19]

The prestige of these collective civil rights claims suffered in the 1980s. Legal changes made class actions more difficult to bring, and by 1988 the official reporter of the Federal Rules of Civil Procedure could opine that "class actions had their day in the sun and kind of petered out."[20] Meanwhile, the Burger Court refused to extend Title VII's disparate-impact theory of discrimination to constitutional litigation in 1976's *Washington v. Davis*, calling its legitimacy into question more generally. Throughout the 1980s, the Rehnquist Court limited disparate impact under Title VII of the Civil Rights Act, insisting that individual discriminatory treatment was the defining civil rights violation.

But in today's job market, collective claims make more sense than ever. Wal-Mart has gained notoriety because it exhibits all of the defining features of the contemporary service-sector employer in an exaggerated form: it has a large, low-wage workforce, high turnover, and a decentralized management structure and evaluates its employees based on highly subjective criteria. Wal-Mart is larger than any other employer, and many of its practices may be more extreme than those of its competitors, but all of the things Wal-Mart's critics hate about it are typical of service-sector employers generally.

These features—especially high turnover, decentralization, and subjective evaluation—make it hard to apply the individual civil rights model that has developed since the 1970s. The main method of proving individual discrimination was established back in 1973, in the context of manufacturing jobs that required objective skills and formal certifications. Percy Green, a black employee of the St. Louis McDonnell Douglas factory who was laid off from his job, sued when McDonnell Douglas rejected his application a year later after it started hiring again. Green insisted that McDonnell Douglas rejected him because of his race; McDonnell Douglas claimed it rejected him because an earlier protest he organized disrupted the company's factory. The Supreme Court in *McDonnell Douglas Corp. v. Green* held that if a plaintiff shows (1) he's a member of a group likely to be the target of prejudice, (2) he applied for and was qualified for the job, (3) the employer rejected him, and (4) the employer continued to seek applications for the position, he has made out a prima facie case of discriminatory intent. At that point the employer must offer a nondiscriminatory reason for rejecting the plaintiff. Finally, the plaintiff can try to convince the judge or jury that the defendant's reason is really a pretext for discrimination: if he does, he wins his lawsuit; if not, he loses.

This method worked pretty well in a manufacturing context, like *McDonnell Douglas*. Employees needed objective skills, such as formal training or certification, to use specific types of equipment, and employers typically were indifferent between employees with the requisite skills. When McDonnell Douglas refused to hire Green, it raised the suspicion that its reasons were unusual. But notice how anachronistic the *McDonnell Douglas* approach is in today's service-sector labor market. Consider factor number 2 of the prima facie case: the plaintiff applied for and was qualified for the job. Today, many jobs are filled by word of mouth or through informal internal promotion processes. The Wal-Mart plaintiffs complained that women were not mentored and groomed for upper-management positions, so they weren't prepared when the better jobs opened up, and sometimes openings weren't even announced. What does it mean, then, to "apply" for a management position at Wal-Mart? And the qualifications for many service-sector jobs are hard to define. The Wal-Mart promotions process was left almost entirely up to local managers, who said they considered factors such as "teamwork, ethics, integrity, and the ability to get along with others" in their decisions. Getting a promotion at Wal-Mart—as in many service sector jobs—isn't a simple matter of being "qualified"; it requires being the best of a large group of aspirants, based on "soft skills" such as demeanor, poise, and personality. It's easy for bias and stereotypes to hide in the fog of subjectivity that such evaluations entail: a manager who thinks women shouldn't be in charge might claim a female candidate lacks "team spirit," or his opinion of a female candidate's people skills might be influenced by his stereotyped views of appropriate feminine demeanor.

The Wal-Mart plaintiffs came close to insisting that decentralization and subjective job criteria are *inherently* discriminatory. This was the weakest part of their case: these are legitimate and effective management styles. A company shouldn't be punished for adopting them, nor should we presume that they are a cloak for bias. In a stereotypical manufacturing job, it might make sense to be suspicious of subjectivity: the main thing the employer should care about is how well and how quickly an employee performs his job on the production line—something that can be objectively measured. But in the service-sector jobs that are the fastest-growing part of the modern labor market, objective performance is only part of the job. A cashier who efficiently completes a transaction but is surly to customers is a bad cashier. A manager who knows how to organize his subordinates but can't manage conflicts among them or inspire them to work diligently is a bad manager. In fact, even in manufacturing, the most successful businesses today know that teamwork, cooperation, and the ability to innovate are important skills for everyone from upper management to the assembly line worker. State-of-the-art management science suggests that giving local managers, who are closest to the specific challenges, the latitude to respond to them often leads to dramatic improvements in productivity and efficiency. These innovations in management may be more "vulnerable" to bias than formal and objective job criteria, but they are becoming more and more prevalent for good reasons.

Decentralized management and subjective job criteria may be

vulnerable to bias, but the real problem for civil rights law is that whatever bias there is will be harder to *detect*, making it nearly impossible to prove specific instances of discrimination, even when discrimination is rampant.

If the Wal-Mart plaintiffs are right about Wal-Mart's pervasive culture of sexism, individual lawsuits can't capture the magnitude of the social injustice, nor can they provide the appropriate incentives for Wal-Mart to change its ways. The evidence of statistical disparity can't tell us whether any *given* woman was harmed by sexism, but it might tell us a lot about the pervasiveness of sexism at Wal-Mart. Since the nature of Wal-Mart's personnel management makes it hard to detect individual discriminatory intent, most of the Wal-Mart plaintiffs would lose individual suits, even if they were victims of discrimination. Judge Frank Easterbrook, of the Seventh Circuit, explained this problem in a race discrimination case:

> Suppose 1,000 employees apply for 100 promotions; 150 of the workers are black and 850 white. If all are equally qualified and the employer ignores race, then 85 white workers and 15 black workers will be promoted, plus or minus some variation that can be chalked up to chance. Suppose only 10 black workers are promoted. Is that the result of discrimination or chance? Econometric analysis may suggest the answer . . . [but] it cannot reveal with certainty whether any given person suffered . . . [Suppose that] but for discrimination, 15 [black employees] would have been promoted . . . Which . . . would have received the other 5 promotions? The statistical analysis does not tell us—and in civil litigation, where the plaintiff's burden is to show more likely than not that he was harmed by a legal wrong, data of this kind will not get a worker over that threshold.[21]

Even when we can be pretty sure a given employer discriminated, it's possible that no individual will be able to prove that *she* was discriminated against. Because individual lawsuits require such proof, they can't address many of the inequities of much of the modern job market. The *Dukes* suit, with its heavy reliance on statistics, was an attempt to bring employment discrimination law into the twenty-first century.

Dukes split the Supreme Court along ideological lines, 5 to 4. Writing for the majority in rejecting the *Dukes* class, Justice Scalia emphasized the lack of any common policy among Wal-Mart stores nationwide and insisted that the plaintiffs had "little in common but their sex and this lawsuit."[22]

Dukes v. Wal-Mart was civil rights litigation for the twenty-first century in the same way the Jena Six protests were a civil rights demonstration for the twenty-first century. In both instances, a fortuitously selected group of individuals became symbols of a larger social injustice: the glaring racial disparities in the nation's criminal justice system in the case of the Jena Six; the enduring fact of workplace gender bias in the case of the Wal-Mart Seven. There's nothing new about this in and of itself. Almost every important civil-rights-based challenge has used an individual to dramatize a collective injury: Linda Brown was one of thousands of black students forced to attend segregated schools in the Jim Crow South; Rosa Parks was one of thousands of blacks forced to sit in the back of Montgomery, Alabama, buses.

But if an individual is to symbolize a larger injustice, she must have in fact suffered that injustice. What's new is that today it's often very hard to tell when an *individual* injustice has occurred, even when we know from looking at society as a whole that a lot of injustices must be occurring *somewhere*. Even if we knew that racism and racism alone had caused the dramatic racial disparities in the criminal justice system, we still couldn't be sure that the Jena Six were in the group of blacks prosecuted because of their race as opposed to the group of blacks prosecuted for legitimate reasons or because of race-neutral prosecutorial overzealousness. Similarly, even if the statistics cited by the Wal-Mart Seven prove that Wal-Mart must have discriminated against women, we may have no way of knowing which women were victims of discrimination and which suffered due to their own poor performance or lack of initiative.

Sex inequality is pervasive in the American labor market. Despite decades of efforts by women's groups, women still earn, on average, roughly 70 percent of what men do for comparable work, and the glass ceiling prevents qualified women from getting many of the most remunerative positions. Wal-Mart may well be worse than average, but it's a prime example of a widespread problem. Wal-Mart makes a good target, not because it's unique, but because it's conspicuous—much like a small town in the American South is a conspicuous target for an accusation of police and prosecutorial racism. The Wal-Mart Seven, like the Jena Six, called attention to a social injustice that they as individuals may or may not have suffered, by zeroing in on a target that may be no worse than many others. In both instances, an individual claim ("Free the Jena Six!" or "Promote the Wal-Mart Seven!") is a potentially misdirected way to address a pervasive injustice. But what's the alternative? It's hard to fault these efforts, as poor a fit as they may be, if there's no other solution to the injustices that such civil rights protests and litigation try to confront.

Against Entitlement

After several well-publicized airline mishaps left passengers stranded on the tarmac for hours without water or access to clean bathrooms, angry travelers began to press for an Airline Passenger Bill of Rights. One proposal would have allowed passengers to sue airlines for flight cancellations, delays, overbooking, lost and damaged luggage, and time "trapped" on the tarmac. Another version, sponsored by Senators Barbara Boxer and Olympia Snowe, was more modest: it required airlines to provide passengers with water, food, and a chance to exit the plane after a three-hour delay, but it wouldn't have required airlines to compensate individual passengers. The Airline Passenger Bill of Rights was grounded in Congress for several years, but

President Obama implemented a similar rule through the Department of Transportation, bypassing the congested legislative runway. Now airlines that let a full plane sit for more than two hours must offer passengers food and water and must let them leave after three hours; violators can be fined $27,500 for each trapped passenger by the Department of Transportation. "This is President Obama's Bill of Rights," said the Department of Transportation secretary, Ray LaHood.[23]

Frequent travelers can only welcome this development, but in what sense is it really a Bill of *Rights*? Of course the bill is designed to help airline passengers, but it doesn't actually create any new rights. A "right" is a legal entitlement that an individual or group can assert against another individual or group. Otherwise, it's just a regulation, no matter how loud the blaring of trumpets and the cheering of crowds that accompany it. By this definition the proposed Airline Passenger Bill of Rights—however commendable as regulation—doesn't live up to its name. Still, the regulations contained in the so-called Bill of Rights are designed to make sure airlines will not keep their passengers stranded on the tarmac for hours on end without food and water—the same goal that an individual entitlement would ideally reach. In this sense, we could think of rights as nothing more than public policies that allow for private enforcement and individual compensation through litigation, rather than for public enforcement by police, prosecutors, or regulatory agencies.

If we think of rights in this way, then we face a practical question of public policy: When are individual entitlements the best way to achieve our goals? The main practical difference between a civil rights lawsuit and public enforcement of regulation is that the former requires the compensation of individual victims while the latter would not. But this difference isn't always as important as it may seem. For instance, in the Wal-Mart class action, individual compensation was almost an afterthought. As Judge Kleinfeld complained in opposing class certification, the trial plan aspired to only rough justice for the millions of putative victims of Wal-Mart; it would almost certainly have given an undeserved windfall to some women who were not victims of discrimination and undercompensated some who were.

This is a damning objection only if individual compensation is the overriding concern. Because we've defined social justice in terms of rights, it's natural to assume that some sort of individual restitution is the ultimate goal. But perhaps individual compensation shouldn't be the main objective; maybe it is a means that has become confused with the end. Consider the idea of the civil rights plaintiff as a "private attorney general"—a sort of desegregation bounty hunter who is deputized to help enforce the law and offered a reward, in the form of monetary damages, for doing so. Viewed this way, private damages are not a moral entitlement designed to compensate individuals but instead an incentive offered to entice people to bring civil rights violations to court. And for defendants, damages are designed to deter discrimination. For purposes of deterrence, it doesn't matter who gets the money as long as the defendant has to pay for violating the law. In this sense civil rights are designed to encourage more responsible behavior so that a lawsuit isn't necessary. Effective regulation can bring about similar changes in behavior directly, making individual entitlements unnecessary.

Suppose we were to suspend—if not abandon—the idea that every victim of discrimination is entitled to an individual remedy. Suppose we shifted our focus from individual entitlements to public policies designed to reduce the prevalence of invidious discrimination and unjust social inequality overall. This may seem unfair if you think that individuals have a right to equal treatment that no collective goal can outweigh. But the American legal system has never recognized such a broad and sweeping guarantee of individual fairness. As people like Jerold Mackenzie know all too well, in the United States most employment is "at will": employers can choose whom to hire, fire, and promote for any reason that isn't explicitly forbidden by law. A lot of bad reasons—nepotism, favoritism, idiosyncratic prejudice (imagine an employer who hates redheads or people with bad skin)—are legally acceptable. Employment at will is controversial, and sometimes it is superseded by other arrangements, such as civil service rules, union contracts, academic tenure, and state wrongful-termination laws. Government could try to guarantee that *all* employment decisions are made for "good cause." But that would require detailed micromanaging of innumerable business decisions: government would need to determine what counts as good cause in a host of different situations and to review every controversial employment decision. Such a reform would be costly, both in terms of direct expenses for regulatory enforcement and litigation and in terms of inconvenience and inefficiency for employers. Employment at will reflects valid concerns about the capacity of government to identify and prevent or remedy unfairness: it can be very hard to tell the difference between unfair treatment and the kinds of difficult judgment calls that every employer must make. Would more aggressive regulation of the employment market be worth the expense? If the labor market is healthy, a good employee who is treated unfairly usually will be able to find employment elsewhere; in fact, many people who could sue their employers for discrimination prefer to cut their losses and find a new job. It's probably wiser to devote scarce resources to unemployment insurance and a robust social safety net to help cushion the blow of unavoidable employment dislocations—whether due to capricious employers or to the unpredictable shifts of a volatile economy.

Civil rights law prohibits only the most severe and socially destructive forms of discrimination—typically those that have become widespread because of misguided laws or social customs in the past. For instance, race discrimination was part of an all-encompassing, legally structured system of racial hierarchy, and many of the habits, attitudes, and effects of that system are still with us today. Similarly, sex discrimination was legally and socially enforced for much of American history, and the bad habits of male chauvinism are not yet extinct. The social injustices and individual harm caused by race and sex discrimination have been much more widespread and severe than those caused by favoritism, nepotism, or idiosyncratic biases. The racial minority passed over because of his race and the woman limited in her advancement because of her sex may not find better opportunities elsewhere; instead, they may well face the same type of discrimination over and over again. But if these kinds of discrimination were less widespread, they wouldn't be as damaging. Public policy that reduced segregation and counteracted irrational prejudice would make race and sex discrimination less widespread and more like the kinds of unfairness we can get beyond without compensation.

Practically speaking, individual rights don't provide every victim of discrimination a remedy anyway. Lots of people are victims of discrimination but don't know it or can't prove it. Plenty of others find that the costs of pursuing their rights—time and expense spent in litigation and a possible tarnished reputation in one's profession—outweigh the benefits. It's expensive and time-consuming to sue for discrimination; as a result, relatively few people do so, even when they have valid claims.

And the people who do sue aren't always those with the strongest claims; instead, they are often those with the least to lose in terms of forgone opportunities and reputation by filing suit. Imagine a competent, conscientious, amiable employee with a good reputation in her field who is fired by a bigoted employer. She could spend the next several years suing her employer for the dubious privilege of returning to work for a bigot, or she could just find another job. Now imagine an incompetent, lazy, and belligerent employee who is fired for her poor performance and disruptive behavior. She is unlikely to find work elsewhere and has no good reputation to put at risk. With nothing to lose, such an employee has every incentive to file a trumped-up discrimination claim.

Individual civil rights can inadvertently encourage weaker claims over stronger ones in other ways. For instance, people are much more likely to sue when they lose a job or are denied a hoped-for promotion than when they are not hired in the first place. This is probably because most people value things that they currently have much more highly than they would value the same thing if they did not have it. This phenomenon is so well-known among psychologists and economists that they have a name for it: the "endowment effect." It's a sort of twist on the idea that a bird in the hand is worth two in the bush. Numerous studies have shown that people will demand much more—sometimes orders of magnitude more—to *sell* an item that they possess than they would offer to *buy* the same item if they did not have it. My colleague Mark Kelman has offered this simple example of the phenomenon: Suppose I were to inherit a rare and valuable bottle of wine, worth $1,000. An acquaintance, who is an obsessive oenophile, would happily pay me $1,000 for the wine. I, by contrast, drink martinis—a relatively plebeian tipple compared with vintage Bordeaux—and would never spend more than $100 on a bottle of wine even for the most special occasion. Still, I'd kind of like to know what a $1,000 bottle of wine tastes like. If I inherited one, it is quite plausible that I would decide to drink the wine myself rather than sell it. This is an example of an endowment effect: I would not relinquish a bottle in my possession even for ten times the price I would be willing to pay for it if I didn't already have it.

The same phenomenon seems to apply to jobs. Immediately after the Civil Rights Act was first passed, many employers had blatantly discriminatory hiring practices and deliberately segregated workforces, and these offered easy targets for litigation. But civil rights lawyers quickly picked off the sitting ducks, and employers began to change their practices. Discrimination in hiring was harder to prove, and few individuals had the information or the incentive to sue over a job that got away. But many people, having landed a job, would fight to keep it. As a result, complaints of termination now outnumber failure-to-hire complaints by almost seven to one.[24]

Devoting such an overwhelming share of resources to investigating and adjudicating claims of discriminatory termination makes little sense. By so heavily favoring discriminatory promotion or termination claims, individual civil rights litigation looks for prejudice where we are least likely to find it while neglecting more promising hunting grounds. Only an employer who has in fact hired members of an underrepresented group can become a defendant in a discriminatory termination lawsuit brought by a member of that group. Such an employer is somewhat less likely to be bigoted than one who has never hired any minority employees in the first place, yet civil rights enforcement spends most of its resources policing the actions of just these employers while paying relatively little attention to employers who discriminate in hiring.

Such lopsided enforcement not only misdirects resources but also creates perverse incentives. A well-crafted civil rights policy would reward employers who hire members of underrepresented groups and punish those who refuse to. But current civil rights litigation does just the opposite: it makes it relatively safe to refuse to hire members of underrepresented groups (because there is little risk of being sued for failure to hire) and risky to hire them (because doing so opens one up to the much more likely lawsuit for discriminatory promotion or termination). As my colleague the law professor and economist John Donohue notes, "A worker who is not hired in the first place is obviously in no position to bring a future firing suit . . . With the enormous increase in discharge cases, the probability that a worker will bring a discriminatory firing suit is now substantially higher than the probability that a worker will bring a failure to hire suit. Consequently, antidiscrimination laws may actually provide . . . a monetary advantage to an employer for rejecting the . . . protected [job] applicant."[25] Supplementing—or replacing— individual entitlements with robust administrative regulation in the public interest and eliminating the most questionable entitlements would change these perverse incentives and lopsided emphases.

Rights and Responsibilities

A right necessarily implies a corresponding duty on the part of someone else: if employees have a right to be free from discrimination, employers have a duty not to discriminate; if disabled students have a right to an adequate free public education, school districts have a duty to provide it; if bar hoppers have a right to equal treatment without regard to sex, bars have a duty to eliminate ladies' night. Rights always imply that there is another party who is able to discharge that duty and who should be required to do so. This makes rights an awkward fit for some purposes. For instance, the English parliamentarian Edmund Burke once asked: "What is the use of discussing a man's abstract right to food or medicine? The question is upon the method of procuring and administering them. In that deliberation I shall always advise to call in the aid of the farmer and the physician rather than the professor of metaphysics."[26] Rights can't feed the multitudes or cure the sick, and it's not clear who would guarantee a right to food or medicine. Farmers and physicians? Should they be expected to contribute their services for free? Why? If not, who will pay them? If the government is to pay, then a right to food and medicine will require a social welfare apparatus, raising difficult policy questions concerning the distribution of scarce resources and the effects of public subsidy on quality and efficiency—all questions on which reasonable people will sharply differ. Declaring a right to food or medicine doesn't help us to work out these details; in fact, a right may make it harder to see the detailed questions involved.

Many issues that have been framed in terms of civil rights—with the implication that some individuals deserve compensation and others deserve to pay—would be better reframed as public policy questions that involve difficult technical and administrative complexities and tricky questions of distributive justice. Consider the problem of long lines at the ladies' room that I discussed in Chapter Two. It's not a trivial problem: longer waits cost women valuable time at work, with the result that they are less productive than men or must work longer. Over the years, this is a real expense— a tax of sorts attached to the female sex. Nor is it simply the natural consequence of biological sex difference; it's also the consequence of bathroom design decisions that could have been different and could be changed. Maybe we've just become inured to the idea that women always have to wait to use the bathroom. Mightn't our acquiescence reflect a silent and insidious belief that a woman's time isn't worth as much as a man's—a belief reflected in and reinforced by the stubborn persistence of a sex-based wage and salary gap? There's a strong argument that these inequities demand attention and redress.

But a civil rights lawsuit is an inefficient, uneven, and unfair solution to the problem. It's inefficient because litigation is costly and time-consuming; it's uneven because only the proprietors who encounter women willing to devote time and effort to a lawsuit will be forced to change; and it's unfair because in many cases the proprietor facing civil rights litigation won't be responsible for the design of the bathrooms, which were built decades earlier and can be changed only at great expense. To a woman sick and tired of wasting her time in long lines, restroom equity may feel like a civil rights issue. But we can make things better without creating a new, inefficient, and costly civil right. The building code is a more promising solution than individual civil rights. Some cities and states require new or remodeled construction to include a specific ratio of men's to women's restroom facilities. This allows proprietors to avoid wasteful remodeling as long as the old restrooms are still in good shape, but requires them to consider gender equity when they are in the process of planning new facilities. Public regulation offers a sensible solution to the problem at a reasonable cost; by contrast, a civil right to sex equity that required monetary compensation and immediate reform regardless of expense would go wrong in terms of both efficiency and fairness.

The current civil rights model—premised on a struggle between individual victims and callous or belligerent perpetrators—pits business against social justice. But many of today's businesses need not be made the enemies of equal opportunity; they could be powerful allies. Today hundreds of businesses try to recruit minority job applicants, improve job conditions for working women, and provide access to people with disabilities. Most do all of this without judicial coercion or the threat of litigation. In fact, large corporations such as 3M, Coca-Cola, General Electric, Hewlett-Packard, Intel, Johnson & Johnson, Kraft Foods, Microsoft, Nike, Pepsi, Procter & Gamble, Reebok, and Xerox urged the Supreme Court to affirm the validity of race- and sex-based affirmative action in 2003's *Grutter v. Bollinger*. They insisted that "today's global marketplace and the increasing diversity in the American population demand . . . cross-cultural experience and understanding . . . Many employers sincerely lament their inability to attract and retain a diverse workforce."[27]

But the antagonistic relationship between businesses and the civil rights community leads some employers to jealously guard information about the race and gender composition of their workforces. For instance, several Silicon Valley high-tech companies, including Google, Apple, Yahoo!, Oracle, and Applied Materials, wanted to keep this information secret so badly that they fought to prevent a *San Jose Mercury News* reporter, Mike Swift, from obtaining this routine workforce data from the EEOC. The companies claimed that the information was a "trade secret."[28]

It's hard to imagine how such data could reveal a firm's recruitment strategy, and we will have to imagine, because when Swift asked for elaboration he was told that the explanation was a trade secret too. But it's not hard to imagine why these companies might prefer to keep the race and gender of their workforces a secret: in 2006–2008, only 1.5 percent of Silicon Valley high-tech workers were black, 4.7 percent were Hispanic, and 23.8 percent were women; by contrast, over half of all Silicon Valley workers are female, and over 24 percent are Hispanic.[29] Of course, this doesn't mean that the firms are discriminating: there are many possible explanations for these figures. Qualification for high-tech jobs varies by race and gender, as does interest and proximity. For instance, although more than 12 percent of the national working-age population is black, only 2.9 percent of working-age Silicon Valley residents are; in this light, the 1.5 percent figure doesn't look quite so bad. Perhaps the statistics simply reflect the qualifications and interest of the available labor force.

Still, it's telling that the businesses of the future are willing to go to such lengths to keep their workplace diversity—or lack thereof—a secret. A more open and cooperative relationship between businesses and civil rights advocates might yield new ideas for improving diversity. Or, of course, it might demonstrate that the firms are as diverse as one could expect, given the available and qualified labor pool.

When Congress debated the Civil Rights Act of 1964, many of its sponsors proposed an administrative approach, modeled on the National Labor Relations Board. Civil rights leaders worried that private enforcement through lawsuits would weaken the new law, because "many of those discriminated against would be poor and legally unsophisticated."[30] As it's turned out, private enforcement has not led to too little enforcement, as liberal civil rights groups feared, nor has it led to too much, as many conservative complaints would suggest. Instead, it has given us some of both problems: many serious offenses go undetected and uncorrected, while minor, innocent, and ambiguous transgressions often receive inordinate attention; many people with strong claims involving widespread injustices do not seek relief or can't prove their cases, while people with weak or dubious claims can extract undeserved settlements from risk-averse businesses. Worst of all, individual civil rights claims are less and less likely to correct the nation's worst injustices.

State and federal agencies charged with setting guidelines for civil rights enforcement, such as the Equal Employment Opportunity Commission, now have decades' worth of experience and information about the nature of unjust inequality. Employers with over a hundred employees are currently required to submit EEO-1 reports that detail the race, national origin, and gender composition of their workforces. The EEOC could use this information to develop antidiscrimination goals and identify and eliminate impediments to equal opportunity. A stronger EEOC could be a clearinghouse for new ideas, assisting businesses that want to improve by offering suggestions based on what has worked elsewhere and allowing employers the flexibility to innovate free from the threat of unpredictable litigation. Employers that met diversity targets or adopted policies known to prevent discrimination might enjoy immunity from civil rights lawsuits.

Of course, tougher measures are in order for repeated and willful noncompliance. Statistical disparities aren't proof of discrimination in and of themselves, but reform is needed when the best information available suggests that concealed or even inadvertent discrimination is distorting the labor market. Effective regulation would have to include cease-and-desist power and fines for the recalcitrant. Armed with enough information about the available applicant pool and with the latest econometric techniques, administrative agencies could determine the likely race and gender composition of an evenhanded employer's workforce. Government could establish realistic expectations and develop rules and incentives that would encourage institutions to eliminate hidden biases and impediments to equal opportunity.

But what of constitutional rights? Most people think of constitutional rights as limitations on the executive and legislative branches, so it may seem contradictory to suggest that such rights might be interpreted, enforced, and even replaced by administration agencies or policies written *by* the legislature. It's a common misconception that the judiciary—in particular the Supreme Court—is in charge of constitutional interpretation. But nothing in the

Constitution gives the judiciary exclusive authority over its meaning or enforcement. In fact all branches of government are responsible for upholding the Constitution. For instance, the Fourteenth Amendment explicitly grants Congress the power to pass "appropriate legislation" enforcing its guarantees. Formally, the Civil Rights Act was upheld as an exercise of Congress's power to regulate interstate commerce, but it could as easily have been justified as an exercise of the power to enforce the Fourteenth Amendment. In fact, many people intuitively think of the Civil Rights Act as an extension of constitutional rights.

Congress and state and local government all have important roles to play in enforcing constitutional rights, because many rights can be guaranteed more effectively through comprehensive regulation than through litigation. For instance, judicial enforcement hasn't ensured the equal educational opportunities sought in *Brown v. Board of Education.* In fact, Southern school districts resisted desegregation for a decade after *Brown,* until Congress reinforced *Brown*'s mandate by tying federal education funding to desegregation as part of the Civil Rights Act of 1964. And things might be better today if Congress, the courts, and civil rights activists had taken up judge J. Braxton Craven's suggestion and allowed federal, state, and local "administrators, [with] some competence and experience in school administration" to take the lead in school desegregation."[31]

Rights are a tool, a technological innovation in the science of law and policy, a means of getting something practical done. Sometimes rights are perfect for the job at hand, just as a hammer is the perfect tool for driving nails. Sometimes rights are just about as good as anything else, as a hammer is as good a means of cracking open a coconut as any other. But sometimes rights are not well suited to the task at hand: a hammer would be a bad tool for removing a cork from a wine bottle, for instance.

To some people carrying a hammer, every problem looks like a nail, and to some people practiced in legal argumentation or social activism, every social problem looks like a civil rights violation. Most of the misdirected rights claims I've discussed in this book were the result of someone hammering away at a real problem. Rights go wrong by trying to address institutional and collective problems as if they were simply a collection of individual injuries. In these circumstances, rights give us moralizing when we need pragmatic solutions; they encourage inflexibility when compromise, cooperation, and sensitivity to concrete stakes are required; they inspire narrow self-interest when we must consider the common good. In such cases, a practical and public-spirited approach to the problem often reveals workable solutions that a claim of individual right obscures from view.

For instance, racial disparities in the criminal justice system are one of the most glaring examples of racial injustice in today's society. Statistical evidence suggests that racial bias plays some role in all stages of law enforcement—investigation, arrest, prosecution, conviction, sentencing, and parole. This has led some to call criminal law enforcement a new Jim Crow. But the evidence suggests that racial bias is relatively mild and somewhat scattered: it can't account for the magnitude of the racial disparity in the imprisoned population. Much of the growth in the American prison population is directly attributable to the war on drugs that began in the early 1980s. According to the Justice Policy Institute, the number of people in jail for drug crimes increased by a staggering 550 percent between 1989 and 2009.[32] In 2005 roughly one-quarter of the people incarcerated in the United States were convicted of a drug offense.[33] And the statistics suggest that racial bias is most prevalent in sentencing for drug-related crimes: for instance, a study in 2000 found that blacks in Kansas City convicted of drug crimes received sentences that were over fourteen months longer than whites convicted of similar crimes, but found no racial disparity in sentencing for violent crimes.[34]

This suggests that we could eliminate much of the racial disparity in law enforcement simply by ending the war on drugs. It's increasingly clear that the war on drugs is a quagmire: it hasn't significantly reduced drug use; it has enriched organized crime both in the United States and overseas, just as Prohibition empowered the Mafia in the 1920s; and it has diverted untold public resources to prisons—resources that could have been used to improve schools and job opportunities in poor neighborhoods where crime is now prevalent. Claims of widespread racial bias in law enforcement will be subject to intractable debate, and bias in individual cases is usually impossible to prove. As a result, a civil rights approach to the problem will indefinitely defer a solution as pundits, politicians, academics, and activists argue over the meaning of the latest statistical evidence. By contrast, ending the war on drugs is a specific and attainable goal on which a growing number of people from across the ideological spectrum agree. Whether they favor decriminalization of most recreational drugs or argue that law enforcement should no longer make drugs a priority, many sensible people now recognize that the current approach to narcotics is extravagantly costly and largely counterproductive.

Students with learning disabilities are only a small fraction of the many students who are disserved by today's educational system. Standardized tests are a necessary part of the evaluative process, and often they yield probative information. But many people read too much into test results that are, at best, a rough proxy for practical competence and skills. This disadvantages everyone who "tests badly"—whether or not a diagnosed learning disability is the cause—and it deprives society of their talents. We'd all be better off if schools and employers took a more nuanced and modest approach to standardized test scores. But a civil right that artificially inflates the scores of a select few only makes the tests even less probative. A better approach would allow disabled plaintiffs to challenge the validity of certain tests generally, as disparate-impact civil rights laws do in the context of employment practices that disadvantage women and racial minorities. If a test doesn't measure the relevant skills, it shouldn't be used to evaluate *anyone*; if it does, it should be administered evenhandedly.

Similarly, too many public schools fail all but the most talented and self-sufficient students; new administrative and pedagogical approaches are desperately needed. The failure of the schools with respect to students with attention deficit disorder and other emotional and learning disabilities is only the most conspicuous example of a more general failure. New research shows that conventional educational methods don't work for a disproportionate number of poor, culturally unsophisticated students, and even many socioeconomically privileged boys are at a disadvantage compared with their developmentally advanced female peers. A civil right that requires cash-strapped schools to divert resources from the general student body to children with mild or vaguely defined disabilities makes things worse for these students and papers over the deeper problem, leaving the underlying rot to spread.

Age discrimination remains a serious problem for elderly *job seekers*, but there's little evidence that age-related bias is widespread for older *workers*, who often actually enjoy preferential treatment. Civil rights prohibiting age discrimination have badly missed their mark, quite possibly worsening the plight of elderly job seekers while forcing employers to give unjustified advantages and windfalls to a small group of relatively wealthy older middle managers and professionals. Age discrimination enforcement should focus on *hiring* discrimination—not termination, promotion, and compensation— and the law should be amended to allow mandatory retirement at some reasonably ripe old age—perhaps seventy or seventy-five— with periodic review to reflect changes in longevity.

Sex discrimination is pervasive in American life: women suffer from antediluvian stereotypes, misogynistic hostility, sexist condescension, and sexual predation. Laws against sex discrimination have made these practices less common and less accepted. But American society is still struggling with the meaning of sex equality. Even committed feminists can't agree on whether equality requires strict equal treatment or demands that we take into account differences between the sexes. Professional women struggle to walk a tightrope between what employers consider unacceptably androgynous and unprofessionally girlish self-presentations. But most women jealously defend certain types of differential treatment based on sex. A law that forbids any and all sex-based distinctions would satisfy a lofty conceptual rigor at the expense of common sense. As a result, judges have no choice but to make tough and inevitably controversial judgments about which distinctions are socially harmful and which are benign or innocent. These judgments don't look or sound like the kind of crisp and decisive logic we have come to expect from legal rights analysis, but at their best they represent the highest form of the judicial art: nuanced and context-specific judgments, inspired by a coolheaded evaluation of the common good and warm-blooded empathy for the individuals involved.

The need for nuanced judgment is no less pronounced in the context of race discrimination. *Brown v. Board of Education* is perhaps our legal system's finest moment, but its aftermath often showed the courts at their worst: stretched beyond their administrative competence and careening back and forth between rigid absolutism and craven capitulation. Civil rights are certainly not to blame for this, but rights analysis did encourage an impractical conceptual approach to the problem of segregation. If, instead, the courts and Congress had simply asked how the nation could most readily and painlessly integrate the public schools, they could certainly have done a better job—even if the effort might have started more slowly and less dramatically. And if desegregation policy had been inspired by such a clearly defined practical goal, no one would be tempted to declare victory and begin winding down the effort when so many of the nation's children still attend racially segregated schools—much less forbid pragmatic integrationist policies that emerge from the democratic process.

Legalistic thinking has spilled over into civil rights activism as well, where it has mixed with rage, nostalgia, and demagoguery to yield a cocktail that stimulates the emotions and depresses the faculties of self-restraint. As a result, today's protest movements too often seem to prefer "speaking truth *to* power" over exercising it. Perhaps that's because exercising power requires one to confront tragic conflicts between compelling goals and to make tough choices: the activist can simply demand that those "in power" free the Jena Six, whereas the person charged with freeing them or keeping them behind bars must ask whether doing so is a good idea for all concerned. But then again, many of today's political activists don't really expect to get what they're demanding anyway: increasingly, they define their objectives in terms of "community building" and "consciousness raising"—a sad admission of the futility of their demands.

It may occur to some readers that I've limited my discussion to a small part of the large hardware store of rights claims: rights to equality that Americans colloquially call "civil rights." Couldn't I make similar arguments about, say, the First Amendment right to freedom of expression, or the Eighth Amendment right against cruel and unusual punishment, or the Second Amendment right to bear arms? Perhaps. I could point out that the First Amendment now prohibits needed campaign finance reform by treating sensible restrictions on corporate spending in elections as restrictions on speech. I could note that the supposed right to be free from cruel and unusual punishment hasn't stopped us from making the threat of rape in prison an implicit part of criminal deterrence. And I could insist that the right to bear arms seems nothing less than a ghoulish approach to population control, firearms being easier to procure than many forms of contraception. But to even begin such an analysis (and *begin* is all I aspire to have done in this book) would require the same kind of context-specific analysis I've offered for the rights claims I've discussed in the preceding chapters. So I raise these tentative observations only to leave them.

This book is part of a long tradition of skeptical commentary on rights. Ever since the French revolutionaries declared the Rights of Man and the Citizen, social critics from both the left and right of the ideological spectrum have questioned the wisdom and efficacy the assertion of rights. Edmund Burke attacked the Rights of Man as a pernicious scholasticism that ignored the complexities of the art of government and the value of tradition.[35] Jeremy Bentham famously attacked the idea of universal and inalienable rights as "nonsense upon stilts" and "bawling upon paper," arguing that rights should yield to changing social circumstances and concerns of social utility.[36] Karl Marx critiqued "bourgeois rights" as a form of alienation that divided humans from each other in society and from their own highest purposes.[37]

In the 1980s, communitarian political theorists worried that the American rights tradition had become corrupted and called for rights to be supplemented with a robust assertion of civic responsibilities. Meanwhile, legal scholars and political theorists associated with the leftist intellectual movement known as critical legal studies advanced a comprehensive critique of rights—work that has profoundly influenced my arguments in this book.[38] They argued that rights offered a false hope of social change through courts and litigation, that they siphoned energy away from more promising political action, and that they distorted political and social consciousness by encouraging people to think of themselves as isolated rights holders rather than as participants in a collective struggle. This inspired a powerful response from many people of color and feminists in defense of rights—civil rights in particular—which they insisted were indispensable to the moral growth of the nation, and a cherished part of the identity of minority groups.

A series of more specific and less sweeping critiques of rights grew out of this debate: instead of making claims about rights generally, the next generation of critiques offered detailed accounts of the costs and benefits of specific claims of right. I have discussed many of the authors of these critiques herein: my colleague Mark Kelman and his coauthor Gillian Lester's work on learning disability claims; my former colleague at Stanford Janet Halley's work on sex harassment and sexual minorities; the Yale Law School professor Vicki Shultz's work on sexual harassment law; Sam Issacharoff's work on age discrimination. One lesson of the debate in the 1980s and the second generation of critiques that followed is that rights imply a distinctive type of analysis, which is better suited to some questions than to others. This suggests that sweeping criticisms of rights are probably mistaken, but that a rights-based approach may well be ineffective or counterproductive in some of the circumstances in which it is currently used.

The law professor Mark Tushnet once insisted that "it is not just that rights-talk does not do much good. In the contemporary United States it is positively harmful."[39] This goes too far. A vandal once threw a hammer through my front window in San Francisco, causing me a lot of trouble and expense, but it would be rash to conclude that hammers are a general public menace. I can, however, certainly say that hammers are sometimes badly used, and perhaps suggest some loose guidelines for their responsible deployment.

Civil rights are indispensable tools, but sometimes they will do more harm than good, like a hammer used to loosen a wine cork or open a window. Luckily, we have other tools: the many injustices that civil rights can't fix—or can't fix at an acceptable cost—can be addressed in other ways. None of this diminishes the significance of civil rights in the slightest. Civil rights serve a vital but limited role. In order to fulfill the practical promise of civil rights, we must acknowledge their limitations. In order to honor the achievement of the civil rights movement, we must move beyond the tactics and ideas of the past.

Righting Rights

Civil rights are remarkably effective against overt prejudice perpetrated by identifiable bigots. But they have proven impotent against today's most severe social injustices, which involve covert and repressed prejudice or the innocent perpetuation of past prejudice. Like an overprescribed antibiotic that kills beneficial microorganisms and eventually encourages resistant strains of bacteria, the civil rights approach to social justice, once a miracle cure, now threatens to do more harm than good.

Americans have been trained to accept and even to celebrate the many costs of rights gone wrong. Like the drinking, brawling, and reckless sex that are supposed to be the necessary by-products of creative genius for a tortured artist, the notorious abuses and misuses of rights are, we're told, a small price to pay for their invaluable virtues. In fact, we've come to embrace some of the worst cases of rights gone wrong, believing that they provide evidence of our society's steadfast commitment to civil rights. Every high school civics student learns that we must allow the Nazi Party to march through a community of Holocaust survivors unless we would have government silence all unpopular speech. The propagandists of unregulated gun ownership tell us that we must allow antisocial militia groups to arm themselves with military assault rifles in order to protect the rights of the small-game hunter and the single woman who keeps a pistol for protection. Resentful single men, overzealous lawyers, and the California Supreme Court instruct us that we must outlaw ladies' night and Mother's Day in order to prevent sexist business owners from keeping women trapped beneath the glass ceiling. But just as addiction rarely contributes to artistic talent, rigidity and extremism are rarely necessary preconditions of human liberty and equality. Rights don't *have* to go wrong: they can and should be exercised in a spirit of responsible civic engagement. Every schoolkid learns that his right to swing his fist ends where his classmate's nose begins. But somehow as adults we forget this simple truth and act as if rights can and should be asserted regardless of the costs to others.

At their best, civil rights can foster socially responsible and altruistic behavior. For instance, Thomas Paine, one of history's most eloquent and sophisticated advocates of human rights, wrote the following in defense of Republican France's Declaration of the Rights of Man:

> While the Declaration of Rights was before the National Assembly, some of its members remarked, that if a Declaration of Rights was published, it should be accompanied by a Declaration of Duties. The observation discovered a mind that reflected, and it only erred by not reflecting far enough. A Declaration of Rights is, by reciprocity, a Declaration of Duties also. Whatever is my right as a man, is also the right of another; and it becomes my duty to guarantee, as well as to possess.

It's no accident that this observation—at once savvy jurisprudence and profound social theory—should come from one of the most passionate defenders of rights. Rights imply duties in a strictly necessary sense: my right to free speech implies the duty of others not to have me jailed for expressing my views; my right to equal treatment implies that other people have a duty to treat me fairly. And more important, as Paine suggests, rights imply a profound reciprocal social relationship between citizens. My right to free speech implies a duty to tolerate speech I find offensive; my right to equal treatment implies a duty to treat others as my equals. Paine envisioned each citizen as not only a bearer of his own rights but also a guarantor of the rights of others. Rights make common sense only in the context of social, political, and economic relationships. To assert rights responsibly, we need to consider how our claims will affect society as a whole.

Think about how far we've moved away from Paine's idea of rights. Today, most people think of rights as a kind of commodity or asset that they can cash in by running to court like an investor redeeming a government bond. Rights go wrong because the civic-minded conception of rights as a social relationship has been replaced by a more miserly and atomistic conception of rights as nothing more than an individual entitlement, to be asserted *against* others and enforced by an omnipresent government.

The work of the civil rights movement is not complete. Although race relations have, in many ways, never been better, overt and vicious racism remains, and inner-city blacks are more socially isolated, desperate, and culturally deprived than they were before the great civil rights reforms of the 1960s. Women have taken their places in the modern workforce, but they suffer from unfairly limited opportunities, depressed wages, demeaning stereotypes, and on-the-job harassment. The disabled have enjoyed significant gains in respect and access to jobs and public spaces, but many needless impediments to their full participation remain. And although older *workers* fare well, jobless older people still face high odds in finding employment. Most of these problems require nuanced and comprehensive institutional changes—not individual entitlements.

Still, despite the numerous instances where rights have gone wrong, many wrongs remain to be righted, including some we as a society have yet to acknowledge. Two examples stand out. Perhaps the most obvious is the now decades-old struggle of gay men and lesbians for respect and basic fairness. Although the inaptly named policy of "Don't Ask, Don't Tell"—in fact a policy that encouraged interrogation and public shaming based on sexual orientation—was repealed in 2010, as I write, the deceptively titled Defense of Marriage Act, a federal law that in fact preemptively attacks marriage, preventing states from extending its full privileges to same-sex couples, remains the law of the land. It tells us all we need to know about these two pieces of legislation—and about the antigay agenda behind them—that their authors gave them names that so directly contradict their purposes and effects. I argued in my book *The Race Card* that opposition to same-sex marriage may not be motivated by antigay bias—even so, the time for people of goodwill to vacillate on these questions is rapidly drawing to a close. Even the argument that the secular state should leave marriage to the church and offer only domestic partnership—a gesture that might have been admirable twenty or so years ago—now can only be apprehended as an insult, akin to the Jackson, Mississippi, decision in 1962 to close its public pools rather than open them to blacks.

Another example should be more obvious than it is. Today, thousands of undocumented immigrants labor in America's factories, fields, restaurants, and office towers, performing necessary work that few citizens of any race care to do. They come here, often packed into the backs of trucks and railcars, smuggled in by profiteers in conditions that recall those endured by African slaves centuries ago. They come voluntarily—that is a big difference, although perhaps not a morally decisive one. They work on farms for subsistence wages, often warehoused in unheated, unlit concrete bunkers or tin shacks without running water—conditions much like those of the black sharecroppers whose places they took at the bottom of America's social food chain. Their plight is not the inevitable consequence of a border between a rich country and its poorer neighbors. We could acknowledge their contributions and the inevitability of their presence here and allow them to work with dignity and without fear. As noncitizens, they have few legal rights, and yet if any group of people can justly lay claim to the legacy of the civil rights movement, they can—they, and whoever will work to improve their lot.

Trumped-up, trivial, and exaggerated claims, based on unrealistic, abstract ideals and inflexible mandates, proliferate, testing the patience of the general public and often actually undermining social justice. But at the same time the valid claims I've just mentioned and many others demand our attention. Of all the risks of rights gone wrong, perhaps the greatest is that the bad habits of opportunism, legalistic conceptualism, and festering ressentiment will slowly take the place of the common sense to recognize injustice when it is staring us in the face, and the common decency to do something about it. Distracted by the wrong rights, we may neglect to right wrongs.

Notes

Introduction

1. Richard G. Jones, "In Louisiana, a Tree, a Fight, and a Question of Justice," *New York Times,* September 19, 2007.
2. Jason Whitlock, "Lessons from Jena, La.," *Kansas City Star*, September 25, 2007.
3. Amy Waldman, "The Truth About Jena: Why America's Black-and-White Narratives About Race Don't Reflect Reality," *Atlantic*, January/February 2008.
4. Craig Franklin, "Media Myths About the Jena 6: A Local Journalist Tells the Story You Haven't Heard," *Christian Science Monitor*, October 24, 2007.
5. Howard Witt, "Questions About Jena Case Funds," *Chicago Tribune*, November 9, 2007.
6. Ibid.
7. Michelle Malkin, "Where Did All the Jena 6 Money Go?" November 12, 2007, http://michellemalkin.com/2007/11/12/where-did-all-the-jena-6-money-go/.
8. Erik Eckholm, "Plight Deepens for Black Men, Studies Warn," *New York Times*, March 20, 2006.
9. Daniel H. Weinberg, "Evidence from Census 2000 About Earnings by Detailed Occupation for Men and Women," Census 2000 Special Reports, May 2004.
10. Kevin M. Clermont and Stewart J. Schwab, "How Employment Discrimination Plaintiffs Fare in Federal Court," *Journal of Empirical Legal Studies* 1, no. 2 (July 2004), p. 432.
11. Ibid.
12. Thomas Paine, *The Rights of Man*, in two parts (New York: Vale, 1848).

1. Entitlement and Advantage

1. Jacques Steinberg, "Savage Stands by Autism Remarks," *New York Times*, July 22, 2008.
2. Kelefa Sanneh, "Party of One: Michael Savage, Unexpurgated," *New Yorker*, August 3, 2009, p. 53.
3. "The Diagnosis of Autism: An Expert Interview with Catherine Lord, PhD," *Medscape*, July 11, 2005, http://www.medscape.com/viewarticle/501469.
4. Individuals with Disabilities Education Improvement Act, H.R. 1350 Sec. 614 (b) (6) (B).
5. Cecilia Kang, "Mothers Rally to Back Breast-Feeding Rights," *Washington Post*, November 22, 2006, http://www.washingtonpost.com/wp-dyn/content/article/2006/11/21/AR2006112101316.html.
6. Anne L. Wright and Richard J. Schanler, "The Resurgence of Breastfeeding at the End of the Second Millennium," *Journal of Nutrition* 131 (2001), pp. 421–25S.
7. Hanna Rosin, "The Case Against Breast-Feeding," *Atlantic*, April 2009.
8. National Women's Health Information Center, "Pumping Breastmilk at Home or Work," http://babyparenting.about.com/cs/pumping/a/pumping.htm.
9. *Sophie C. Currier v. National Board of Medical Examiners*, No. 07-J-434 (Mass. 2007).
10. Dahlia Lithwick, "Express Yourselves," *Slate*, September 28, 2007, http://www.slate.com/id/2174934/pagenum/all/#p2.
11. MamaBear, "Breastfeeding Accommodations," September 18, 2007, http://www.breastfeedingsymbol.org/2007/09/18/breastfeeding-accommodations/.
12. http://massachusettsmom.blogspot.com/2007/09/sophie-currier-part-2.html, accessed August 7, 2010.
13. Ibid.
14. Mark Kelman and Gillian Lester, *Jumping the Queue* (Cambridge, Mass.: Harvard University Press, 1997), p. 47.
15. H. Rep. 101–485 (1990), pt. 2, p. 32.
16. Matthew S. Moore and Linda Levitan, *For Hearing People Only*, 3rd ed. (Rochester, N.Y.: Deaf Life Press, 2003); www.deafculture.com.
17. Brief for Petitioner at 9, *Board of Education of City of New York v. Tom F.*, 552 U.S. 1 (2007).
18. Nanette Asimov, "Extra-Special Education at Public Expense," *San Francisco Chronicle*, February 19, 2006, p. A1; Julie Rawe, "Who Pays for Special Ed," *Time*, September 17, 2006, http://www.time.com/time/magazine/article/0,9171,1535854-1,00.html; Alison Leigh Cowan, "Amid Affluence, a Struggle over Special Education," *New York Times,* April 24, 2005.
19. Brief of the Council of the Great City Schools and the National Association of State Directors of Special Education as Amici Curiae in Support of Petitioner at 24, *Board of Education of City of New York v. Tom F.*, 552 U.S. 1 (2007).
20. Brief for the National Disability Rights Network and the New York Lawyers

for the Public Interest as Amici Curiae in Support of Respondents at 12, *Board of Education of City of New York v. Tom F.*, 552 U.S. 1 (2007).

21. Amicus Curiae Brief of Autism Speaks in Support of Respondent at 14, *Board of Education of City of New York v. Tom F.*, 552 U.S. 1 (2007).

22. Brief for the National Disability Rights Network and the New York Lawyers for the Public Interest as Amici Curiae in Support of Respondents at 14, *Board of Education of City of New York v. Tom F.*, 552 U.S. 1 (2007).

23. Brief of the Council of the Great City Schools and the National Association of State Directors of Special Education as Amici Curiae in Support of Petitioner at 20, *Board of Education of City of New York v. Tom F.*, 552 U.S. 1 (2007).

24. Brief for the National Disability Rights Network and The New York Lawyers for the Public Interest as Amici Curiae in Support of Respondents at 12, *Board of Education of City of New York v. Tom F.*, 552 U.S. 1 (2007).

25. Kelman and Lester, *Jumping the Queue*, p. 101.

26. Ibid., p. 99.

27. Dan Keating and V. Dion Haynes, "Special-Ed Tuition a Growing Drain on D.C.: Basic Needs Take a Hit to Cover Costs of Sending Kids to Private Schools," *Washington Post*, June 5, 2006.

28. Marcus A. Winters and Jay P. Greene, "Debunking a Special Education Myth," *Education Next* (Spring 2007), p. 70.

29. Kelman and Lester, *Jumping the Queue*, pp. 74–75.

30. Ibid., p. 75.

31. Brief of the Council of the Great City Schools and the National Association of State Directors of Special Education as Amici Curiae in Support of Petitioner at 26, *Board of Education of City of New York v. Tom F.*, 552 U.S. 1 (2007).

32. Sharon Otterman, "Class Sizes Rise, Mostly Due to Budget Cuts," *New York Times*, December 1, 2009, p. A30.

33. Michael Montgomery, "Class Sizes Begin to Rise Again in California Schools," *California Report*, November 19, 2009, http://www.californiareport.org/archive/R911190850/b.

34. Brief for Petitioner at 14, *Board of Education of City of New York v. Tom F.*, 552 U.S. 1 (2007).

35. Paul Steinberg, "Attention Surplus? Re-examining a Disorder," *New York Times*, March 7, 2006.

36. "Google's I.P.O. Five Years Later," DealBook, *New York Times*, August 19, 2009, http://dealbook.blogs.nytimes.com/2009/08/19/googles-ipo-5-years-later/.

37. *Reid v. Google*, 66 Cal. Rep. 3d 744 (Cal. App. 2007).

38. See U.S. Department of Labor, Bureau of Labor Statistics, "Unemployment Rate by Sex, Race, and Age, 1947–1979," *Handbook of Labor Statistics* 67 (1980).

39. *Age Discrimination in Employment: Hearings on H.R. 3651, H.R. 3768, and H.R. 4221 Before the General Subcommittee on Labor of the House Committee on Education and Labor*, 90th Congress 7 (1967) (statement of William D. Bechill, commissioner on aging), p. 154.

40. Michael Luo, "Longer Unemployment for Those 45 and Older," *New York Times*, April 12, 2009.

41. U.S. Department of Labor, Bureau of Labor Statistics, February 2010, http://www.bls.gov/news.release/pdf/empsit.pdf; Luo, "Longer Unemployment for Those 45 and Older."

42. Laura Nielsen, Robert Nelson, Ryon Lancaster, and Nicholas Pedriana, *Contesting Workplace Discrimination in Court: Characteristics and Outcomes of Federal Employment Discrimination Litigation, 1987–2003* (American Bar Foundation, 2008), p. 6.

43. *Age Discrimination, in Employment: Hearings,* supra note 39 (Norman Sprague, director, Employment and Retirement Program, National Council on Aging), p. 69.

44. Ibid.

45. Ibid., p. 155.

46. Samuel Issacharoff and Erica Worth Harris, "Is Age Discrimination Really Age Discrimination? The ADEA's Unnatural Solution," *New York University Law Review* 72 (1997), p. 830.

47. *Age Discrimination in Employment Act*, 81 Stat., sec. 12, p. 604.

48. Issacharoff and Harris, "Is Age Discrimination Really Age Discrimination?" p. 803.

49. Steven Greenhouse and Michael Barbaro, "Wal-Mart Memo Suggests Ways to Cut Employee Benefit Costs," *New York Times*, October 26, 2005.

50. *Hazen Paper Co. v. Biggins*, 507 U.S. 604 (1993).

51. Issacharoff and Harris, "Is Age Discrimination Really Age Discrimination?" p. 803, citing Alan Auerbach and Laurence Kotlikoff, "The Impact of the Demographic Transition on Capital Formation," in *Demography and Retirement: The Twenty-first Century*, ed. Anna M. Rappaport and Sylvester J. Schieber (Westport, Conn.; Praeger, 1993), p. 174.

52. Issacharoff and Harris, "Is Age Discrimination Really Age Discrimination?" pp. 815–16.

53. Ibid., p. 816.

54. New York State Bar Association, Special Committee on Age Discrimination in the Profession, *Report and Recommendations on Mandatory Retirement Practices in the Profession* (January 2007).

55. See *EEOC v. Kelley, Drye & Warren, LLP*, Civil Action 10-CV-0665; Anthony Lin, "Sidley Austin Settles Age Bias Suit; No Determination of Merits," *National Law Journal*, October 8, 2007, http://www.law.com/jsp/llf/PubArticleLLF.jsp?id=1191834192615.

56. Lin, "Sidley Austin," p. 819.

57. Paul Krugman, "Always Low Wages. Always," *New York Times*, May 13, 2005.

58. Richard Posner, *Aging and Old Age* (Chicago: University of Chicago Press, 1995), p. 320.

59. Paul Brest, "In Defense of the Anti-discrimination Principle," *Harvard Law Review* 90 (1976).

2. Discriminating Tastes

1. *Michael Cohn v. Corinthian Colleges Inc.*, 169 Cal. App. 4th 523, 528 (2008).
2. Lauren Collins, "Hey, La-a-a-dies!" *New Yorker*, August 6, 2007.
3. *Koire v. Metro Car Wash*, 40 Cal. 3d 24 (1985).
4. Joanna Grossman, "The End of 'Ladies' Night' in New Jersey," FindLaw, June 14, 2004, http://writ.news.findlaw.com/scripts/printer_friendly.pl?page=/gross man/20040615.html.
5. "Denver Man Files Complaint to Bar 'Ladies Night,'" 7 News, September 14, 2006, http://www.thedenverchannel.com/entertainment/9852164/detail .html; "'Ladies Night' Under Fire in Colorado," 7 News, January 7, 2007, http://www.thedenverchannel.com/news/10683429/detail.html.
6. Steve Friess, "A Las Vegas Gym Faces a 'Ladies' Night' Bias Case," *New York Times*, December 12, 2007.
7. *Angelucci v. Century Supper Club*, 41 Cal. 4th 160 (2007).
8. Charisse Jones, "Many Scoff at N.J. Ruling over 'Ladies' Nights,'" *USA Today*, June 4, 2004.
9. Carrie Lukas, "Last Call on Ladies' Night: $5 Beers and Government Overreach," *National Review Online*, June 4, 2004.
10. Jones, "Many Scoff at N.J. Ruling," supra note 8.
11. Brittany Bacon, "'Ladies' Night' Lawsuits on the Rocks?" July 25, 2007, http://abcnews.go.com/TheLaw/story?id=3412561&page=1.
12. Lis Wiehl, "Constitutional Dilemma Surrounding Ladies' Night," Lis on Law, Fox News, http://www.foxnews.com/story/0,2933,292255,00.html.
13. Lukas, "Last Call on Ladies' Night," supra note 9.
14. Grossman, "End of 'Ladies' Night' in New Jersey."
15. Lukas, supra note 9.
16. Owen Fiss, "Groups and the Equal Protection Clause," *Philosophy and Public Affairs* 5, no. 2 (1976).
17. Paul Brest, "In Defense of the Anti-discrimination Principle," *Harvard Law Review* 90 (1976).
18. https://www.harrahsreno.com/casinos/harrahs-reno/casino-misc/nightlife -detail.html.
19. "Five Cocktail Servers Agree to Settlement," *Las Vegas Review-Journal*, July 8, 2000, http://www.reviewjournal.com/lvrj_home/2000/Jul-08-Sat-2000/news/13928641.html.
20. Sharon Gerrie, "Servers Rail Against High Heels," *Las Vegas Review-Journal*, June 16, 2001, http://www.reviewjournal.com/lvrj_home/2001/Jun-16-Sat-2001/business/16337479.html.
21. "Harrah's Dress Rules Draw Protest," *Las Vegas Review-Journal*, February 17, 2001, http://www.reviewjournal.com/cgi-bin/printable.cgi?/lvrj_home/2001/Feb-17-Sat-2001/business/15468450.html.
22. *Jespersen v. Harrah's Operating Company Inc.*, 444 F.3d 1104 (2005).

23. *Craft v. Metromedia Inc.*, 766 F.2d 1205 (1985).
24. Hooters Employee Handbook, http://www.thesmokinggun.com/archive/0915051 hooters1.html.
25. *Wilson v. Southwest Airlines*, 517 F. Supp. 292, 294 (N.D. Tex. 1981).
26. "Hooters Settles Suit by Men Denied Jobs," *New York Times*, October 1, 1997.
27. "Texas Man Settles Discrimination Lawsuit Against Hooters for Not Hiring Male Waiter," April 21, 2009, http://www.foxnews.com/story/0,2933,517334,00 .html.
28. *Jespersen*, supra note 22.
29. Campbell Gibson and Kay Jung, *Historical Census Statistics on Population Totals by Race, 1790 to 1990, and by Hispanic Origin, 1970 to 1990, for Large Cities and Other Urban Places in the United States*, Population Division Working Paper 76 (Washington, D.C.: U.S. Census Bureau, 2005).
30. U.S. Census Bureau, State and County QuickFacts, New Haven, Connecticut, http://quickfacts.census.gov/qfd/states/09/0952000.html.
31. Nicole Allan and Emily Bazelon, "The Ladder," *Slate*, June 25, 2009, http:// www.slate.com/id/2221250/entry/2221298/.
32. Ibid.
33. Melissa Bailey, "Latino Group Backs White Firefighters," *New Haven Independent*, February 6, 2009.
34. Allen and Bazelon, supra note 32.
35. Paul Bass, "Kimmmm—BERRRRRR! Why the Mayor Needs to Ax the Rev.," *New Haven Advocate*, June 13, 2002.
36. Alyssa Rosenberg, "To New Haven and Back Again," Ta-Nehisi Coates, Atlantic .com, http://ta-nehisicoates.theatlantic.com/archives/2009/06/to_new_haven _and_back_again.php.
37. *Ricci v. DeStefano*, 557 U.S. (2009).
38. Ibid. at 19–20 (slip op.).
39. Ta-Nehisi Coates, "Rules for Ricci," *Atlantic*, June 29, 2009, http://www.the atlantic.com/entertainment/archive/2009/06/scotus-rules-for-ricci/20285/.
40. John McWhorter, "Thinking About 'Ricci': When Black People Don't Peform As Well on Standardized Test, What Should Be Done," April 22, 2009, http:// www.tnr.com/blog/john-mcwhorter/thinking-about-ricci-when-black-people-dont-perform-well-standardized.
41. Abigail Thernstrom and Stephen Thernstrom, "New Haven's Racial Test: Merit Doesn't Matter for City Firefighters" *Wall Street Journal*, April 21, 2009.
42. Allen and Bazelon, supra note 32.
43. Complaint for Damages and Injunctive Relief, *Michael Briscoe v. City of New Haven*, October 15, 2009.
44. *Romer v. Evans*, 517 U.S. 620 (1996).
45. Michael Klarman, *From Jim Crow to Civil Rights* (New York: Oxford University Press, 2004), p. 391.

46. Mary Dudziak, *Cold War Civil Rights: Race and the Image of American Democracy* (Princeton, N.J.: Princeton University Press, 2000), p. 29.
47. Patricia Williams, *The Alchemy of Race and Rights* (Cambridge, Mass.: Harvard University Press, 1991), 159.
48. Robert Post, *Prejudicial Appearances: The Logic of American Antidiscrimination Law* (Durham, N.C.: Duke University Press, 2001), p. 22.
49. Alexander Bickel, *The Least Dangerous Branch: The Supreme Court at the Bar of Politics* (Indianapolis: Bobbs-Merrill, 1962), pp. 16–17.
50. Jeffrey Toobin, "After Stevens," *New Yorker*, March 22, 2010, p. 46.

3. The Unintended Consequences of the Law

1. *Brown v. Board of Education of Topeka*, 347 U.S. 483 (1954).
2. Erica Frankenberg, Chungmei Lee, and Gary Orfield, *A Multiracial Society with Segregated Schools: Are We Losing the Dream?* Civil Rights Project, Harvard University, January 2003.
3. Derrick Bell, *Silent Covenants* (New York: Oxford University Press, 2004), p. 4.
4. Gary Orfield, *Reviving the Goal of an Integrated Society: A Twenty-first Century Challenge*, University of California, Civil Rights Project, January 2009, p. 13.
5. Herbert Wechsler, "Toward Neutral Principles of Constitutional Law," *Harvard Law Review* 73 (1959–60).
6. Ibid., p. 34.
7. See generally Daryl Michael Scott, *Contempt and Pity: Social Policy and the Image of the Damaged Black Psyche, 1880–1996* (Chapel Hill, N.C.: University of North Carolina Press, 1997) p. 128.
8. Risa Goluboff, *The Lost Promise of Civil Rights* (Cambridge, Mass.: Harvard University Press, 2007), p. 244.
9. Ibid., pp. 154–56.
10. *Turnstall v. Brotherhood of Locomotive Firemen*; *Railway Mail Association v. Corsi*; *James v. Marinship Corp.*
11. *Plessy v. Ferguson*, 163 U.S. 537 (1896).
12. *Green v. County School Board of New Kent County*, 391 U.S. 430 (1968).
13. *Brown V. Board of Education of Topeka* (Brown II), 349 U.S. 294, 300–301 (1955).
14. *Swann v. Charlotte-Mecklenburg Board of Education*, 402 U.S. 1 (1971).
15. Ibid.
16. Michael Klarman, *From Jim Crow to Civil Rights* (New York: Oxford University Press, 2004), p. 326.
17. Ibid., pp. 389–401.
18. Ibid., p. 392.
19. J. Anthony Lukas, *Common Ground: A Turbulent Decade in the Lives of Three American Families* (New York: Vintage, 1986); Henry Hampton and Steve Fayer,

Voices of Freedom: An Oral History of the Civil Rights Movement (New York: Bantam, 1990), pp. 601–5.

20. Derrick Bell, "Serving Two Masters," *Yale Law Journal* 85 (1976), p. 483.
21. Daryl Michael Scott, *Contempt and Pity: Social Policy and the Image of the Damaged Black Psyche, 1880–1996* (1997), p. 128.
22. Stuart Buck, *Acting White: The Ironic Legacy of Desegregation* (New Haven, Conn.: Yale University Press, 2010), pp. 87, 89.
23. *Bradley v. Milliken*, 484 F.2d 215, 298 (6th Cir. 1973).
24. *Swann*, 243 F. Supp. 667, 668.
25. *Parents Involved in Community Schools v. Seattle School District No. 1*, 127 S. Ct. 2738, 2768.
26. Transcript of oral argument in *Brown I*, p. 7 (Robert L. Carter, December 9, 1952).
27. *Parents* at 35, quoting *Metro Broadcasting*, O'Connor dissenting.
28. Ibid. at 36, Thomas dissenting.
29. *Brown*, 347 U.S. at 494.
30. *Robinson v. Jacksonville Shipyards*, 760 F. Supp. 1486 (1991).
31. Susan Estrich, "Sex at Work," *Stanford Law Review* 43 (1991), p. 820.
32. Laura B. Hoguet, "Seinfeld Goes to Work," Hoguet Newman Regal and Kenney, LLP (1999), http://library.findlaw.com/1999/Jun/1/127781.html.
33. Gillian Flynn, "Love Contracts Help Fend Off Harassment Suits," *Workforce Management* 78, no. 3 (March 1999), pp. 106–8, http://www.workforce.com/archive/feature/22/18/74/223281.php.
34. Janet Halley, "Sexuality Harassment," in *Left Legalism/Left Critique*, Brown and Halley, eds. (Durham, N.C.: Duke University Press, 2002), p. 82.
35. Phyllis Schlafly, "'Yale Five' Challenge College Coed Dorms," Eagle Forum, August 26, 1998, http://www.eagleforum.org/column/1998/aug98/98-08-26.html.
36. Vicki Schultz, "The Sanitized Workplace," *Yale Law Journal* 112 (2003), p. 2064.

4. Civil Rights Activism as Therapy

1. "Farrakhan Inspires and Infuriates at Once," *USA Today*, February 16, 1996.
2. Eric Pooley, "To the Beat of His Drum: Like It or Not, Louis Farrakhan Is Once Again Forcing the Nation to Focus on Him and His Message," *Time*, October 23, 1995, http://www.time.com/time/special/million/1023time.html.
3. "Who's In and Who's Out: Which Black Leaders Supported the March," *Time*, October 13, 1995.
4. CNN, "Minister Farrakhan Challenges Black Men: Transcript from Minister Louis Farrakhan's Remarks at the Million Man March," October 17, 1995, http://www-cgi.cnn.com/US/9510/megamarch/10-16/transcript/index.html.
5. Eric Pooley, "To the Beat of His Drum."
6. James Dobson et al., *Seven Promises of a Promise Keeper* (Colorado Springs: Focus on the Family, 1994), pp. 79–81.

7. "Myths and Facts About the Promise Keepers," National Organization for Women, http://www.now.org/issues/right/promise/mythfact.html.

8. Alvin Klein, " 'Day of Absence' Offers Fantasy on Prejudice," *New York Times*, October 17, 1993, http://theater.nytimes.com/mem/theater/treview.html?res =9F0CE0D91F3AF934A25753C1A965958260.

9. "SFPD to End Critical Mass?" *SF Gate*, March 2, 2010, http://www.sfgate.com/ cgi-bin/blogs/green/detail?entry_id=58252&o=7&gta=commentslistpos #commentslistpos#ixzz0j3FzCuNh.

10. Cornel West, in "Tavis Smiley Presents, State of Black America," C-SPAN, February 2008.

11. Scott Raab, "The Battle of Newark," *Esquire*, July 16, 2008.

12. Gloria Steinem, "Women Are Never Front-Runners," *New York Times*, January 8, 2008.

13. Katherine Q. Seelye and Julie Bosman, "Ferraro's Obama Remarks Become Talk of the Campaign," *New York Times*, March 12, 2008.

14. Toni Morrison, "Comment," Talk of the Town, *New Yorker*, October 5, 1998.

15. "Andrew Young: Obama's Time Will Come," NPR, December 7, 2007, http:// www.npt.org/blogs/newsandviews/2007/12/andrew_young_obamas_time_will .html.

16. Rachel L. Swarns, " 'African-American' Becomes a Term for Debate," *New York Times*, August 29, 2004.

17. Debra Dickerson, "Colorbind: Barack Obama Would Be the Great Black Hope in the Next Presidential Election—If He Were Actually Black," *Salon*, January 22, 2007, http://www.salon.com/news/opinion/feature/2007/01/22/obama.

18. Sara Rimer and Karen W. Arenson, "Top Colleges Take More Blacks, but Which Ones?" *New York Times*, June 24, 2004.

19. John Ridley, "The Manifesto of Ascendancy for the Modern American Nigger," *Esquire*, November 2006.

20. Nathan Glazer, *Affirmative Discrimination: Ethnic Inequality and Public Policy* (New York: Basic Books, 1975).

22. Nathan Glazer, "In Defense of Preference," *New Republic*, April 6, 1998.

23. Chandran Kukathas, "Are There Any Cultural Rights?" *Political Theory* 20, no. 1 (1992), p. 105.

24. E. Franklin Frazier, *Black Bourgeoisie* (Glencoe, Ill.: Free Press, 1957).

5. Righting Rights

1. Harold Meyerson, "In Wal-Mart's Image," *American Prospect*, September 11, 2009, http://www.prospect.org/cs/articles?article=in_walmarts_image.

2. Dan Frosch, "African Immigrants Accuse Wal-Mart of Discrimination," *New York Times*, February 2, 2010.

3. Abigail Goldman, "Young to Quit Wal-Mart Group After Racial Remarks," *Los Angeles Times*, August 18, 2006.

4. Meyerson, "In Wal-Mart's Image," supra note 1.

5. Reed Abelson, "6 Women Sue Wal-Mart, Charging Job and Promotion Bias," *New York Times*, June 20, 2001.

6. Al Norman, "Wal-Mart Exposed for 'Outdated and Sexist' Hiring Practices," *Huffington Post*, March 2, 2010, http://www.huffingtonpost.com/al-norman/wal-mart-exposed-for-outd_b_483334.html.

7. www.ipodnanosettlement.com/pdfs/AIN_Notice.pdf.

8. *Hall v. Werthan Bag Corp.*, 251 F. Supp. 184 (M.D. Tenn. 1966). See also *Jenkins v. United Gas Corp.*, 400 F.2d 28 (5th Cir. 1968); *Bowe v. Colgate-Palmolive Co.*, 426 F.2d 711, 719 (7th Cir. 1969).

9. Abelson, "6 Women Sue Wal-Mart," supra note 5.

10. *Dukes v. Wal-Mart Inc.*, No. 04-16688, CV-01-02252-MJJ (9th circuit, 2008) at 16227.

11. Steven Malanga, "The Tort Plague Hits Wal-Mart: A Federal Judge Dignifies a Flimsy Claim," *City Journal*, June 24, 2004.

12. *Dukes*, supra note 10, at 16251–52.

13. Malanga, "Tort Plague Hits Wal-Mart."

14. Plaintiffs' Third Amended Complaint, *Dukes* at 7.

15. Ibid.

16. *Dukes*, supra note 10, at 16242.

17. Mark Fischer, "*Dukes v. Wal-Mart*: A New Interpretation of the Class-Action Model," 2007, http://works.bepress.com/mark_fischer/1.

18. *Dukes*, supra note 10, at 16258.

19. See Robert Belton, "A Comparative Review of Public and Private Enforcement of Title VII of the Civil Rights Act of 1964," *Vanderbilt Law Review* 31 (1978), p. 907.

20. Douglas Martin, "The Rise and Fall of the Class-Action Lawsuit," *New York Times*, January 8, 1988, p. B7.

21. *Baylie v. FRB*, 476 F.3d 522 (7th Cir. 2007).

22. *Wal-Mart Stores, Inc. v. Dukes*, 564 U.S.———(2011), quoting J. Kozinski, 603 F. 3d at 652 (dissenting opinion).

23. Matthew Wald, "U.S. Limits Tarmac Waits for Passengers to 3 Hours," *New York Times*, December 21, 2009.

24. Laura Nielsen, Robert Nelson, Ryon Lancaster, and Nicholas Pedriana, *Contesting Workplace Discrimination in Court: Characteristics and Outcomes of Federal Employment Discrimination Litigation, 1987–2003* (American Bar Foundation, 2008), p. 6.

25. John Donohue and Peter Siegelman, "The Changing Nature of Employment Discrimination Litigation," *Stanford Law Review* 43 (1991), pp. 1024–27.

26. Edmund Burke, *Reflections on the Revolution in France* (New York: Oxford University Press, 2009/1790).

27. Brief for Amici Curiae: 65 Leading American Businesses in *Grutter v. Bollinger*, U.S. Supreme Court, 2003.

28. Mike Swift, "Tech Firms Fight to Keep Workforce Make-up Hidden," *San Jose Mercury News*, February 15, 2010.

29. Mike Swift, "Blacks, Latinos, and Women Lose Ground at Silicon Valley Tech Companies," *San Jose Mercury News*, February 13, 2010.

30. Paul Burstein, *Discrimination, Jobs, and Politics: The Struggle for Equal Employment Opportunity in the United States Since the New Deal* (Chicago: University of Chicago Press, 1985), pp. 27–28.

31. *Swann*, 243 F. Supp. 667, 668.

32. Justice Policy Institute, *Pruning Prisons: How Cutting Corrections Can Save Money and Protect Public Safety* (Washington, D.C., May 2009), p. 6.

33. Justice Policy Institute, *Substance Abuse Treatment and Public Safety* (Washington, D.C., January 2008), p. 1.

34. Cassia Spohn and Miriam DeLone, "When Does Race Matter? An Analysis of the Conditions Under Which Race Affects Sentence Severity," *Sociology of Crime, Law, and Deviance: Volume 2*, ed. Jeffery T. Ulmer (Bingley, U.K.: Emerald Group, 2000).

35. Edmund Burke, *Reflections on the Revolution in France* (1790).

36. Jeremy Bentham, *Anarchical Fallacies: Being an Examination of the Declarations of Rights Issued During the French Revolution* (1795, 1816).

37. Karl Marx, "On the Jewish Question," in *Marx: Early Writings: The Marx Library*, 234 (1975).

38. See, e.g., Mark Tushnet, "An Essay on Rights," 62 *Texas Law Review* 1363 (1984); Duncan Kennedy, *A Critique of Adjudication (fin de siècle)* (Cambridge, Mass.: Harvard University Press, 1997), pp. 299–338.

39. See *Palmer v. Thompson*, 403 U.S. 217 (1971).

Acknowledgments

I was first introduced to the "critique of rights" as a law student, more years ago than I care to admit. Before I started law school, scholars associated with the critical legal studies movement, such as Duncan Kennedy, Morton Horowitz, and Mark Tushnet, had developed a deep and sophisticated jurisprudential critique that I found (and still find) very convincing. This inspired many thoughtful and impassioned responses, of which Patricia Williams's work is exemplary. At the same time, scholars such as Mary Ann Glendon and Amitai Etzioni developed critiques of "rights talk" from a communitarian perspective. Meanwhile, the legal scholar Frank Michelman, the political theorist Michael Walzer, and the political scientist Robert Putnam all did probing and insightful work on the origins and contemporary relevance of the civic republican tradition in American political thought—work that had profound implications for the critique of rights even if that was not its primary concern. This book borrows insights from all these lines of study and analysis—my attempt has been to temper the insights of the various critiques of rights with the most compelling responses.

What I would call a second generation of rights critique emerged later as scholars explored the unintended consequences and misfiring of specific legal entitlements. My colleague Mark Kelman was one of the first and most comprehensive of such critics—his work on antidiscrimination law was characteristically synoptic, daring, and logically airtight. Janet Halley's work on gender and sexuality has redefined what legal critique could be and provided a model for my work on race and civil rights law. I learned a great deal from Vicki Schultz's work on harassment law and Samuel Issacharoff's work on age discrimination.

As always, my thoughts on race relations and legal controversies have been influenced by Randall Kennedy, who has written consistently probing and courageous work about race and the law. Robert Post's insistence on a sociological approach to antidiscrimination law has been an indispensable theoretical foundation for my thinking about civil rights law. And I've profited from the work of countless others, including Kim Yurako, Julie Suk, Tristin Green, Devon Carbado, Kimberle Crenshaw, Katherine Franke, and Susan Strum.

I profited greatly from comments on and discussions about various chapters of the book in lectures and workshops at Stanford Law School, Harvard Law School, the Harvard Inequality and Social Policy Seminar Series, Yale Law School, Cornell University Law School, and the IIT Chicago-Kent College of Law.

This book is part of an ongoing series of projects about the future of civil rights law, for which I have enjoyed the generous support of an Alphonse Fletcher, Sr., Fellowship and the equally generous support and hospitality of the Fletcher family. I have also been fortunate as a Fletcher Fellow to have made the acquaintance of other Fletcher Fellows past and present, and to have had the chance to renew my acquaintance with Henry Louis Gates Jr., one of the most insightful, energetic, and personable scholars in academia.

Index